$70 BILLION IN THE BLACK

$70 BILLION

D. Parke Gibson

IN THE BLACK

AMERICA'S BLACK CONSUMERS

A Revised and Updated Version of *The $30 Billion Negro*

Macmillan Publishing Co., Inc.
NEW YORK

Collier Macmillan Publishers
LONDON

For my wife, PATRICIA, for her love and understanding; for my associates ELLEN HALL, MARY MURRAY, BILL BRIGHT, HELEN JONES, and VINCENT HALL for their continuing support in the building of bridges; and for those who have believed in me.

For my editor, BETH RASHBAUM, and her keeping the faith.

Above all, for HIM from Whom all good flows.

Macmillan Publishing Co., Inc.
866 Third Avenue, New York, N.Y.   10022
Collier Macmillan Canada, Ltd.

Library of Congress Cataloging in Publication Data
Gibson, D   Parke.
   $70 billion in the Black.
   "A revised and updated version of The $30 billion Negro [published in 1969]"
   Bibliography: p.
   1. Afro-Americans as consumers. I. Title.
HC110.C6G5   1978   339.4   78-2662
ISBN 0-02-543160-9

First Printing 1978

Designed by Jack Meserole

Printed in the United States of America

CONTENTS

PART III
Developing the Market

PART IV
How Some Companies Developed
Black-Oriented Campaigns

 FOREWORD

IN THE TEXT of this book, the terms *black* and *Negro* are often used interchangeably. The terms *Negro and other races* and *nonwhites* describe persons of all races other than white, and are used whenever data for blacks alone are not available for the period shown. Generally, government statistics for the national population of "Negro and other races" reflect the condition of the black population, since about 90 percent of the population of "Negro and other races" is black. When *The $30 Billion Negro* was written in 1968, that term was the most widely used, and is still used today in the names of some organizations, in conversation, and in certain research.

PREFACE

THE 24.1 MILLION BLACKS and the 3.2 million other non-white residents of the United States comprise the ninth largest consumer market in the world, bigger than that of 114 member countries of the United Nations, buying an estimated $70 billion of goods and services—enough to make the difference between profit and loss for many companies.

Because of the growing affluence and power of nonwhite consumers, it will be important to the future of American and multinational firms selling to the American marketplace to learn how to sell effectively to this relatively new consumer group with its own unique set of needs and desires.

The growing power of nonwhites in America has affected virtually every area of the nation's life—government, education, business and industry, health and welfare, urban development—yet, perhaps nowhere has it had or could it have as much effect as in the marketplace for goods and services.

This book, like its earlier version, *The $30 Billion Negro*, takes a look at one aspect of black life in America: how nonwhites act and react in the marketplace, and what those who would sell goods and services or seek to shape thought or opinion should know about effectively motivating this consumer.

An effort has been made to separate the black consumer's thoughts and actions as a consumer from other aspects of his or her life, but this is often not possible, because the attitudes one brings to the marketplace are part of the whole fabric of life.

I have attempted to put down those theories that my firm, D. Parke Gibson International, has either proved or observed in successful practice, as well as guidelines that can make marketing to nonwhite consumers more effective. While many companies and service organizations have operated successfully without such guidelines, and still others who have attempted to put them into practice have failed at it, I do think it is both possible and, increasingly, necessary to educate the American business community about how to relate to one of the most powerful consumer groups in this country.

I have included a chapter on the Hispanic market, although this book is primarily about black consumers. Black and Hispanic consumers have many similar characteristics, as I have indicated in illustrations of programs. By no means is this book an attempt to thoroughly cover this growing market segment, but rather to give some insights into it.

Government and Census data, on which I rely extensively, have defined such characteristics, and I have tried to include them in an effort to give further information on the growing importance of racial markets.

The principles and guidelines put forth here have resulted from some twenty-six years of observation, study, and practice. I believe that they will be a significant contribution to the understanding of the nonwhite as a consumer.

D. PARKE GIBSON

New York City
January 1978

PART I

Understanding the Black Consumer

CHAPTER 1

Why There Is a Black Consumer Market

THE AMERICAN SOCIETY today is, as it has been for centuries, divided into two basic groups, the white and nonwhite populations; as a result the two groups tend to reveal distinct and separate patterns of behavior in the basic areas of economics, housing, and social activity.

There is little likelihood in the foreseeable future of the black community in the United States being assimilated into the white community. And this must be the basis upon which business and industrial management will have to operate in the sale of goods and services to this expanding market segment.

The ramifications of such a division in American society will continue to have impact upon government, institutions, and business and industry, and will continually confront us with the need for more effective communication.

Samuel Johnson said, "A nation's ideals are judged by its advertising." The lack of black orientation in the majority of the nation's advertising indicates a lack of marketing know-how or understanding on the part of American business and others selling in American markets, and reflects the ideals not only of the nation, but of those responsible for creating the advertising.

It will be some time before there can be any full integration of advertising, yet in the meantime there is a group whose recognition as consumers can be meaningful and profitable in the sale of goods, services, and ideas. This is the black consumer market.

There are four basic reasons why the black consumer market exists as an identifiable group:

(1) Blacks, unlike white ethnic groups, have not been absorbed

3

into the American "melting pot," and their high visibility results in "forced identification."

(2) This group of consumers has definable purchasing patterns.

(3) The 25 million consumers in this group make it not only an identifiable market but a sizeable one.

(4) This market is not evenly distributed throughout the United States, but is concentrated primarily in urban areas.

At 25 million, American blacks constitute over 92 percent of the nonwhite population in the United States, and 11.1 percent of the total population.

It is estimated that by 1985 blacks will make up 12.1 percent of the nation's total population, or 29.1 million. Over 75 percent of blacks live in cities, 41 percent of which have black populations of 100,000 or more.

This large population group has very distinct purchasing patterns which can be isolated and analyzed quite effectively. What black consumers buy with their money is, of course, the key question for business people, and the question I have been most frequently asked in speeches to businessmen throughout the United States.

Among other findings, research indicates that blacks, with 11 percent of the total U.S. population, have a 50 percent higher per capita consumption rate of imported Scotch whisky than whites; that these consumers at one time accounted for 70 percent of the entire output of the Maine sardine industry; consume more than 49 percent of all the grape soda produced in America; spend 23 percent more per capita for shoes than does the majority white population; and spend up to 12 percent more for food sold in supermarkets to be consumed at home.

To effectively sell this market, it must be analyzed—how it has been shaped historically, where it is today—but far too few companies have either understood or tried to correctly develop the black consumer market.

One reason for this insensitivity, this failure to effectively appeal to such a powerful portion of the market, is the often expressed belief that segmented marketing—customer-oriented programming directed to black consumers—is segregation in reverse.

Customer-oriented programs aimed at black consumers are not segregation in reverse but are a highly desirable form of recognition. With the widely acknowledged concept that advertising and other means of communication, in order to achieve maximum identification, should be tailored as closely as possible to the interests of the consumer, it is surprising that marketing and communications executives still need to be made aware that this same concept applies in the black consumer market.

The black consumer wants the same recognition that other unique consumer groups get. To understand why this is true, one must understand why there continues to be a separate black community, and how it differs from other, more readily assimilated communities.

The black community exists in America largely because of the economics of business and industry in America during the seventeenth and eighteenth centuries. Slavery had existed in all parts of the world, and was, at that time, as prevalent in South America as it was in the United States. However, the scars upon blacks in North America were unusually deep because the United States did not recognize the slave as a human being. Black slaves were treated as property, the same as animals or other chattel.

South American slavery, in contrast, recognized every human being as having a soul and at least a potential right to freedom. This freedom included the right to own and to inherit property. Thus any slave could work his way to complete freedom, and also could inherit property from his legal forebears.

In North America, however, in order to protect the economic interests of the slaveholder, many artificial legal means were employed to preserve the economic institution of slavery. Though slavemasters had many children with their slaves, the assimilation of these offspring into the mainstream of white America was prevented by the fact that anyone with any Negro blood was defined as a Negro before the law. Thus, progeny from interracial contact automatically was classified as Negro, disqualified from inheriting property, and effectively isolated from white life with all its advantages.

The churches were no more advanced or humane than the law. The practice of American churches to exclude black Americans was born of the need to consider the slave a creature without a soul. If he were not human, the logic went, why should he need the church? Thus the church, one of our major institutions for social ideals and goals, joined the law in perpetuating the racist system that condemned black Americans to exclusion from the mainstream. So deep have the effects of this separatism been that to this day communication between blacks and whites is affected by vestiges of the North American system of slavery.

The history of black people in America has also affected their identity—and their perception of that identity. As social psychologist Dr. Thomas F. Pettigrew pointed out,

... slavery in all its forms sharply lowered the need for achievement in slaves. Negroes in bondage, stripped complete of their African heritage, were placed in a completely dependent role. All of their rewards came, not from individual initiative and enterprise, but from absolute obedience—a situation that severely depresses the need for achievement among all people.*

Dr. Pettigrew goes on to say that "strong traces of these effects of slavery, augmented by racial discrimination, have persisted since Emancipation"; and he shows how the self-image and self-esteem of the Negro (which are needed in order to compete in business or industry) are still depressed via the pictures projected by the media, directed primarily to white Americans. Pettigrew explains:

We learn who we are, what we are like, largely by carefully observing how other people react to us. But this process is highly structured for the Negro by the role he is expected to play. When he attempts to gain an image of himself on the basis of his typical contacts with white America, and the general culture, he often receives a rude jolt. While he is totally American in every conceivable meaning of the term, he finds that most Americans are white and that somehow the mere color of his skin puts him into a unique and socially-defined category. And, when the Negro looks around him—except in the spheres of athletics and entertainment—he discovers very few Americans with his color who hold important positions in society.

Save for the mass media expressly tailored for Negro audiences, he sees only white models in advertisements and only whites as heroes of stories. When he does see Negroes in other mass media, they are likely to be in low-status roles. . . . Little wonder, then, that the question who am I?, raises special difficulties for him.

American business and industry of the twentieth century are not responsible for the creation of a segregated America. The enlightened management of today knows that it is always more profitable to employ the most efficient means, be it black or white, human or machine, to do the job. But only because of the protests of black Ameri-

---

* Thomas F. Pettigrew, *Profile of the American Negro* (New York: Van Nostrand, 1964).

cans over the years and the resultant government pressure to alter the system has it been possible for business and industry to abandon the practices of segregated America.

It is now recognized that segregation and separatism have been enormously costly to American business and industry, depriving them of both workers and consumers. And it is beginning to be understood that unless all Americans are offered the incentive to achieve, the skills to produce, and the opportunity to compete on equal grounds with all other Americans, we are all going to be sharing equally in the subsidizing of millions of people through the relief rolls, Aid to Dependent Children, and many other services that don't in fact work very well but do add enormously to our total tax burden, thus further reducing profits.

The whole world is rapidly changing its attitudes because of interdependence; and the speed of communication heightens the need for better understanding. Dark-skinned nations have risen. Maturity of the colored people of the world—and their predominance with over 75 percent of world population—should make business and industry here in America far more concerned about their relationship with darker-skinned people here. The tide of events both at home and abroad makes it extremely expensive in this age of automation, increased technology, and rising new political power centers, for discrimination, real or symbolic, to continue.

Black Americans must change their attitudes toward themselves and their attitudes toward business and industry before they can ever expect white American institutions and people to change.

CHAPTER 2
Migration and Urban Concentration

THE MOVEMENT of blacks from the South, beginning in World War II, has had considerable significance, much as the opening of the American West.

In 1910 nearly 90 percent of blacks in the United States lived in the South. In the period from 1940 to 1960, three million moved from the South to other parts of the United States. The proportion of blacks living outside the South swelled from 30 percent in 1947 to 44 percent by 1967, and has leveled off at 47 percent. Recently there has also been a slight trend of black migration back to the South. Overall, however, the trend had been away from the South, and it has been significant.

Black movement and concentration in urban centers of the North, Midwest, and West marked the beginning of a black consumer market that was to become identifiable and take on many of its present forms. Had blacks distributed themselves evenly throughout the United States, there might very well have been no distinct black consumer market as we know it today.

What caused the migration?

The main reason nonwhites left the South, or moved to the big cities, was to improve in the three basic areas of human activity. They had either been led to believe or come to believe that by moving into urban areas they could improve their *economic* position, expand their *social* activity, and obtain better *housing*.

These dreams were to come true, for the most part, but within the framework of *continuing* to be black. While blacks had better opportunities to find employment, obtain housing, and enjoy certain social privileges, they would do so while becoming more aware than ever *of being black*.

8

As *Ebony* magazine pointed out in its booklet "The Urban Negro Market Potential" some years ago, "The Negro in nearly every field of employment must rationalize the opportunity—not by a comparison of technical skills—but by the limitation of being a Negro. In economics—job and employment possibilities—the Negro must *think* and *respond* as a Negro."

Although the new immigrant was in a major city, he soon learned that social activity would continue to be limited to predominantly nonwhite social affairs, private entertainment, public dances, or invitation affairs. For the most part, the church, social club, or other outlet within the community would still provide the greatest nexus of social contact.

The black would also learn that whether he was in the Northeast, the Midwest, or the West, he could not easily obtain desirable housing, and when he did so, it would be concentrated in clearly defined neighborhoods in the central cities. This concentration has brought problems in race relations, but it has also produced a highly identifiable, geographically delimited group of consumers who now comprise a significant portion of today's downtown shopping traffic. Central-city businessmen are well aware of this concentration and, as blacks themselves become more aware of it and of the power it gives them, the businessmen will become more responsive to the needs and wishes of their black customers.

Because of their distinct migration patterns and their concentration of population, it would appear to be easier to locate, identify, and sell nonwhite consumers. More companies and advertising agencies now are taking the time to learn and understand the new customers for their products and services.

The following are the top one hundred black metropolitan population areas in the United States, according to Standard Rate and Data, 1977:

Top One Hundred Black Metro Population Areas, 1977

		BLACK CONSUMERS
1	New York	2,347,885
2	Chicago	1,472,134
3	Philadelphia	977,351
4	Los Angeles–Long Beach	961,535
5	Detroit	938,316

		BLACK CONSUMERS
6	Washington, D.C.	865,234
7	Baltimore	555,234
8	Newark, New Jersey	464,476
9	Houston	462,921
10	St. Louis	415,456
11	San Francisco–Oakland	406,178
12	Atlanta	393,071
13	Cleveland	371,724
14	Dallas–Fort Worth	363,805
15	New Orleans	360,117
16	Memphis	305,070
17	Miami	224,312
18	Norfolk–Virginia Beach–Portsmouth	203,861
19	Birmingham	202,411
20	Kansas City	179,591
21	Pittsburgh	171,797
22	Cincinnati	160,424
23	Indianapolis	158,526
24	Boston (Official S.M.S.A.)	156,626
25	Milwaukee	147,699
26	Nassau–Suffolk (NY)	143,777
27	Jacksonville, Florida	139,699
28	Richmond, Virginia	139,531
29	Tampa–St. Petersburg	137,364
30	Greensboro–Winston Salem–High Point	134,506
31	Gary–Hammond–East Chicago	132,704
32	Buffalo	130,487
33	Columbus, Ohio	118,605
34	Nashville–Davidson	117,744
35	Mobile	117,328
36	Charlotte–Gastonia, North Carolina	115,916
37	Louisville	111,518
38	Shreveport	109,397
39	Raleigh–Durham	107,104
40	Dayton, Ohio	103,380
41	Baton Rouge	103,161
42	Jackson, Mississippi	99,519
43	Fort Lauderdale–Hollywood	96,446
44	Charleston–North Charleston, South Carolina	95,097
45	Columbia, South Carolina	90,734
46	Greenville–Spartanburg, South Carolina	88,474
47	Newport News–Hampton, Virginia	82,531
48	Orlando	81,114
49	San Diego	79,752
50	Rochester, New York	79,334
51	Jersey City	79,309
52	Flint	77,323
53	Montgomery, Alabama	75,975

		BLACK CONSUMERS
54	Beaumont–Port Arthur–Orange	73,831
55	West Palm Beach–Boca Raton	71,017
56	Macon	70,270
57	Augusta, Georgia	69,561
58	Columbus, Georgia	68,881
59	Paterson–Clifton–Passaic	68,072
60	Denver–Boulder	68,026
61	San Antonio	67,699
62	Savannah	67,196
63	Toledo	66,476
64	Wilmington, Delaware	66,243
65	Oklahoma City	63,773
66	Trenton	63,758
67	Hartford (Official S.M.S.A.)	63,708
68	Little Rock–North Little Rock	63,079
69	Riverside–San Bern.–Ont.	61,196
70	Akron	59,441
71	Youngstown–Warren	53,441
72	Fayetteville, North Carolina	53,161
73	Sacramento	51,953
74	New Haven–West Haven (Official S.M.S.A.)	51,488
75	Chattanooga	48,079
76	Seattle–Everett	46,498
77	Omaha	46,442
78	Tulsa	46,369
79	Lakeland–Winter Haven, Florida	44,081
80	Pensacola	43,458
81	Petersburg–Colonial Heights–Hopewell	39,894
82	Phoenix	38,561
83	Minneapolis–St. Paul	38,457
84	Long Branch–Asbury Park, New Jersey	38,105
85	Greenville, Mississippi	37,889
86	Austin	36,905
87	Albany, Georgia	36,834
88	Wichita	36,180
89	Bridgeport (Official S.M.S.A.)	35,639
90	Harrisburg, Pennsylvania	33,605
91	Atlantic City	33,552
92	Galveston–Texas City	33,420
93	Lake Charles, Louisiana	33,417
94	Alexandria, Louisiana	33,090
95	Saginaw	32,950
96	Syracuse	32,704
97	Pine Bluff	31,781
98	Huntsville	31,415
99	Las Vegas	31,186
100	Biloxi–Gulfport	30,588

It is believed that the 1970s may have seen the end of the migration to Northern cities, and a trickle of reverse migration has begun. Whether this trickle becomes a stream is, of course, dependent upon the economy of both sections. It is obvious, for example, that the North will lose some black population if it cannot provide work for it.

There is, however, little doubt that large numbers of blacks will continue to remain in the metropolitan areas where 75 percent of them now live. Although blacks have been relocating to other than their traditional sections, black population in the centers of the largest cities has continued to grow in the past two years.

In 1974, according to Standard Rate and Data, the total black population of the top twenty cities was 11,862,300. By 1976 this population had risen to 12,471,037.

In the two-year period, the New York City area increased its black population from 2,174,700 to 2,347,885; Chicago increased from 1,410,400 to 1,472,134; Philadelphia went from 947,200 to 977,351; Los Angeles–Long Beach from 880,000 to 961,535; and, Detroit from 884,000 to 938,316.

Marketing management will have to take black population and its center-city concentration into account for current and future marketing planning. Any shifts in migration patterns will also have to be monitored closely, as will the rapid population growth due to a high black birthrate. The black population continues to remain a younger population—median age of 23.5 years versus 29.6 for whites—as well as a more prolific one—2.44 children per black woman versus 1.80 per white woman. While these comparative birthrates are important to any accurate marketing study, it's the shifts that are news.

In its July 21, 1975, issue, *Sales & Marketing Management* magazine announced: "The black population's massive migration to the industrial centers of the North has about run its course."

Updated county statistics, developed by Market Statistics, the research division of Bill Communications that prepares the Survey of Buying Power data, show that the movement of blacks is taking dramatic new turns in the 1970s. On the one hand, as more blacks move into the middle class, they are making the traditional move to the suburbs. On the other hand, as life becomes unbearable in Northern ghettos, they are returning to the South, where civil rights laws, economic growth, and black political power have made life much different from what it was in prewar days.

You get glimpses of the suburban trek when you note what's happening in the Washington, D.C., and San Francisco–Oakland metro areas. Although the District of Columbia's black population has decreased by almost 20,000 since 1970, suburban Prince Georges County, Maryland, has gained over 10,000. Out West, San Francisco County has almost 6,000 fewer blacks than at the start of the decade, but neighboring Alameda County has gained more than 10,000.

The bustling economies of the South's principal growth cities— Houston, Miami, and Dallas—are inducing many blacks disaffected with life up North to return home. Thus the biggest numerical gains in black population in the current decade have occurred in Harris County, Texas—up 35,400; Dade County, Florida—up 33,000; and Dallas County, Texas—up 15,500. Compared with this are the sharp reductions taking place in Northern manufacturing counties—down 35,300 in Philadelphia, Pennsylvania; down 23,400 in New York, New York; down 21,800 in Kings, New York; down 15,200 in Wayne, Michigan; and down 14,600 in Cuyahoga, Ohio.

The following chart reflects shifts by counties:

Black Population in Dramatic Market Shifts

COUNTY	1974 POP. (THOUS.)	CHANGE 1970–74 (THOUS.)	CHANGE 1969–70 (THOUS.)	BLACK % OF TOTAL POP.	RANK 1974	RANK 1970
Cook, Ill.	1,195.4	+11.9	+322.3	21.6	1	1
Los Angeles, Cal.	776.0	+13.2	+301.3	11.2	2	2
Wayne, Mich.	705.9	−15.2	+191.5	26.8	3	3
Kings, N.Y.	633.2	−21.8	+283.6	24.8	4	4
Philadelphia, Pa.	618.5	−35.3	+124.6	33.0	5	5
Dist. of Columbia	518.1	−19.6	+126.0	72.2	6	6
Baltimore City, Md.	415.4	−4.8	+94.6	47.3	7	7
Harris, Texas	386.1	+35.4	+104.3	20.3	8	10
New York, N.Y.	356.4	−23.4	−17.3	24.4	9	8
Bronx, N.Y.	352.6	−5.1	+193.8	23.9	10	9
Cuyahoga, Ohio	313.8	−14.6	+73.1	18.8	11	11
Essex, N.J.	284.1	+5.0	+98.4	30.3	12	12
Shelby, Tenn.	276.7	+10.5	+38.7	36.7	13	14
Queens, N.Y.	267.8	+9.5	+112.5	13.6	14	15
Orleans, La.	266.4	−.9	+33.8	45.4	15	13
Fulton, Ga.	236.3	−1.1	+44.4	39.3	16	17
Dallas, Texas	236.0	+15.5	+82.6	16.9	17	18
St. Louis City, Mo.	223.5	−30.7	+39.8	39.9	18	16

COUNTY	1974 POP. (THOUS.)	CHANGE 1970–74 (THOUS.)	CHANGE 1969–70 (THOUS.)	BLACK % OF TOTAL POP.	RANK 1974	RANK 1970
Dade, Fla.	223.0	+33.3	+52.4	15.7	19	20
Jefferson, Ala.	210.7	+4.2	−13.1	32.6	20	19
Alameda, Cal.	171.8	+10.5	+49.9	15.3	21	21
Allegheny, Pa.	147.1	+2.6	+10.4	9.4	22	23
Hamilton, Ohio	145.8	+.5	+21.9	15.8	23	22
Marion, Ind.	137.0	+2.5	+34.6	17.0	24	24
Duval, Fla.	124.0	+5.8	+12.5	22.0	25	25
Jackson, Mo.	115.4	+2.5	+28.8	17.4	26	26
Lake, Ind.	114.2	+2.2	+24.9	20.6	27	27
Franklin, Ohio	112.3	+7.9	+24.2	12.9	28	31
Milwaukee, Wis.	109.1	+3.1	+43.0	10.2	29	28
Mobile, Ala.	108.1	+5.7	+1.4	32.8	30	32
Suffolk, Mass.	106.4	+1.1	+41.6	14.5	31	29
Erie, N.Y.	105.2	+6.0	+24.4	9.5	32	33
Prince Georges, Md.	102.6	+10.8	+60.8	14.5	33	36
Jefferson, Ky.	99.7	+4.1	+17.2	14.0	34	35
Richmond City, Va.	98.7	+6.1	+12.8	42.5	35	30
Westchester, N.Y.	92.1	+7.1	+24.6	10.2	36	39
East Baton Rouge, La.	92.1	+10.3	+8.8	30.4	36	44
Mecklenburg, N.C.	91.9	+7.6	+17.6	24.5	38	41
Nashville–Davidson, Tenn.	91.6	+3.7	+11.4	20.1	39	37
Hinds, Miss.	91.2	+7.1	+9.3	39.5	40	42
Broward, Fla.	90.7	+13.3	+22.6	11.3	41	47
San Francisco, Cal.	90.4	−5.7	+17.2	13.6	42	34
Caddo, La.	89.3	+4.9	+2.9	37.3	43	40
Charleston, S.C.	87.4	+9.5	−.6	33.7	44	46
Tarrant, Texas	85.9	+4.9	+22.0	11.8	45	45
Montgomery, Ohio	85.2	+1.5	+21.8	14.0	46	43
Norfolk City, Va.	81.6	−5.7	+8.5	29.0	47	38
Richland, S.C.	79.4	+6.0	+8.6	32.7	48	48
San Diego, Cal.	74.8	+12.0	+22.6	4.8	49	54
Nassau, N.Y.	74.0	+8.6	+26.1	5.2	50	50

SOURCES: Market Statistics Div. of Bill Communications; Census Bureau: *Negro Populations in Selected Counties*, PC(S1)-2. © Sales Management.

CHAPTER 3
The Growing Hispanic Market

THE SECOND LARGEST minority consumer market in
the United States is the Hispanic market, which has been estimated
at $25 billion—and growing. Many of the techniques of segmented
marketing work as effectively with Hispanics as with blacks. Those
who hope to gain a bigger share of the Hispanic market should look
closely at what the statistics reveal about it.

According to the Census, as of March 1974 about 10.8 million
persons of Spanish origin were residing in the United States, including 6.5 million persons of Central American, South American, or
other Spanish origin. (The Community Relations Service, U.S. Department of Justice, estimates Hispanics at 12 million, and swelling
to 20 million with illegal aliens.)

Background on persons of Spanish origin includes such facts as
the following:

- The majority of persons of Spanish origin (6.3 million) live in
  five Southwestern states: Arizona, California, Colorado, New
  Mexico, and Texas.
- The greatest concentration of the Spanish-origin populace is in
  New York State, mainly metropolitan New York.
- Most Spanish-origin persons live in metropolitan areas.
- The Spanish-origin population is a young population, with a
  median age of 20.1 years, compared to 28.5 years for the total
  U.S. population.
- There are significant differences among the subcategories of
  Spanish-surname persons in median age, occupation, income, resi-
  dence, and educational attainment.

These facts should be examined very closely by companies seeking to sell their goods and services to an expanding Hispanic market.

Spanish-surname persons are most likely to reside in metropolitan areas. Approximately 83 percent, or 2.0 million families were living in metropolitan areas in 1974, compared with 68 percent for the general population. Some 1.2 million Spanish-origin families live in central cities. Interestingly, almost all Puerto Rican families—94 percent —and 75 percent of families of Mexican origin live in metropolitan areas.

Census figures show that one of every 8 persons of Spanish origin in 1974 was under five years old, but only about one of every 13 persons in the total population was in that age group. On the other hand, only about one of every 29 Spanish-origin persons was sixty-five years old and over, but one of every 10 persons in the overall U.S. population was sixty-five years old and over.

These figures are particularly significant when it is considered that persons of Cuban origin living in the United States had a higher median age—35.7 years—with only about 5 percent of all Cuban residents under five years old in March 1974 and 11 percent sixty-five years and over.

The size and median age of the Mexican-American and Puerto Rican subcategories, however, contributes to the overall lower (20.1) median age. Persons of Mexican origin, for instance, had a median age of 18.9 years and those of Puerto Rican origin 19.4.

The average Spanish-origin family—with more than four persons per family—is larger than the average family in the United States (which has just over three persons per family). About 5 percent of all families in the United States had seven or more persons per family; the proportion of Spanish-origin families with seven or more persons per family was about double, 11 percent.

Because of the size of the average Hispanic household, Hispanics buy greater quantities of consumer products and services than non-Spanish-speaking families. In New York, for instance, the Spanish home spends 10 percent more than the average non-Spanish household in food stores. In Los Angeles, Spanish-speaking families spend more than 6 percent above the average, and in certain Southwest markets account for more than a 50 percent higher per capita expenditure in food stores than Anglos.

Family size is of course just one of the demographic factors that marketing analysts will want to take into account. The youthfulness of the Hispanic market, its geographic concentration, family income, etc., must also be examined carefully. But what is most strikingly characteristic of the Hispanic market—the fact that it is a foreign culture, speaking a foreign language and observing foreign customs—is not revealed in these statistics.

Marketing specialist and advertising executive Eduardo Caballero, who has consulted with our marketing/communications publication *The Gibson Report,* goes beyond statistics to point out that, "Latins have not been assimilated into the existing Anglo-American population at the rate expected in the early 1960s. To the contrary, they have manifested a life-style which serves to maintain their own special character and culture." Generally, Caballero said, Latins tend to reside in close proximity to one another. Further, nearly 80 percent of Spanish-Americans speak only Spanish in the home, a fact that has given considerable impetus to a variety of Spanish-language news and advertising media.

Quality- and brand-consciousness are particularly noticeable in Spanish consumers' purchasing selections, perhaps in part because the Hispanic consumer perceives himself as a foreigner. One major advertising-agency study pointed out that Latins "have a strong desire for quality, coupled with the insecurity of the newcomer that leads logically to a high level of brand loyalty. . . ."

Comparing Hispanic buying patterns with majority population buying patterns provides evidence that there is no necessary relationship between them. While some of this evidence points up the influence of Spanish traditions and customs, there are also indications that particular marketing strategies can have a significant effect. For example, Pepsi-Cola started its promotion in the New York Latin market before Coca-Cola and continued to outspend Coke about 2 to 1. As a result, Pepsi enjoyed a 52 percent market share in this area, compared to Coke's 33 percent, although shares were almost equal in the majority market.

A similar situation existed with Schaefer beer, which was unknown to Puerto Ricans until they came to New York. Good Spanish-language advertising, promotion, and public relations within the Spanish community gave Schaefer such a position that sales in this market could have represented about 40 percent of their total sales in this marketing area.

A particularly good campaign, out of BBDO's* ethnic marketing department several years ago, was a targeted program on radio,

---

* Batten, Barton, Durstine & Osborn advertising agency.

"Memories of Puerto Rico," which touched a sensitive spot in the community, as most Puerto Ricans always nurture the dream of going back home. Coupled with music from Puerto Rico, which in itself evoked memories, were "bulletin board" notices from communities throughout Puerto Rico.

Another example illustrates what can happen to an advertiser who enjoys a good share of the Spanish-speaking market, but does nothing to maintain his position while competition actively seeks out these potential customers—as Palmolive soap learned.

A study of the Spanish community in New York showed that Palmolive enjoyed a 37.4 percent share of the Hispanic market, while Ivory had 11 percent and Camay 10.2 percent. Palmolive did nothing in Spanish media, while Ivory and Camay both went into Spanish-oriented television.

A similar study five years later showed Palmolive had slipped to a 7.3 percent share of market, while Ivory climbed to 33.2 percent, and Camay to 23.6 percent.

The same earlier study showed that Bayer aspirin had 21.7 percent of the Hispanic market, and Bufferin 9.8 percent. Both subsequently went into Spanish television. In the later study, Bayer had increased its percentage to 42 percent, and Bufferin had climbed to 15.8 percent after only a few months of advertising in Spanish media.

In another situation where two product brands were both advertised in Spanish media, the pulling power of TV was revealed. The earlier study showed Mazola oil had a 61.2 percent share of the Hispanic market, and Wesson oil an 8.4 percent share. Mazola went into Spanish-language radio and newspapers—and a later study showed Mazola maintained its level with a 62.5 percent share. Wesson, however, almost tripled its previous share with 24.3 percent share of market.

Later studies by Wesson in New York showed that by a year later, it had overtaken Mazola, primarily because of its TV participation and increased distribution in New York's *bodegas* (Spanish food stores) from around 50 percent to nearly 99 percent.

Advertisers are becoming increasingly conscious of the need to create targeted material and utilize Spanish-language media.

It is estimated that there are about 250 radio stations and sixty television stations in the United States with part or complete Spanish programming (which often is heard on both sides of the Mexican border). In addition, there are an estimated twenty Spanish-language newspapers and five Spanish-language magazines. Moreover, "network" opportunities exist in this market. Caballero Spanish Media syndicates "Lo Mejor del Cine Espanol" ("The Best of Spanish Movies") to some twenty-five TV stations in the United States. The movies are hosted by actor Ricardo Montalban, and sponsored by Bristol-Myers.

It is estimated further that 95 percent of the Spanish-speaking market in the United States can be reached by radio, and that Hispanics spend 51 percent more time listening to Spanish radio than their Anglo counterparts do to English-language radio.

It appears likely that the Spanish-speaking market will remain a separate entity for some time, with the desire and/or the necessity to retain customs and culture, to communicate in their native language, and to concentrate in metropolitan areas. Anyone wanting a share of the Hispanic market will want to take these factors into account.

CHAPTER 4

The Consumer and Use of Economic Withdrawals

WHEN we had finished talking about God and about Jesus—I'm going to tell you just like it was—we came down out of our pulpits and talked about Tastykake," summarized a minister, one of four hundred in Philadelphia who participated in what was the beginning of the largest "selective patronage" program ever staged in the black community. It later became the model for such programs in major cities throughout the United States.

Boycotts had been staged before, but none with the degree of sophistication that was developed in Philadelphia in the 1960s.

The ministers who organized the Philadelphia Selective Patronage Program chose the term selective patronage, rather than boycott, because it had more positive connotations. "Selective patronage" was a positive act—choosing to do business with those who cooperated in reaching the goals of the group. That guiding philosophy, of taking a positive approach, became the basis for all such programs that followed.

The goals of the Selective Patronage Program were to gain employment and upgrading of blacks, particularly among those companies having significant shares of the black consumer market, and to give consumer support to those companies who demonstrated their concern for blacks.

The success of the Philadelphia technique, and its use in other areas of concentrated black dollars, was striking: as a result, thousands of jobs were opened up to blacks. Consequently, millions of dollars were added to available income in the nonwhite community.

The selective patronage program has drawn attention to the value of the black consumer to a wide range of product and service lines.

It has been used primarily to open up new jobs, which in turn have enriched the communities in which this type of activity has been used.

Selective buying on the part of blacks and other minorities (often with white support) will continue for some time to come as a tool of the minority consumer to achieve recognition and equity. One reason selective buying has been so successful is that management and marketing executives have been unfamiliar with the processes involved. Thus it is apparent that the how and why of selective buying techniques should be examined in depth.

Managements against which campaigns were used tended to feel that (1) demands were unreasonable; (2) the threat of economic withdrawal was a bluff and could not be carried out; and (3) if they simply ignored the situation it would go away.

These assumptions proved to be misconceptions on the part of management executives. Historically, selective buying campaigns have been carried out through the most effectively organized structure in the black community—the church. The combination of church membership, the church's influence on non–church members, and the resulting word of mouth has a swift, extended reach in these communities; it is unlikely, therefore, that the problem will simply go away.

Management must educate itself to the realities of selective buying because, both as a technique and as a threat, it has been successful. When management has either failed to react to it at all or has overreacted, the results have proved costly to their companies, not only in direct sales volume, but in embarrassment and—even worse—tarnished reputations, which have produced long-term business slumps for the affected companies in areas with heavy black consumer traffic. Since both the threat and the reality of these "don't buy" campaigns continue, management executives across the board must be prepared to address themselves to these confrontations.

In order to get the best possible focus on the technique of economic withdrawal, it is necessary to give some background as to why it is effective and how it got started.

As far back as the 1930s, there were "buy black" or "don't buy where you can't work" campaigns, and straight boycotts against companies whose attitudes and practices toward nonwhites were objectionable. These campaigns did bring about some change, but for the most part they were not as effective as later economic withdrawals, usually because there was not the right combination of factors present.

Several ingredients were missing in the 1930s, including: (1) an understanding of business operations on the part of black leadership, (2) the concentration of population that allows the underground communications network to flourish in a limited area, and (3) the necessary financial strength and buying power to bring about an effective withdrawal.

Today, high concentrations of nonwhites in urban areas combined with the billions of dollars they spend are enough to bring powerful pressure on the business community. All of these factors were present in Philadelphia in the early 1960s.

The story of the Philadelphia Selective Patronage Program was told in detail for the first time at an all-day seminar sponsored by our firm, on behalf of *The Gibson Report*, our marketing/communications publication on minority markets. The Reverend Leon H. Sullivan, one of the "Philadelphia 400" ministers, told management and marketing executives how selective patronage works.

Reverend Sullivan pointed out the conditions existing in Philadelphia three years previously. The fact that no blacks were driving soft-drink trucks. That black white-collar workers were missing from bank-teller windows, and in the crowds of employees leaving insurance companies.

In addition to the soft-drink trucks, blacks were not driving ice cream trucks, newspaper delivery trucks, and major oil-company trucks as driver-salesmen.

Philadelphia, it was determined, was no more than an example of what existed in every large urban city in the North, South, East, and West. The realization was that in Philadelphia, where blacks comprised 27 percent of the total city population, less than one percent of all employees in private industry were black, or other persons of color.

"You could walk Walnut Street and Chestnut Street in Philadelphia and you would hardly see a colored girl walk out of an office building with a job of any sensitive nature in the entire City of Philadelphia," Reverend Sullivan said. "Just a handful hired as tokens of some symbol, an effort of some company to appease its conscience." (A "sensitive" job is one that has high visibility in the community or company.)

It was determined that "economic slavery" existed, and the traditional civil-rights groups had their hands tied—that a new technique had to be found to erase the existing conditions.

Meeting informally, the ministers in Philadelphia determined that each Sunday morning they spoke, collectively, to more than 250,000 people. At their meeting they decided to launch a "demonstration of the emancipation, economically, of persons of color in a major community in America." They were amazed that of 468 ministers contacted, all 468 agreed to participate in the program.

The ministers based their movement on a simple statement: "We cannot in good moral conscience remain silent while members of our congregation patronize companies that discriminate in the employment of our people." This concept remained the total philosophy behind selective patronage.

The program's effectiveness depended upon the ministers' ability to influence the majority of their congregation membership to stop buying a given product and to pass the word on to non-churchgoers as well.

The developers of the Philadelphia Selective Patronage Program also realized that each minister had to appear to his own congregation as a leader, not a follower taking orders from someone else. It was agreed that there would be no minister singled out for leadership in the program. It was further decided that there would be no formal organization, no bylaws, no officers, no treasury, no dues, and no staff. (This later was to prove frustrating to legal counsel for the opposition, as it prevented them from initiating suits for restraint of trade, unfair practices, and so forth, because technically and legally the group did not exist.)

In most selective buying programs, such as this one and, later, "Operation Breadbasket" in Chicago, priorities committees are formed to determine in what order industries, and then companies within an industry, should be approached. Usually the committee is rotated. No minister calls on more than one company, and the group calling on Company A would not call on Company B.

This technique, of course, has had advantages. It has averted factionalism because there is nothing for anyone to take over, which could lead to a division within the group. It has also enlarged the white community's idea of leadership available in the black community.

The church congregations were quick to accept this idea of selective patronage. There were no meetings to attend, no carrying of protest signs, and no fear of reprisals for switching from product A to product B. As one minister said, "The easiest thing in the world is to switch brands in the comfort of a supermarket in the black community, and to tell anyone why you are doing it." A certain pride exists with minorities participating in economic withdrawal, since the reasoning for the campaign is considered just.

In the first three years of the Philadelphia Selective Patronage Program, thirty companies became targets for withdrawal campaigns.

Few companies, however, drew as much unfavorable publicity as did the Tasty Baking Company of Philadelphia, the first company approached.

It was Tasty Baking Company's refusal to meet the demands of the Selective Patronage Program that gave the campaign all the impetus it needed, and the opportunity to demonstrate what could be accomplished by the economic-withdrawal techniques developed by the ministers.

Tasty Baking Company was selected by the ministers because in their opinion it "had a flagrant record of discrimination and non-employment of blacks in sensitive positions. Strangely enough, this company employed more than 400 blacks, but limited them to the same job categories that have been assigned to blacks for the past fifty years." The ministers considered "sensitive positions" to be driver-salesmen, office workers, and other semiskilled and skilled jobs.

The Selective Patronage Program visitation committee assigned to Tasty Baking called on the president of the company, according to a policy of approaching only top management of any company.

According to Reverend Sullivan, the position of the group was, "We want to know from the company its own sense of intention. We want from the company what it does on its own. Because we believe it would be in error to rupture an economic situation of a single industry or company simply because of hearsay. In spite of the fact that often enough we knew what we heard was true. We wanted it from management itself."

Tasty Baking Company executives told the ministers what the company was doing concerning minority employment, and the ministers returned to report to the priority group concerned with Tasty Baking.

A *priority group* in a selective buying campaign is made up of involved leaders of various denominations. These people determine for the visitation committees what the minimum requests will be in each case. The priority group also determines whether or not it is necessary at all for a selective patronage campaign to be launched against a given company.

The ministers did not ask Tasty Baking for quotas for employees, but they did ask for a minimum number of blacks to be employed, and requested that equal employment opportunity be practiced, thereafter, particularly in hiring for so-called sensitive positions.

The visitation committee asked Tasty Baking for seven positions, all of them new for blacks. They included two driver-salesmen, two clerical workers, and three or four women in the icing department.

The ministers waited to learn if their demands would be met. They gave Tasty Baking two weeks in which to reply.

After the two weeks passed and the minimum request had not been met, the ministers—all 468 of them—returned to their pulpits and "talked about Tastykake." They urged their congregations to stop buying Tasty Baking Company products. In a week's time, Tastykakes began piling up on the counters in retail outlets. Unfavorable publicity began to appear in black-oriented newspapers, and with the support of word of mouth, spread throughout the community. Handbills advising against purchasing Tastykakes and pies were distributed.

The experience was a totally new one in the Philadelphia black community. The word was spread quickly, within almost a matter of hours, by church members. When a publication distributed solely in bars came out two days after the church announcement, it told of the church program, and called for full-scale support of the campaign against Tasty Baking. It helped to make the campaign effective.

During the seven-week campaign that followed, Tasty Baking Company ran two full-page advertisements in the *Philadelphia Tribune*, the city's leading black publication. The ads stated that there had been a misunderstanding, and that there was "integration of all of the facilities" (lunchrooms, washrooms, etc.), that blacks were already employed in some categories, and were considered along with other employees for advancement.

The ads had little effect, because by this time support was overwhelming among all levels of the black community for the withdrawal campaign. It was demonstrating, perhaps for the first time, what could happen when purchasing power was used collectively.

Tasty Baking Company's sales dropped off as the campaign continued. According to estimates, Tasty Baking lost 40 percent of its sales during the seven-week period it was under a selective patronage program.

At the end of that period, Tasty Baking Company capitulated and hired from the community two driver-salesmen, two clerical workers, and six women as icers, thus ending the campaign against the company.

Now a standard technique for adding to the community's income in cities across the United States, for giving evidence of the black consumer's value to companies, and a practice that is likely to continue, selective patronage began with Tasty Baking Company's refusal to hire or promote blacks into *seven new jobs*.

The Philadelphia program proved that: (1) concentrated purchasing power could prove effective when withdrawn from a given company; (2) the church continues to be the most organized network for communication in the black community; and (3) the use of the economic-withdrawal technique could change companies' attitudes and practices toward minorities.

White support can also be counted on, and often generated, in many selective buying campaigns. A number of religious organizations have gone on record stating they will not buy from firms practicing discrimination in their hiring and promotional practices. White ministers have exerted their influence in white and interracial congregations to join the practice of selective buying.

Selective patronage campaigns and the threat of boycotts are realities with which companies will have to live. They are here to stay—until equal employment opportunity, sincere corporate support, and equitable consumer practices are more than superficial goals. While consumer-product companies are most readily subject to the withdrawal of economic support, other pressures can be applied to businesses that do not sell directly to the consumer.

Here are some steps companies might take to effect a positive result from selective buying approaches:

(1) Management should make sure it is advised immediately of the threat of a boycott or selective buying campaign. Usually, the president (or head of a field unit) is contacted by letter or telephone and an appointment is requested. The request should be granted. If possible, at the initial meeting the president (or senior executive) should attend and inform the representatives of the group to which individuals he is assigning responsibility in the matter.

(2) The public relations officer of a corporation should review and examine avenues through which the company's story can be truthfully told to the group's representatives. Silence by companies often is an assumed sign of guilt, and rumors, true or false, are allowed to flourish.

(3) The personnel department (and urban affairs personnel), certainly, has a major stake in negotiations and should review employment policies and practices, affirmative action plans, goals and

timetables, and results, and keep management briefed on opportunities for employment and upgrading.

(4) Marketing executives should be ready to advise retailers of the company position and any action it plans to take. Sales losses become greater when retailers cooperate with selective buying programs.

(5) If a "don't buy" campaign is launched, management should seek expert counsel to determine how it should begin rebuilding its tarnished image and sales position. The presence of nonwhite counsel may create better understanding and a better image, thus lessening the chances of a selective buying campaign.

Effective corporate measures can forestall loss of sales or reputation. Usually it has taken years of goodwill to build a reputation among nonwhites—a reputation that can be lost overnight. Obviously, those firms that have not made efforts to understand nonwhite consumers and the economic sanctions available to them, are at great disadvantage when threatened with selective buying programs.

CHAPTER 5
The Need to Create a Black Consumer Reaction

STUDIES and selected surveys of buying repeatedly reveal that nonwhite consumers do react differently in the marketplace. *Black consumer reaction,* or the way blacks *qua* blacks react to a given set of circumstances, can have a significant influence on black activity in the marketplace. If this important factor is capitalized on to positive effect, and is woven as a thread throughout a marketing campaign, the campaign stands an excellent chance of succeeding. If it is not capitalized on, a market effort could be a complete waste.

The black consumer reaction—or "BCR" response—that a company, its products, or its services produces in the black community can determine the success of a product. The BCR factor can be used effectively in advertising, public relations, sales promotion, and in personal selling; and it can be either positive or negative—can influence a consumer to buy, or not to buy.

How to use the BCR factor effectively gets prime consideration whenever we take on a new client, and as public affairs counsel, we keep this in mind while reviewing all programs. It is an old technique, but not as widely used as it should be. Though discussed a good deal, it has suffered in practice.

As far back as 1956, the *Public Opinion Index for Industry,* published by the Opinion Research Corporation, pointed up the need to consider the BCR factor. A study in that volume, "The Controversy Over Equal Rights for Negroes," pointed out that blacks, in their buying attitudes, are considerably more sensitive than others to a company's racial practices. When blacks felt that a company was discriminatory in its practices, their interest in that company's product lessened, the *Index* pointed out.

28

A follow-up study, "The Growing Power of the Negro Market," was published in the November 1961 *Public Opinion Index*. This study revealed that five years later, the same attitude prevailed—"Negroes nationwide say they are inclined to buy from companies that are known for their fairness toward Negroes, and to withhold patronage from those said to be discriminatory."

In a study conducted by the Center for Research in Marketing, released in 1962, it was revealed that a growing number of blacks were boycotting specific products and stores because of what *they* believed to be discriminatory practices. In fact, it is possible for many companies to suffer from a lack of communication that produces a *belief* that they are discriminatory and unfair in their race relations practices, even if that is not in fact true.

A 1976 study by the Foote, Cone & Belding advertising agency, as well as studies by some other agencies, concluded that while the black consumer market is similar to the white in many ways, it is different in many others. What often sets it apart is "black pride and identity."

What contributes to the kind of communication gap that can be harmful to a company's interests in the black consumer market? The lack of black-oriented programs, the absence of blacks in sensitive positions with a company, and the lack of nonwhites in print and television commercials, the white-dominated media—all these are important contributing factors. They say to the black consumer that since a company evidences no interest in him as a consumer, it must be hiding its race-relations practices. The black consumer then voices his response in the marketplace.

The black consumer reaction factor—what blacks think of a company, its policies, and its products vis-à-vis black—becomes an important part of a company's public relations programming, and a necessary step in influencing and winning consumers.

Too often, we have found that the BCR factor is only taken into consideration in one area—in public relations alone; in advertising alone; or in sales alone. To be truly effective, BCR thinking must be used and tested from the planning of a campaign to its hoped-for successful conclusion throughout all marketing and sales areas.

To spur the nonwhite into a positive buying action, as studies and case histories have indicated *can* be achieved, two factors must be present: (1) consumer familiarity with brand names, and, (2) more important, belief and conviction in the company's message. Yet without a favorable BCR, an apparently successful campaign is still not doing all it could. When a company disregards the favorable-image factor in advertising and in public relations, and strives to achieve it only through the use of black sales personnel, it is like three people pulling a loaded wagon, but with two letting the third do the work; if all three worked together, the potential for a successful pull would be increased.

To effectively sell the black consumer he must be reached and motivated—whether directly through media or indirectly through word-of-mouth—but he must get the message that blacks are wanted.

Advertising in white-oriented media does not contribute to a company's credibility with blacks; only when an advertising message is projected in black media does it convince the black consumer that he or she is wanted and included.

Prentice-Hall's *Executive Report* summed it up on October 20, 1962: "To be judged are your advertising campaigns, promotional drives, community contributions and hiring policies." All of these can contribute to the achievement of a favorable BCR for the company that is sincere in wanting to increase or protect its share of the black consumer market.

From all indications, the black population's growing awareness of its buying power is making for more selective customers. In both the short and the long terms, black consumer reaction to a given company, product, or service will become even more meaningful; thus, when properly used, a more favorable image can mean increased sales for a company and strong consumer awareness of its products.

At D. Parke Gibson International (DPGI), we have used the technique of black-oriented programming to produce favorable BCR for most of the clients and projects in which we have been involved.

A case in point was our association with Ex-Lax, Inc., in the early 1960s. William Safire, at that time president of Safire Public Relations, called us in to discuss how we might work with his firm for Ex-Lax in the black community. Safire's firm provided public relations counsel and services to the client in the majority market.

In preparing our suggestions for areas of opportunity for Ex-Lax, we first took a look at the community in terms of the company's interests, as is DPGI policy.

Studies showed that blacks, who make up 11 percent of the nation's population, represented 25 percent of the market for laxatives, and in Ex-Lax's sales a significant share of the market.

Our work for Ex-Lax was less to improve the client's already healthy share of market than to return to the community some of the benefits of the success the company enjoyed. This in turn would provide the company with a sound platform for its public relations activity.

After initial meetings with Bill Safire and Len Safire of the public relations firm, Roy M. Goodman, president of Ex-Lax, and Robert A. M. Petersen, Ex-Lax vice-president for marketing, some directions became clear.

We wanted to find a worthwhile activity in the black community for the client to engage in. We determined that this activity should both benefit the black community and enhance Ex-Lax's black consumer reaction rating. Our job was to find a need in the community that Ex-Lax could fill. And we wanted that problem to be in some way related to the business of the client. With all these factors in mind, we decided that Ex-Lax would underwrite a nurse-recruitment program among minority students.

Our research had indicated that there was a critical shortage of nurses in the minority community. Although the shortage was also national, it was more acute among blacks. Nationwide, less than 3 percent of doctors and 5 percent of nurses are black.

Further research in the Ex-Lax project indicated that while there were few black nurses, there were still fewer (only 3 percent) in training. At the time all recruiting materials used to attract young women and men to the profession were white-oriented.

It was decided to enlist the cooperation of New York's Harlem Hospital School of Nursing to help develop a brochure for recruiting purposes that would be black-oriented.

The School of Nursing was having its own problems in recruiting and welcomed the opportunity to cooperate with and have the support of a business firm. The school provided facilities, personnel (including students) and time for the development of a brochure. An attractive black student nurse was "advanced" through the training program to graduate for purposes of the brochure.

The nurse was photographed for the cover with the headline: "How YOU Can Become a NURSE." To the thousands of black young women who would eventually see this brochure, it would be obvious whom "YOU" referred to.

The brochure described the advantages of a nursing career, the qualifications of a student nurse, costs, scholarships available, and other pertinent information.

On the back page, which also included photographs of several white nurses, the bottom half of the page was given over to a letter from Roy Goodman, addressed to prospective nurses. On reproduced Ex-Lax stationery, he outlined the company's concern with the nurse shortage. There was no commercialism in the letter, and coincidentally the name of the company is the name of the product as well. No repercussions developed.

The National Urban League had done a good deal of research into health and welfare matters and cooperated by distributing the brochures through their affiliates throughout the United States as a tie-in with the League's educational program.

The Ex-Lax company also underwrote campus seminars at five predominantly black colleges, under the League's program, and brochures and speakers were furnished for these programs.

Some 13,000 copies of the brochure were distributed to nonwhite high school students and graduates through the active program of Ex-Lax. News releases were distributed to black media nationally, and each ended with a mention that additional copies of the brochure were available by writing to the company's headquarters in Brooklyn, New York. Numerous requests for additional copies were received, which were promptly mailed from Ex-Lax.

At the time of the program effort, Ex-Lax was one of the largest advertisers on black-oriented radio. Thus, it was decided to seek public service assistance for the recruitment effort. The student nurse who was our model and an attractive registered nurse made one-minute commercials, through the cooperation of WWRL Radio in New York. The station itself aired the public service announcements for two months, pointing up the nurse shortage and encouraging young people to enter the field. Copies of the public service announcements were sent to fifty-eight other radio stations in twenty states and received excellent air play.

Here was a marketing campaign, doubly effective with the targeted public service program, impacting on black consumers with a commercial message and the fulfillment of a community need.

The favorable black consumer reaction we had planned for initially was beginning to make itself felt. Contact had been established with organizations in nursing, including the magazine *Nursing Outlook*, which later ran a two-page spread on the Ex-Lax program.

With the cooperation and approval of the National League for Nursing, a one-hour seminar for black high school women and men was set up at Harlem Hospital. It served as a pilot program to be repeated in other major cities.

An estimated two hundred students attended the seminar and

asked questions of a panel of distinguished social workers, nursing educators, and doctors. The panel discussed the need for nurses, their role in the hospital and the community, and the personal satisfaction to be gained from the nursing profession.

Following the question-and-answer period, the young people were taken in groups on a tour of the hospital, and given refreshments.

Thirty-two black-oriented newspapers carried news on the seminar, and gave exposure to Ex-Lax's interest in helping to meet the shortages of nurses.

WWRL Radio taped the seminar, and it was edited down to one half hour. A transcription was distributed to all of the radio stations that had been using the public service announcements. Each of the stations was to play the seminar transcript at least once, and some more than once.

Meanwhile, the brochure was being used at career day conferences, at schools with predominantly black enrollment, and in other ways to reach young women, and men.

A second seminar was conducted at Howard University in Washington, D.C., with the cooperation of a black women's organization, the District of Columbia League for Nursing, and Freedmen's Hospital. This seminar attracted over two hundred high school students, as well as counselors, who later reported it as one of the few times they had known a company to perform a public service for black high school youngsters. Similar seminars were held in other cities, as part of this approach for the client.

From the program was to come the first "integrated" recruitment efforts. Ex-Lax designed (and contributed ten thousand copies of) a poster headlined: BE A NURSE—AND WALK WITH PRIDE, showing white and black women nurses, and a white male nurse walking down a hospital corridor. The credit line, "Contributed to Nursing Careers, National League for Nursing, as a Public Service by Ex-Lax, Inc." was the only identification with the company.

The posters appeared in high school classrooms across the United States, were featured in *Nursing Outlook*, and were distributed to professional and black-oriented media.

More than five thousand handwritten requests for the recruiting booklet were received from students in urban and rural areas. These were followed up by nursing school officials, and many of the inquirers took pre-nursing school examinations.

An additional sixteen thousand copies of the booklet were sent, at the request of groups involved, to nursing schools, high schools, community centers, and job-training centers.

The Ex-Lax campaign *recognized* a need in the community, *identified* with the community, was particularly sympathetic to community needs, and *invited* community participation.

Because of its handling of issues important to the community to which it was trying to appeal, Ex-Lax established itself as credible and concerned, thereby producing a favorable black consumer reaction and protecting a significant share of its market.

PART II

Planning for
the Black Consumer
Market

CHAPTER 6
Where the Business Is

WHILE the overall expenditure pattern by black families continues to be typical of that generally found among low-income groups, there is evidence of emerging middle-class spending habits. The freedom to move about, the access to housing and to public and private facilities, the new opportunities in private and public employment, the ability to express opinions and participate in the decision-making process, the power of education, and the desire for the material goods that represent well-being and status for white Americans are values increasingly reflected in black spending patterns.

In the foregoing chapters, the rationale and efficacy of the black consumer market has been described; other theory and practice will be developed in subsequent sections. All of this material is presented in the context of developing and sustaining a marketing effort, and identifying business opportunities becomes an important consideration. Business with minority consumers can be found in two areas: the existing franchise among black consumers, and growth areas of black expenditures.

A company that already has a significant franchise in the market presents an opportunity to maintain and build upon an established market. On the other hand, emerging areas of growth in black consumer expenditures offer business an opportunity to consider these consumers in current and projected marketing programs. Obviously, the company that is aware of current expenditures by blacks for its products or services, and the company that develops vigorous marketing programs to attract new consumers, will gain competitive advantage.

Demographic profiles of blacks, particularly families, should be

37

examined and understood from a marketing perspective. For example, white-collar employment among blacks and other minorities is growing at a faster rate than that of whites. Between 1963 and 1973, the proportion of men of black and other minority races employed in white-collar jobs grew from 15 to 23 percent, while similar employment for whites remained static at 40 percent.

Black families continue to be larger, an average of 3.90 persons compared to 3.32 for whites. This may have important implications for marketers of youth-oriented products who see a general decline in consumer demand.

College enrollment among blacks has doubled since 1970, according to the U.S. Census Bureau. Only 370,000 blacks attended college in 1966, compared to 522,000 in 1970 and 1,100,000 in 1976. Better education will mean a better informed consumer, whose tastes closely approximate that of the majority market.

Housing is another factor contributing to black consumer demand for a variety of products and services. The home-ownership rate for black households increased from 38 percent, or 1,974,000 units, to 43 percent or 3,024,000 units between 1960 and 1973. The biggest increase occurred outside metropolitan areas. However, blacks continue to predominate in metropolitan areas, and as pointed out previously, this factor has significant impact on purchasing patterns.

The proximity of housing to downtown shopping areas makes blacks urban customers. The response of central city businesses to the concentration of blacks in the cities has been mixed. Many have either adjusted their merchandise to meet the tastes and preferences of customers, or moved their businesses out of downtown areas to suburban shopping centers and malls.

Another factor affecting black expenditure patterns has been the growth of minority business. Blacks owned 194,986 businesses in 1972, according to the Census Bureau. Receipts of these firms amounted to $7.2 billion. Although still far from being a major force in American business, the trend toward entrepreneurship is expected to continue, spurred by federal assistance programs and the need for local community services.

Estimates of total black consumer spending vary according to the individual or agency doing the estimating. A variety of projective techniques that have been used by economists have resulted in 1976 estimates that run as high as $80 billion. The Department of Commerce computed minority expenditures at $64.7 billion in 1973, the latest government estimate available.

Minority share-of-market estimates and personal consumption expenditures were developed by the U.S. Department of Labor for 1973 based upon detailed data collected in 1966. Since blacks constitute more than 90 percent of the minority population in the U.S., the data can be described as generally reflecting black spending habits.

An examination of historical spending patterns of minorities shows that the proportion of minority spending on food, alcohol, tobacco, clothing, and personal care has been declining. On the other hand, expenditures for housing, medical care, personal business, transportation, recreation, and education have been increasing—which means that black spending patterns are coming to resemble those of the white population in many areas.

The higher share of the minority dollar going to some of these categories reflects the lifting of discriminatory barriers. It also reflects increased income, with an increased ability to buy, and higher educational attainment, which makes the minority consumer more aware of differences among competitive products and more demanding of higher quality and more variety in merchandise and services.

The proportion of personal consumption monies spent for food by minorities dropped from 28.3 percent to 25.8 percent between 1966 and 1973, the largest decline in all categories listed. But nonwhite families continue to spend a larger portion of their money for food than do white families, who spend only 22.4 percent in this category.

Medical care expenses rose from 5.3 percent to 6.2 percent of minority personal consumption expenditures over a seven-year period. Blacks spent less than whites (8.2 percent) in this area. A lack of access to medical care or a conscious choice of spending on other categories may account for this difference.

Low-share areas have great potential market-growth possibilities because of their low market saturation. In the next decade, there is a strong growth potential among minority markets, as minority income rises and discretionary-income spending patterns emerge.

The impact of minority spending on the sale of specific goods and services and market saturation can be determined by an industry-by-industry share-of-market analysis.

Detailed information on minority spending and consumption patterns is provided in the Appendix. Table Five, in particular, details dollar expenditures, percentage of consumption expenditures, and percentage of minority share of market.

Obviously, black consumers constitute a heavy user category for a number of products. An interesting study by the Leo Burnett Company, Chicago, selects 33 examples that show black women buy more convenience foods and home cleaning products than do whites. The table below represents a comparative index of black to white purchases for a small selection of consumer products. One hundred is the median figure; figures above 100 indicate heavy consumption, while figures below 100 indicate lighter consumption.

Index of Purchase

	WHITE WOMEN	BLACK WOMEN
HOME CLEANING PRODUCTS		
Disinfectant cleaner	98	123
Aerosol rug shampoo	93	175
Oven cleaner	94	160
Air freshener	93	180
Insecticide	93	176
Paper towels	98	129
Large plastic garbage bags	94	168
PERSONAL CLEANLINESS PRODUCTS		
Skin-care lotion	98	116
Deodorant/antiperspirant	100	105
Deodorant soap	99	113
Ladies' disposable blades	98	111
Facial tissues	99	121
Toilet tissues	99	118
Paper napkins	98	134
Beauty soap	97	137
Mouthwash	97	135
CONVENIENCE FOODS		
Prepared gravy	98	129
Canned stew	97	163
Canned tuna	99	114
Cheese sauce	98	128
Spaghetti sauce	100	103
Chili sauce	98	119
Refrigerated store-bought cookies	97	166
Ready-to-eat store-bought cookies	97	142
Refrigerated biscuit dough	96	163
Refrigerated turnovers	95	144
Refrigerated dinner-roll dough	97	167
Refrigerated Danish	95	142
Pancake/waffle mix	95	151
Frozen French toast	92	164
Weiner wrap (weiner in dough)	97	169
Layer-cake mix	99	120
Ready-to-serve canned frosting	92	210

When information like this is available, it can help companies develop more efficient, accurately targeted marketing programs.

Procter & Gamble's Tide detergent campaign is one of many examples of how an effective minority marketing and media strategy can be developed.

Procter & Gamble and its advertising agency, Compton Advertising, Inc., learned that white consumers used Tide primarily as a laundry detergent, and that black consumers used Tide as an all-purpose detergent.

It was decided that a new strategy would be developed for the black consumer, and the white strategy would remain the same.

While whites looked at commercials for Tide on television or in white-oriented print media, the message referred only to Tide as a laundry detergent.

At the same time, nonwhites were made aware, through media keyed to their interests, that Tide was an all-purpose detergent and could be used for dishes, in the bath, or for washing fine fabrics, *as well as* the family laundry. The approach paid off in increased Tide shares of the black consumer market. A subsequent study of the Tide campaign showed:

On a national basis, 86.4 percent of the black households used soap—liquid or powder—for dishes. Of these users, 22.4 percent of black households used Tide for dishes, compared to 3.4 percent of white households. There was also a strong relationship between the size of the black population and this particular consumption pattern.

In those markets where blacks were 10 percent of the population, 42.3 percent using Tide for dishes were black, and 57.7 percent were white.

In markets where nonwhites were 30 percent, 62.7 percent of the households using Tide for dishes were nonwhite, and 37.8 percent were white.

In markets where blacks were 40 percent of the population, 73.8 percent of the households using it were black, and only 26.2 percent were white households.

This clearly indicates that knowing where the business exists is the basis for developing a marketing strategy and a media mix that can increase a product's share of market among black consumers, and possibly result in expanded uses for products.

Johnson & Johnson with its Baby Oil has certainly discovered this; its product is supported in black magazines as a multipurpose product used by the entire family.

All estimates place the nonwhite consumer market in a continuing growth pattern, and it will be important for management and marketing executives to be alert to new opportunities. For those who have significant shares of the black consumer market, it will mean protecting those shares.

According to a 1975 *Progressive Grocer* article on black shoppers, blacks are traditionally said to have an above-average loyalty to national brands. A special *Advertising Age* issue in 1974 on blacks points out that although strong brand loyalty and the status appeal of the number-one brand is expected to continue, there will be shifts in product and brand preference within certain consumer-goods categories.

With a growing black middle class and the evolution of new black perceptions and values, changes may take place in brand preferences for cosmetics, liquor, automotive products, tobacco, and appliances. Blacks are becoming more venturesome and independent, with less interest in impressing whites and a greater inclination to express themselves among their peers.

The business exists, and targeting marketing programs to nonwhite consumers will result in bigger shares of the black dollar.

CHAPTER 7
How to Plan a Minority-Market Campaign

ARKETING MANAGEMENT will want to focus on the nonwhite consumer for one or more of the following reasons: (1) to increase its share of the market for its products or services; (2) to increase its profit; (3) to increase its volume; (4) to protect an already existing share of market.

In planning a marketing approach, a company must take into consideration that the black consumer market is a constantly evolving market; that market conditions are changing; and that there is usually competitive activity taking place. Having taken these factors into account, a company can develop a sound plan to sell this market effectively. It can execute this plan, and evaluate it.

Some years ago, we developed what we called the *Negro Market Checklist*, which we believed could insure a successful program in developing the black consumer market. We have used the checklist in planning nonwhite marketing campaigns, and also as an aid for determining the effectiveness of an existing program.

Through the years we've been providing counsel and services, the checklist has stood the test of time and, with revisions for updating and a new name, *Marketing and Merchandising Guidelines for Inner-City Market Development*, it still serves as an important guide. I have reproduced it here, and added some comments:

(1) *Determine the potential market (size, income differentials) among minority consumers for the product or service.*

(2) *Know what makes the market identifiable and what sets it apart.* If marketing management knows this, it can all the more effectively tailor its campaigns to the markets it is trying to sell.

(3) *Determine if the current total marketing program is creating*

43

a favorable climate within the black and Hispanic communities. Some campaigns could be effective in the minority market, and others with some creative development could become so.

(4) *Determine how well informed the entire marketing team is on minority consumer markets.* Too often, both the company and its account group at the public relations agency have not been as fully informed on the market as they could be. More briefings are needed and fuller exploration of the market.

(5) *Understand the needs and desires of the minority consumer as stated in authoritative studies; do not accept stereotype or hearsay opinions.* Much more research exists today than ever before, and personal experiences and prejudices should not enter into what could be important opportunities.

(6) *Know what competition is doing in this market.* One of the best methods of getting people interested in the black and Hispanic markets has been to point out what competition is doing.

(7) *Know what competing brands of services are now being developed for this market.* Some companies have created new products especially for this market, and have determined other existing needs. This factor could be most important as we move into the 1980s.

(8) *Become familiar with competition's advertising, merchandising, and public relations.* Black-oriented media should be reviewed periodically to determine what products or services compete with your own, or are being developed, and how these are being promoted. Point-of-sale materials and product publicity should be compared.

(9) *Determine how much should be spent to develop minority markets effectively.* Underspending is often a failing in this market. Few companies are spending commensurate with potential. Remember, token efforts will produce token results.

(10) *Determine media strategy for the minority markets.* The media mix is highly important, and white-oriented media cannot be as effective. Know how to use minority media to support overall marketing mission.

(11) *Employ specialized advertising, marketing, and public relations counsel to offer guidance and assistance in program development.* If the minority marketplace is unfamiliar, get some counsel. Paying for some advice up front is much less costly than making a significant investment and receiving an unsatisfactory return on that investment.

(12) *Give specialized advertising and promotional support to*

distributors and dealers where it will effectively support the campaign. Time and again, taking the local retailer into consideration haś proven itself in making minority consumer campaigns successful. Black and Hispanic point-of-sale material usually gets a higher percentage of use than comparable material in white retail outlets.

(13) *Conduct research adequately, giving it proper analysis and interpretation against market potential and objectives.* Not enough research money is being spent in the minority consumer markets, and much of what exists is not given proper analysis and interpretation when considering market development. This is an extremely important factor in today's marketing.

(14) *Know the structure of the black and Hispanic communities —leadership influence, merchandising opportunities, and cooperation available.* The reasons why there are separate structures are important to know, and how the leadership groups impact on consumer understanding and purchasing is also significant in total communications. Reprints of relevant articles, advertisements, and so forth can be merchandised to this leadership.

(15) *Establish corporate representation at minority conventions, and share experiences with other executives.* Visibility at these gatherings and participation in them could be invaluable in building good relations, and in getting firsthand experience with organizations. It is important, too, that these exeeriences be shared with other executives.

(16) *Determine if current programs and new-product development programs can be adapted for use in the black consumer market.* For some companies, the extension of ongoing efforts to include this market can be extremely beneficial. Products can be developed for this market and, in some cases, expanded outward.

(17) *Determine what community-service programs your company could become involved in.* There are needs in the minority community that companies can help meet, which will result in goodwill and marketing dividends. These opportunities for involvement exist almost nationwide.

(18) *Know physiological as well as psychological needs among minority consumers.* Personal-care needs, for example, are more easily understood than those associated with "black identity." Time needs to be spent studying the latter in campaign development.

(19) *Determine minority-vendor involvement, and its relationship to total marketing strategy.* In recent years, the inclusion of

minority vendors in corporate marketing programs, and those of corporate social responsibility nature, have grown. Determine how they can fit into your marketing activities. Available resources may be going to waste through ineffective use.

(20) *Determine if minority groups are included in public speaking programs, film presentations, and so forth.* Few companies use this technique among black-interest organizations. Consumer protection, consumer education, product development, support on particular issues make this technique one to be considered for development.

One of the questions we have frequently been asked is whether it is important to place blacks and other minorities in sales and marketing positions. We have, almost without exception, recommended that blacks and Hispanics be employed in advertising, sales, marketing, and public relations positions. On more than one occasion, we have also indicated that executives who happen to be black or Hispanic might function well heading up programs targeted to minority consumers. But I have long supported the idea that minorities should be employed in a wide range of jobs, and not just those keyed to a company or an agency's minority market efforts.

Title VII of the Civil Rights Act of 1964 prohibits the denial of job opportunity with regard to race, sex, or national origin. It has caused some confusion in the matter of special markets, in that many minorities do not want to work in such areas. Nonetheless the function must go on, and some of the best minority-oriented campaigns have been conceived by executives and creative people who happen to be white. Yet for those who want to work in this market area, minorities are more likely to understand the problems; they can move about more easily in the market; they can easily spot and correct mistakes; and they can help establish the necessary conviction and believability in programming to the minority markets.

We have developed job descriptions for clients interested in creating that position frequently known as special markets manager. Though companies use a variety of titles today, including assistant to the vice-president, manager of market development, inner-city marketing manager, etc., the preferred title seems to be director or manager of special markets. Whatever it's called, the work is the same—specially tailored marketing activity directed at blacks and Hispanics.

Here is a prototype of the job description we have provided clients:

Manager of Special Markets

BASIC RESPONSIBILITY

Development and recommendations of policies, programs, practices, and procedures of marketing for the nonwhite market at the company. Development of, and participation in, sales-promotion activity toward increased sales of products in minority markets.

GENERAL RESPONSIBILITIES

Maintenance of liaison with sources of marketing information and community activity for promotion purposes, so as to make this market an integral part of the overall sales efforts of the company.

ORGANIZATION RELATIONSHIP

(1) Reports to: vice-president, sales

(2) Supervises: assistant; clerk-stenographer

(3) Other significant relationships: Headquarters officers and sales-management staff, on minority-market matters.

FUNCTIONS AND DUTIES

(1) Develops ways and means to stimulate new and additional profitable business in nonwhite markets.

(2) Recommends and assists in the development of target market advertising and sales-promotional aids specifically to attract these markets.

(3) Reviews and studies geographic areas and other aspects of the market and makes recommendations for greater development of the potential for the company.

(4) Coordinates the performance of all supervisors in target market areas.

(5) Establishes and maintains contact with various media, sales-promotion organizations, and other development organizations in minority community to keep sensitive to opportunities, changes in conditions, attitudes, and needs that can influence sales of the company's products.

(6) Conducts and participates in meetings to present and discuss policies, programs, and practices of the company in order to coordinate these into nonwhite market activity.

(7) Participates in interviews and assists in training new employees in the target markets field, or whose responsibilities will include these markets.

(8) Makes periodic trips through the field sales organization to coordinate more effectively the company effort in minority markets.

(9) Performs special assignments and other duties as directed by the vice-president for sales.

At some companies, the functions are integrated into the overall marketing effort, and at others, separate structures exist. A determination will have to be made on what will be the most effective way of doing it.

Some advertising agencies maintain a task-force approach, and others have persons directly assigned to minority market activity.

In the task-force approach, blacks and other minorities might be working on any given account. When a client wants a particular type of campaign, they may be withdrawn temporarily to work on this assignment and then return to their other duties.

Some excellent campaigns have resulted. One outstanding example was the campaign created by the black group at Young & Rubicam, Inc. for Eastern Air Lines, which focused on an advertisement with the slogan, "Come Home to a Place You've Never Been," calling attention to the West Indian/Caribbean heritage of many black Americans. It is unlikely that the sensitivity shown in this advertisement could have been created other than by the technique Y & R used for Eastern.

Most executives can reach up on a shelf and extract a variety of marketing plans and support data, yet rarely a well-developed minority market plan. If one has not been developed, it should be.

The master plan should include a step-by-step procedure the company will establish and follow in more effective marketing to nonwhite consumers. The plan should cover advertising, sales, sales promotion, market research, public relations, and community relations, and include plans and guidelines in each area.

Copies should be disseminated to all persons who are even remotely concerned with the market. More advertising agencies today are providing their clients with information on minority demographics, spending profiles, and rationale on why the client should be involved.

The plan should be reviewed periodically, and changes made as the need arises.

Once a minority consumer market plan has been developed along the recommended lines, it will become very clear why nonwhite efforts may not have succeeded as they should have.

CHAPTER 8

Creating Products for Black Consumers

ROM TIME TO TIME, as counsel on marketing to minorities, we are asked: "Should products be created for black consumers?"

The concentration of population, the consumption patterns, as well as perceived and real needs, and the available opportunities for targeted advertising and sales promotion indicate that products can be created for this market.

At the same time, however, we say that limitation of a product's consumption should not be built into the planning. On occasion, a product initially created for black consumers has expanded distribution and sales into white consumer usage as well. Yet this is the ideal.

In creating a product especially for the black consumer market—as opposed to planning for expanded usage of an existing product among these consumers—there is a tendency to concentrate too hard on nonwhite marketing of such products. This creates the danger of rejection by the market, a possible result of associating the product with a "less than first class" label.

In some cases where the black-oriented product failed, it was clearly because the product had been promoted with overtones of a "second-class-citizen syndrome."

Certain categories of products designed for the black consumer have met with a greater rate of success: personal-care items, special tastes in the food category, and products that obviously filled a need, real or imagined, existing in the market.

Examples of the wrong way to proceed in introducing a new black-oriented product abound. For instance, most toy companies at one time or another have manufactured dolls for the nonwhite market. But most have not been good sellers, because they were either in bad taste—such as the "mammy" dolls—or lacked sensitivity to black consumer appeal—as with the obviously white Anglo-Saxon doll given a brown paint job.

When one toy company took its top-of-the-line doll, painted it brown, and called it their "black version" of the doll, it met with little success. The would-be purchasers, black parents, concluded that if the manufacturer took dolls from its best line and painted some of them brown to create a black version, then these dolls must have been rejects or substandards from the regular line that could not be sold to white customers.

How did the company arrive at this marketing decision? Instead of using its research-and-development team to conduct an orthodox program of determining consumer interest, marketability of such a product, and correct research techniques, management asked black production-line workers if the doll would sell to blacks. This unsophisticated approach was the beginning of the end for the doll.

Another company, however, was to begin marketing a complete line of black dolls. Remco Industries commissioned a black artist to make the dolls as correct ethnically as possible in all details. This in itself represented a serious attempt to understand the market and its needs.

Hair-care products for the black consumer market are highly successful, and fill a particular need in the community. In this market area needs exist for a wide range of products. From the day in 1905 when Madame C. J. Walker, a black beautician, produced a hair-straightening comb designed to remove the excessive curl from a black woman's hair, companies have earned a comfortable living from such products. Many products have expanded markets among other nationalities whose hair-care problems are similar to those of nonwhites.

A plan to create a product especially for this market should have built into it uses over and above the target consumer. Although the initial thrust might be to this market, the long-range view should be for developing additional consumer markets.

In one instance, a nonwhite market for a product developed unexpectedly. A cosmetic firm withdrew its sun-tanning product from the market because of poor sales performance, only to discover a prime market among blacks—but not for the original use as a sun-tanning agent.

After the product's withdrawal from the market, the company

received repeated requests from retailers in the Southeastern United States. Upon investigation, it was determined that nonwhites working in the fields were using the sun-tanning products to keep from becoming darker while working out in the sun. (While no product can make blacks lighter, this product helps clear blemishes and other skin problems, which gives a clearer skin.)

Based on this discovery, an entirely new marketing life was developed for the product, targeted to the black consumer market. Today the product, which met a need existing in the black community, is well advertised in this market, and enjoys sales success. It has also been subsequently expanded in its sales and distribution into the white market.

Many needs existing in the nonwhite market can be met through effective product research, development, and testing. With the proper techniques, the nonwhite community represents an important marketing segment for the firm willing to invest in it and, importantly, give it the necessary follow-through to introduce the new product.

Several areas, including health, personal care, and motivation, offer opportunities for product development.

The marketing and media strategies that a company uses may determine whether nonwhites believe a product to be strictly for them, and how the approach will be interpreted. Extreme caution, therefore, should be used in developing the strategy.

Some years ago, a baking company made a determination about the black consumer market that led to the creation of a product especially for this market. The company discovered that blacks not only bought more bread per capita than did whites, but that they preferred a sweeter loaf of bread. Based on this knowledge, the company decided to meet this taste preference among nonwhites.

The company made a sweeter loaf of bread, packaged it in a clear cellophane wrapper, named it "Honey-Sweet," and marketed it only in black consumer areas. The sales of this "new" product were good, and continued strong for years in this market.

To determine the advisability of introducing a new product to the nonwhite consumer market, begin by answering the following questions:

(1) Are blacks a group of consumers which would constitute demonstrably different product usage and consumption?

(2) Will the product fill a need, real or imagined, in this market?

(3) Should a new product be created, or is there an existing product that could be adapted to this market?

(4) How large is the potential market for the product, in terms of dollar volume to be achieved both in an initial market and in a long-range market?

(5) Is there a similar product available from a competitor that could be improved upon?

(6) Would there be a market potential for the product among other nationalities (e.g., darker-skinned people of other countries)?

(7) Is there an effective method of pretesting the new product?

(8) If there is reason to believe that a profitable market potential exists, can effective marketing techniques be employed?

(9) Can a significant competitive advantage be achieved?

A need does exist within the market for products having particular benefits. Some alert companies are meeting this need, and others have the opportunity of considering doing the same for sales and profits.

The minimum benefit for a company that is sincerely interested in researching and developing this market is an enlightened attitude toward the nonwhite as a consumer. Enough current information and marketing data is available for any company to begin developing new products for this consumer.

CHAPTER 9

Introducing the New Product

UNLESS a product is specifically targeted for the black consumer market, that market is rarely considered when a new product is introduced. Most new product introductions are white-oriented efforts, a reflection of "mass" thinking and execution.

Several studies have shown that blacks are slow to purchase new products. As a result, the idea has developed that new products should not be introduced to nonwhites.

I personally feel that if new-product campaigns included the black consumer from the beginning, then the differences between white and nonwhite new-product purchases would be substantially reduced.

We had an opportunity to test this theory in the introduction of Gablinger's beer in the Northeastern United States.

Gablinger's Beer, a product of Rheingold Breweries, Inc., was introduced as the first low-carbohydrate beer. It was brewed under a process developed by a Swiss chemist, Hersch Gablinger. (Not only was the product named for him, but it carried his picture on every bottle. This did not impede product identification with the nonwhite market, however.)

Robert Windt, an executive with the Vernon Pope Company, the public relations counsel to Rheingold, called us in to hear how we could work to get the product introduced at the same time it was introduced to white consumers in the Northeast.

We developed a plan for the market; it was accepted, and we began our work assignment.

The Pope Company had also asked us to take on the Puerto Rican market for this introduction. This marked our first venture into Spanish-speaking markets in the Northeast. While there are similarities in marketing to blacks and Spanish-speaking consumers, the latter group has its own characteristics that we had to address ourselves to.

Our objective in the work assignment was to make black and Spanish-speaking consumers aware of Gablinger's beer, establish rapport for the product, and create the climate for its acceptance.

The two groups comprise nearly 25 percent of the total New York City population, and more than 32 percent of the market for beer. Some estimates placed blacks and Spanish-speaking consumers in the classification of "heavy" beer drinkers, which represents 50 percent of the beer-drinking market.

Although Spanish-speaking consumers in New York are of Puerto Rican, Dominican, Cuban, Colombian, and other South American and Latin extraction, they have come to be identified as Puerto Ricans. This is true of Spanish-speaking blacks, whether of African heritage or from the West Indies.

Working with us in the Spanish-speaking community was Manuel R. Roque, who in addition to consulting with us, worked for such firms as Batten, Barton, Durstine & Osborn, Consolidated Edison, and other clients concerned with the Spanish-speaking market. Manny provided us with special insight into the Spanish-speaking community.

The theme had been developed that Gablinger's beer "Doesn't Fill You Up," and we were to hit hard with that theme in our efforts with minority-group consumers.

Our efforts were also to be keyed to the take-home market through implementation of community-interest organizations' ongoing activities. One reason for this strategy was that our target audience spent more for beer to be taken home, while on-premise consumption was lower.

Studies have established that the Puerto Rican people, and for that matter, the entire Spanish-speaking community of New York City (referred to as *El Barrio* or the Spanish market) require a highly specialized and skilled approach on the part of advertising agencies and their clients. Generalities and standard procedures fail to reach this group effectively. For example, advertising copy cannot simply be literally translated from English to Spanish, as is the common practice, and get a favorable reaction from this ethnic group to the advertising claims.

The Spanish market consists largely of newcomers to the U.S. mainland, people separated from the rest of the citizens by a very different culture and by a massive language barrier. Hispanics refuse to give up their heritage, and anyone who wishes to win their loyalty and support must be willing to tune in to their way of life and thought.

Although we did not have responsibility for advertising, we did on occasion meet with Doyle Dane Bernbach's account group to discuss advertising strategy in the black and Spanish-speaking markets. Some translating was done, and advertising guidelines for both markets were provided.

As stated, part of marketing strategy was to concentrate on the ongoing social activity in the minority-group markets. We were also able to concentrate on women in the target audiences.

Minority group members, particularly Puerto Ricans, tend to form their own communities for reasons of security, status, social well-being, and convenience. In New York, there are about twenty Puerto Rican enclaves or barrios, with Spanish-language theaters, clubhouses, recreation centers, and service establishments.

Similar structures exist in the black community. In both minority communities there are numerous social, civic, fraternal, sports, and professional organizations. These became the target audience for the introduction of Gablinger's beer to the minority markets.

Having established the objectives of the campaign, and the strategy we were going to employ to reach them, we set the program in motion, with a four-month introductory period. We knew that ethnic media support would be an important factor, so we held two get-togethers for the working press of this media, at locations convenient to the specific group whose cooperation was sought.

Publicity materials had been provided earlier; the press get-togethers were for the purpose of further explaining the program and, importantly, sampling the product.

Product sampling at meetings, picnics, and club meetings would be the basic thrust of the introductory campaign.

The Spanish buttons read, "Me gusta Gablinger's porque no llena," or, "I like Gablinger's because it doesn't give you that full feeling."

Both the English and Spanish buttons, with a foaming beer stein as background, carried out the Gablinger's colors (dark brown and beige), which were also used in the dresses worn by the models who helped promote the product.

In addition, we created a pamphlet of summer recipes, keyed to the interests of both markets, featuring recipes of particular appeal to blacks and Hispanics. There were two versions of the pamphlet, one in English and one in Spanish.

The buttons and the recipes were widely distributed in high-traffic supermarkets—where store owners and managers welcomed the Gablinger's Girls to stand near huge displays of Gablinger's beer—as well as at group meetings and sampling parties.

We met with black and Hispanic salesmen of Rheingold Breweries to outline our program to them and to help build their enthusiasm in opening up new outlets for the product. This enthusiasm turned out to be one of the most effective forces in our campaign. Like so many others, the salesmen, too, had become convinced that black and Spanish-speaking markets would not "go for anything new." We managed to change their minds, and together proved that if new-product introductions are well supported, minority markets will indeed "go for them."

Minds were also changed at the point-of-sale. Retailers themselves told us that their minority-group consumers relied on premium brands of beer, and would hardly be switching to a new beer like Gablinger's. After being advised of our campaign, many who would not ordinarily have placed an initial or repeat orders did so. This was crucial to our success, since retailers are key in the introduction of new products in these markets as in the majority community.

As part of the campaign, we made a heavy promotional pitch to women, based on the lightness of the beer, and the claim that it "does not fill you up." Although we never made any claim or intended to suggest that it was low in calories or that it could be used to control weight, many women read that into it and bought the product on that basis.

We knew that if such a demand could be created among women in our markets, by appealing both to their "black consumer reactions" and their feminine interests, there would be initial and repeat orders for Gablinger's. This, in fact, happened in the introductory period of the campaign.

Since it would have been impossible to reach all of the hundreds of minority-group organizations in the Northeast during the introductory campaign, we concentrated on the largest groups. But in an attempt to reach all groups, a letter was sent to the president or secretary of all minority-group organizations, with a description of the campaign, a sample of the recipe booklet, and an invitation to write us for additional copies. Many organizations did this, and thousands of booklets were distributed.

Minority-oriented media publicity was a primary consideration throughout the four-month introductory campaign. Initially, black and Puerto Rican models were shown holding the new product bottle, and the beer was described in captions. These photographs were serviced with excellent pickup to target media, including newspapers and magazines serving these communities. Subsequently, almost every part of the campaign was publicized through these media: the appointment of the Gablinger's Girls; their custom-made outfits; the recipe booklets; product publicity; and, the company's involvement in various community activities.

At the press gatherings, we also photographed members of the press with Rheingold executives, ethnic-market salesmen, and the "Girls." These photos got unusual pickup by the media.

Women's talk shows on minority-oriented stations included appearances by those involved in the Gablinger program to talk about the program and the product.

The Gablinger's Girls also appeared at amusement parks, shopping centers, and other gathering places where they distributed recipes and buttons.

The campaign for the introduction of Gablinger's beer to minority markets in the Northeast was successful in its goal of reaching all of the primary market for the product in its debut in the marketplace.

It helped to disprove the idea that blacks and Spanish-speaking consumers are slow to respond to new-product introductions. It demonstrated the importance of including minority markets in the campaign from the beginning if maximum sales and profits are to be realized.

When including the minority markets in new product introductions, the following guidelines can be helpful:

(1) Decide whether the marketing strategy should be the same or separate from the primary marketing strategy.

(2) Consider the effectiveness of using a complete marketing mix of black and other minority-oriented media in the new-product introduction.

(3) Determine what public relations and community relations activity should be utilized in the introductory stages of the campaign to achieve maximum consumer awareness.

(4) Investigate opportunities to get additional retail support in

stores located in minority areas; this support can materially contribute to the introduction.

(5) Explore the possibility and advantages of using blacks and Hispanics in product sampling activity in their respective communities (though not limited to them).

(6) Make certain that the marketing effort provides minority groups with the basic information on the product, and gives them the *recognition, identification,* and *invitation* that must be present to effectively sell them.

(7) Build in feedback systems that will allow measurements to be made on the inclusion of minority consumers in introductory programs, and improve upon techniques as determined.

CHAPTER 10

Brand Positioning in the Black Consumer Market*

BY KELVIN A. WALL

*Kelvin A. Wall is president of Kabon Consulting, Inc.,
former senior consultant at Arthur D. Little, Inc., and vice-
president of market development at Coca-Cola USA.*

LET'S START by accepting the proposition that positioning is the most important decision you can make in your advertising. David Ogilvy has stated the case eloquently. Al Ries and Jack Trout have documented it extensively (in AA Features).

What your product is and what you say about it are secondary to the position it occupies in the consumer's mind. That proposition leads to four corollaries on the black consumer market:

(1) If positioning is the most important decision, it is the one most ignored by advertisers aiming at blacks.

(2) The special characteristics of the black consumer market magnify the importance of positioning there.

(3) It is quite possible to develop a position that is tops in the white market and weak in the black market.

(4) It is also possible to establish a strong position in the total market—and then to find a position in the black market that is

---

* Reprinted from *Advertising Age*, June 18, 1973.

compatible with the general theme. In that way, you achieve the full return from your dollars investing in black media.

Positioning in the black consumer market begins with the recognition of a whole set of differences from whites, starting, of course, with physical differences, but also including social class, demographics, environment, life style and habits. Brand preferences and purchase behavior are important major differences, too.

Any one or any combination of those factors may be vital to your positioning in the market.

For example, a cardinal rule of positioning begins with the rank of products or brands on the ladder in the consumer's mind. It is foolhardy to advertise head-on against the No. 1 product or brand, because your advertising tends to reinforce the leader. This fact of life is even more significant among blacks, because they are more rank-conscious and they use rank for more deep-seated reasons. More than whites, they tend to select brands in the No. 1 positions and to use them as signals to their peers—and to whites.

Automobiles, of course, are the most prominent signal available to blacks, who are often restricted from suburban homes and other expressions of rank. The ultimate has been the Cadillac, and it would not make sense to challenge the Cadillac's position head-on. Yet the Cadillac's No. 1 position in the mind is being eroded somewhat by a slight change in its image—and image is also important to blacks. The Cadillac image is tending to be that of the got-rich-quick black.

Substantial upper-class blacks—doctors, lawyers, business men—are trending away from the Cadillac and to the Continental, Mercedes and Imperial.

This segmenting of blacks is becoming increasingly important as more of them move up the economic scale. Approximately 1,000,000 of them now have incomes of $10,000 or more, and their values are changing. A decade ago, the typical successful black adopted the white man's middle-class style. The black from Tuskegee was more Ivy League than the Brahmin from Yale. Blacks are no longer emulating whites. They are expressing their black consciousness. More important, they are not monolithic. They are using products to differentiate among themselves.

Such segmentation offers advertisers new opportunities within the market through positioning. In segmented markets, there can be several number ones. This is particularly true of products that blacks use in their conspicuous consumption, such as clothing, alcoholic beverages, travel and appliances, as well as automobiles.

One advertiser obviously aware of this fact is Smirnoff. Its ads in black media ask, "Are you still drinking scotch? Smirnoff is slowly getting next to everybody."

Recognizing that scotch has been the top status symbol, the Smirnoff ad suggests that there is an alternative. It doesn't try to leapfrog up the position ladder—it positions itself beside the leader, much like Seven-Up with the Un-Cola campaign.

Conversely, another ad for liquor in black media says, "What cheese did for Wisconsin, Old Crow did for Bourbon."

Apparently, many advertisers think they are positioning their products in the black consumer market when their advertising uses black models with Afros and the copy includes strained references to "natural" and "cool."

This approach did work in the past, when blacks were responsive to advertising that acknowledged their existence in a positive way. But it is now vulnerable to competitive advertising based on a keen sense of positioning.

For example, for years black women used Vaseline on their hands, knees and elbows for cosmetic reasons. Dry skin that is invisible on whites appears "ashy" on blacks. All-purpose Vaseline enjoyed this market virtually by default. Then in moved Ash-Away from Posner Laboratories. The brand name itself establishes a strong position.

As a product positioned specifically within the black market, Ash-Away is a significant exception. Here is a $50-billion market, soon to amount to one-fifth of the U.S. population increase with discernible differences, and relatively few products are positioned against them, although because of their crowded conditions and social awareness they are more conscious than whites about body odor.

The facial skin of black men tends to be bumpy from ingrown hairs. Yet no shaving product is strongly positioned against them. (The Personna Face Guard could be, but it hasn't made the effort. What better way to move alongside Gillette in the black man's mind?)

In general, marketing today is in the *Guess Who's Coming to Dinner?* stage. Where it should be is illustrated by *Cotton Comes to Harlem*. Blacks go to movies more than whites. Film-makers at long last are learning that it is profitable to position themselves with products that reflect the black perspective and are true to the black experience. Blacks no longer want white hand-me-downs.

As a result, blacks are rapidly segmenting themselves. The segmentation starts with income. The top 20 percent of black population accounts for 45 percent of black income. They share some common characteristics with the other 80 percent of blacks and other characteristics with upscale whites. Most of all, they are themselves.

They are not good prospects for boats. Nor would they find much identification with a scotch ad showing a boat, even if the skipper were black. And, as George Lois suggests, to them the Cutty Sark looks like a slave ship. Thus symbols and images are often totally different.

Positioning requires an understanding of both motivations and images. For example, upscale blacks are traveling abroad, but with their own set of motives. Conspicuous consumption is perhaps uppermost. But it is not consumption of history. Blacks are less interested than whites in historical sites and more concerned with the friendliness of local people. Travel ads in black media touting castles are using the wrong images to establish the wrong position.

Much of the advertising directed at blacks obviously is based on hunch and superficial assumptions. Motivational research is needed to understand all the segments of this market. No marketing effort directed at blacks for any product can be considered serious unless it starts by learning why blacks buy the product, how they use it and where competition stands on the position ladder. The black psyche is changing, as is the black market, so that periodically position strategy and its advertising must be reviewed and in some cases updated.

Problems and inadequacies of current ad planning usually result from lack of marketing direction. Or more specifically, lack of a sophisticated marketing plan, with specific black market objectives, with special black product position statements. This is not to deny the place of creativity in advertising to blacks. But too often we see advertising strategy to blacks as a *non-strategy*. Here is the usual (wrong) approach:

(1) *Use black media.* This is necessary, obviously, to reach the black consumer, but the evaluation of black media is not as important as the evaluation of message in that media. For many advertisers, black media become the message.

(2) *Use black models.* Black models alone do not sell a product, particularly if it's a black model substituted in a currently running white ad. Is the ad environment meaningful to your black target group?

(3) *Use black English.* This places more emphasis on how to

say it than on what to say, and often the words are already outdated as a cliche, in addition to being condescending to many blacks who don't speak that way.

(4) *Use product ad.* No people. Is the ad missing the personal human touch required to sell blacks?

The following generalizations illustrate why positioning against segments of the black market must be approached as a separate marketing problem:

- Given equal income, black spending patterns are different. There may be reasons to ignore the black market (boats) or to direct proportionately more attention to it (movies).

- Blacks are considerably younger, with a median age of 21 against the white median of 29. Most advertising for food is aimed at the 35-year-old housewife. What does it mean to the 25-year-old black housewife? Should products be positioned against black teenagers? What media should be used?

- Blacks are growing in numerical importance and will account for one-fifth of the net population gain between 1970 and 1980.

- Black families are not only younger and larger, they are more closely knit. Black fathers are involved more in child-rearing and household tasks. For many products, positioning in the black man's mind is much more important.

- Black mothers are more concerned about nutrition. They have less faith in the lunches their children get at school. They put more emphasis on breakfast.

- While proportionately more black mothers work and would seem good prospects for instant or easy-to-prepare foods, there is a counteracting factor. Black mothers will not sacrifice nutrition or taste.

- Black tastes are different and reflect Southern origins. Black consumption of soft drinks in Chicago follows the same patterns as in the South. Colas, grape and orange drinks are favored. Root beer doesn't exist. Kool cigarettes capitalized on the desire for a richer taste and have a lucky name.

- Blacks use products differently. Black mothers use meals to a much greater extent as a reward system and as a means of keeping the family together. They put more of themselves into food preparation and varying and personalizing recipes. Spare rib sauce is used for more kinds of meat than spare ribs. Hot cereals are used more. A meal without gravy or sauce doesn't look appetizing.

- Blacks are more insecure when shopping. They respond to re-assurances such as guarantees—and, of course, the perceived position.

- Blacks are more skeptical and suspicious. Are so many products named Ajax really good for so many different tasks? Different brand names, rather than line extensions, would establish better positions.

- Two-thirds of blacks live within the inner city. Cramped apartment life, shopping on foot, less open space create different conditions. Smaller packages and products appeal to them. They use mass transit for work and leisure. Black kids play on concrete, not on grass or the wooden floors of gymnasiums. Where do you position sneakers?

- Even the climate is different for blacks. Whether they live in the urban North or rural South, they see less snow. (It melts faster and is removed faster in the city.)

All of those differences, plus others, are becoming more pronounced as blacks are veering toward their own life styles. Obviously, the advertiser who wants to develop a strategy within the market, the fastest-growing in the U.S., must consider the full special marketing needs of the product. Today this can be accomplished through:

(1) Proper motivation research.
(2) Proper definition of target customer.
(3) Proper selection of product benefit.
(4) Proper positioning selection.

Because an increasing number of advertisers are beginning to develop a strategy, those who coast along with hunches and non-strategies will find their products positioned outside the market—somewhere between hair curlers and vacation trips to South Africa.

CHAPTER 11

The Strategy in Developing Good Press Relations

IN ORDER to build good minority-group public relations, especially in the black community, it is necessary to first effect good press relations.

Any group, organization, or institution, any business or industry, that wishes to build more positive relations can use the following methods, which have already been proved successful.

It is important for company public relations people to establish dialogue between their management and the management of black-oriented media. Black-oriented newspapers, for the most part, are controlled by an active ownership whose personal viewpoints dominate editorial policy. Conferences between companies and minority media leadership help to establish some rapport between black and white groups—both of which have often misunderstood each other. The personal participation of company executives would build goodwill among the leadership of nonwhite-oriented media.

Conferences between media management and company executives should not be limited to the corporate headquarters city, but should also include cities where the company has substantial operations, such as plants employing a sizeable number of minorities. Plant tours for black press representatives have become an important means for helping companies to establish good press relations for future material usage.

Nothing should be staged, of course, and it should be the regular tour given to all visitors. However, a public relations executive should go along to answer any questions that might arise. It should not be a "see how many minorities" in a department, but rather a concentration on the company's products, processes, or services. If nonwhites are highly visible, the press representative will readily observe this fact.

Black-oriented news media should be invited to all functions open to other newsmen, and provided with the same material. This would cover such events as new product introductions, new plant openings, and similar events.

We do recommend, however, that if the event has significant interest to the black community, such as if the new operation will employ so many minority group members, or is being built near the community, this information should by all means be included in the material for the black press.

Here are some guidelines for servicing black-oriented media:

(1) Prepare material with the publications in mind (most are weekly, for example). From the time we distribute a news release, we have found that it takes from two to three weeks for it to appear throughout the United States, which is a normal news-release usage pattern.

(2) Publications and broadcast media are usually understaffed, so the right material prepared with the media's format in mind has an excellent chance of being used. Anything that would cut down rewriting has a better-than-average chance of being used.

(3) Do not send routine business announcements on promotions unless they pertain to minorities. Most media do not have a business news page or section as such, so there is not much chance of it being used.

(4) If you continually send product publicity, your advertising department or agency can expect to be solicited. The theory is that if the press is good enough for your product publicity, it is good enough for your company's advertising.

(5) Releases with photographs of blacks have a better-than-average chance of being used. Even product publicity with black models has better acceptance, because it reflects that someone took time to consider the media receiving such material.

(6) Ethnic media are more personalized, so it is important to keep names of editors updated. Do not send releases addressed impersonally.

(7) Invitations should be extended to all press functions to which other media are invited.

(8) Because of weekly deadlines, consider servicing nonwhite media before the release date for white-oriented media. This is particularly true for news and publicity involving nonwhites. An editor

reading news involving his readership in a daily newspaper could become resentful, when a little extra effort could let the editor know what is happening, and win friends for an alert publicist.

(9) Subscribe to a good cross section of black-oriented print media in order to be familiar with format, editorial philosophy, type of material used, and general approach. This is particularly important in cities where the company has sizeable operations.

(10) Be sure to know when corporate advertising is being considered or scheduled to be placed in black-oriented media on such occasions as new plant openings, Brotherhood Week, or Black History Week. Editorial copy should be prepared by the public relations department to go to this media, in support of the advertising message. Special opportunities exist in any specific issues the media may develop.

(11) Deal frankly and honestly with representatives of the media. Don't be patronizing, but do be understanding.

(12) Understand that most black-oriented radio stations carry international, national, local news, *and* news of particular interest to minority groups. In addition, two networks—Mutual Black Network and the National Black Network—feed news to member stations.

(13) The needs of magazine and supplement editors should be thoroughly analyzed *before* they are approached for story consideration. Remember that the story must have a *positive* black interest angle, or one that can be developed.

(14) Feature stories should be prepared on black and other minority-group employees in responsible positions, including company awards or recognition given to such employees. While other media might not normally carry such material, the ethnic press welcomes such material. Also, material on company executives involved in activity in minority communities that would reflect well on the company or other organization should be sent to this media.

(15) Remember why minority-oriented media exists, and help fill the need that exists for properly tailored information and publicity.

Filling a particular need of nonwhite media can also pay dividends, as we advised our client, the B. F. Goodrich Company, in support of the company's marketing mission. Although retained by the marketing department at BFG, we also did counsel with the internal public relations department and with BFG's counsel, Carl Byoir & Associates.

In our research of black-oriented media nationally we determined that no automobile company, parts manufacturer, or rubber company placed a column on car care in the national black press.

We felt there was a need for such a column, especially since marketing statistics indicated that on a percentage basis blacks bought more used cars.

We recommended this to BFG's public relations department, and a column, "Car Care," was initiated, using a black model (as a car specialist) at the head of the column.

The column was devoted to problems drivers usually encounter in first-line maintenance. Only when appropriate was the BFG name mentioned.

On a given week of the column's distribution (it was not sent weekly), as many as fifty-five black-oriented newspapers would carry it, an estimated 25 percent of the nation's black papers. It clearly provided a service.

Of course, whenever possible, we pointed out to advertising managers of the papers that with such a column the BFG store in their area was a possible client for advertising, and that a section could be built around the column. We also mentioned other rubber companies, used-car dealers, parts suppliers, and service stations as possible advertisers in a section concerned with car care.

CHAPTER 12

Educating Marketers About Low-Income Consumers

IN THE UNITED STATES, the major thrust of marketing has been toward middle- and upper-income consumers. But today more attention must be focused on the marketing opportunities in low-income areas and on the impact of those marketing practices on our total society. This conclusion was reached by the National Marketing Advisory Committee, Task Force on Commercial Services to Low-Income Urban Areas, established by the U.S. Department of Commerce and composed of representatives from business, industry, and community organizations.

The committee agreed that customer practices toward nonwhite consumers, as well as other low-income groups, have led to a credibility gap between these consumers and the business sector. "Low-income consumers present a challenge to marketing because marketing plays a critical role in making the benefits of our economic system available to all," concluded the committee.

Along with employment, marketing, especially in the retail area, is one of the main contacts between the business system and the individual citizen. Low-income consumers, despite their income disadvantages, buy relatively large shares of the total output of some products and services. The products and services available, their prices, and the stores in which they are bought are vital, everyday concerns for the low-income consumer. These variables affect the consumer's standard of living, the way he or she spends time, and attitudes toward the community and the society.

While it is proper here to allude to the positive social gains to be made through better marketing practices to low-income consumers, it goes without saying that the primary thrust is indeed marketing.

69

Although not all disadvantaged consumers live in urban areas, a high percentage of them do. And not all of these consumers are black. Moreover, central city markets, particularly in densely populated low-income neighborhoods, may mean the difference between profit or loss in many retail markets. Marketing methods must reflect these perceptions, and business must understand the hidden costs to itself and society for ignoring this market segment.

The following checklist can be used in evaluating potential marketing activities in low-income areas, whether these projects are aimed at immediate or long-term improvements in the awareness and welfare of these consumers. The checklist can also be used in judging programs that might be continued or expanded. Bold new approaches are needed. Marketing improvements must be made to better serve low-income consumers. Accepted marketing ideas and methods do not provide an adequate basis for evaluating this market segment, and innovations can be tested only by trial and error. But decisions must be made about which ideas to try and how to evaluate the results.

(1) Is there adequate demand for the goods or services to be made available to low-income consumers? A consideration might be the development of new products to meet the needs and desires of low-income consumers. Such products have been successfully developed, and some have found uses in middle-income markets.

(2) Is there a good range in the choice of facilities, goods, and services offered such consumers? Often low-income consumers have no real alternatives in the marketplace and it is frequently assumed that they desire only one type of product or service mix, usually the most inexpensive line.

(3) Are low-income consumers as a group getting an even break in the marketplace? It is alleged, and it is sometimes true, that the poor pay more for certain products and services. Exposure of such retail practices can be very embarrassing to a company, even if the company is not directly responsible, and ways should be explored to reduce this possibility.

(4) Is the consumer getting satisfaction from the personal marketing experience? Consumer satisfaction does not depend solely on lower prices. Increased sense of self-esteem, dignity, and involvement with the local community and society at large are by-products of the personal marketing experience. By a variety of means, particularly the media and advertising, low-income consumers contrast the facilities, products, and services in their immediate environment with those

in other parts of the community. Are your products marketed with the same fundamental taste and appeal in all areas?

(5) Are the people to be served involved in the planning? Few companies bring a product or service into a middle- or upper-income neighborhood without obtaining reaction or feedback from the potential consumer. Too often the low-income consumer is overlooked in this regard. Market research, for example, frequently bypasses these communities because of hazards or difficulties for interviewers. It is true that such communities may have higher crime rates, fewer telephones, and more high-rise apartment buildings. Nonetheless, experience has demonstrated that participation by residents of low-income areas can play an important role in overcoming suspicion and in properly designing the program to fit the community.

(6) Is basic marketing information available about low-income consumers, and can it be put to better use? Marketing decisions should be made on an adequate data base, and the first step in defining and reaching this segment is accumulating such a base. Moreover, can this information enhance the consumer's understanding and benefit from buying the product or service? Imaginative programs are needed to increase low-income consumers' familiarity with, and use of, sound buying practices. And simply making information available is not enough. Marketing and public affairs executives must be actively involved in both the planning and the implementation of programs.

(7) Is the low-income consumer victimized by unethical and illegal business practices, such as overcharging, underweighing, misrepresentation of quality or quantity, mislabeling, false and misleading advertising, bait-and-switch advertising? Such practices have bad psychological and economic effects.

(8) Do facilities in low-income areas need improvement? As observed above, changes in appearance may seem superficial, but do contribute to customer satisfaction. Changes may be required in operation, as well. Further, the upgrading of commercial facilities in a locality often stimulates improvements in other facilities nearby.

(9) Are financial resources available to expand marketing in low-income areas? Frequently, these areas are treated inadequately in capital and marketing budgets. Programs are needed which will attract investments to help build the community, rather than merely offer a quick profit to the investor. Long-range financial planning will build customer goodwill.

(10) Can the drain of resources out of low-income areas be

reduced? Money earned by low-income residents often passes quickly into higher-income areas (in the black community it's estimated that this takes about twenty-four hours). Low-income communities can benefit from positive programs that increase the use of resources within those areas, and increase the circulation of money there.

(11) Can improved use be made of existing facilities? Expanding or improving established facilities often brings faster results than does creating new facilities. The use of existing facilities also may enhance the sense of participation by area residents and increase their acceptance of new marketing services.

(12) Are employment and job-training opportunities for residents of low-income areas being provided? Marketing activities that provide jobs for poverty-area residents that require little or no extended training or remedial education have obvious merit. There may be even greater value in practical projects in which low-income citizens with adequate skills can assume managerial and entrepreneurial positions. Marketing programs in low-income areas should include specific plans for at least some of the higher-level jobs to be filled by area residents.

(13) Can managerial skills be provided? The best-looking store with the widest selection of merchandise will fail if it is not properly managed. Projects that do not provide for adequate management should be avoided.

(14) Are the costs of operating in low-income areas being considered realistically? Elements that contribute to high cost and risk in low-income areas are: relatively small value of purchases per shopper; use of costly selling methods; expensive credit administration; high insurance costs; pilferage; and damage. Programs and experiments aimed at cutting these costs are obviously highly desirable. Such costs should be taken into consideration in planning new ventures in order to avoid failures that will result in a drain on the low-income areas rather than a contribution to them.

Some years ago, Theodore Levitt, a prominent marketing-research specialist, defined "the real challenge to marketing people." He said it is crucial to "firmly get hold of the idea that changing a business—finding it new roles, new customers, new markets—is even more important than operating it efficiently. If corporations are to outlive the market on which they were founded, then marketing must replace the lost function of the entrepreneur in the business planning process." This holds true today.

While this chapter has addressed areas of concern for the marketer, much more needs to be undertaken to provide consumer education for low-income communities. In nonwhite communities of the United States media, organizational meetings on national, regional, and local levels, and community-based programs could be effective channels of such educational programs.

Seminars, workshops, films, and materials can be targeted to the needs of nonwhite and other low-income consumers.

Many companies, trade associations, and government agencies have speakers' bureaus, program aids, and similar consumer education materials that often are not effectively used in nonwhite communities, but could be.

A consumer-information and education program, built to support the marketing program, could prove highly desirable.

PART III

Developing the Market

CHAPTER 13
Media and Their
Effective Use

MEDIA in America have contributed as much as any other institution to the duality in our society. That is not to say, of course, that blacks do not read white-oriented media, listen to white-oriented radio programs, or watch television; studies reveal that, in fact, they do. But a medium that in many respects ignores the concerns, and at times even the existence, of a group of consumers faces a serious challenge when it wants to turn around and establish believability and conviction with the group and effectively sell it.

The "mass communications complex" reflects the audience for which it is mainly intended—white Americans. Yet beyond that it tends to ignore vital dimensions in the lives of nonwhite Americans, usually by talking *about* nonwhites and not *to* them.

Black-oriented media, on the other hand, offer communication with this market by reflecting the life-styles and concerns of its black audience with a message of conviction and believability difficult to achieve in other media. Therefore, to ignore the use of black media in a total marketing mix is, in most instances, to ignore a vital medium that can effectively reach and sell a consumer segment through the success formula of *recognition, identification,* and *invitation.*

In recent years, several advertising agencies have examined the media habits of blacks and the impact of various media on their consumer behavior. Many of these studies have been conducted as part of ongoing media studies and are therefore identified only by the advertising agency conducting it, as in the case of the two examples which follow. All too often, however, advertising and media research tends to overlook racial and ethnic media in its studies, which often contributes to false impressions about the relative influence these media play in selling consumers.

Grey Advertising, Inc. outlined in an agency study five different methods of communicating with the black consumer market. Since they are especially useful, we will paraphrase them here:

GENERAL MESSAGES IN GENERAL MEDIA

This direction assumes the black community does not comprise a special market segment apart from the general, or majority, market. It assumes that mass appeals will have equal impact with the entire audience.

"TAILORED" MESSAGES IN GENERAL MEDIA

By "tailoring" a message, copy and/or layout is adjusted to avoid exclusion of any market segment, or to explicitly include segments considered to be special target audiences. "Tailoring" may be accommodated by special creative approaches, manipulation of word and picture symbols, and the use of black talent in so-called integrated advertising. The premise is to make the message acceptable to all races by catering to common motivations influencing purchasing behavior, and constructing the message so that each audience segment *selectively perceives* only those portions of the total communication intended for it.

A by-product of "integrated" advertising may be to strengthen the advertiser's nondiscriminatory image in the black community. Black-oriented and "integrated" advertising are discussed in other chapters of this book.

"TAILORED" MESSAGES IN BLACK-ORIENTED MEDIA

It is generally agreed that blacks consciously or unconsciously find it difficult to identify with white models, white products, white appeals, and sometimes white-oriented media per se. Black media will surround a black-oriented message with an atmosphere that should heighten message impact.

USING A COMBINATION OF WHITE- AND BLACK-ORIENTED MEDIA

Blacks are relatively heavy users of white-oriented media, especially television. White-oriented media with realistically "tailored" messages combined with black-oriented media as a secondary overlay are likely to maximize reach while capitalizing on the increased impact of specialized media. Moreover, to the extent that there is a synergistic effect (i.e., a combination of media reinforcing each other to make the whole greater than the sum of the parts), this combined-media approach may be highly effective.

Such a media mix must create a commercial message that selectively appeals (without alienation) to all marketing segments.

A "TOTAL-COMMUNICATIONS PACKAGE" DIRECTED TOWARD THE BLACK COMMUNITY AND THE BLACK CONSUMER MARKET

This communication goes beyond advertising. It involves a total program of advertising, merchandising, and public relations similar to majority market approaches—with one important addition. It means hiring and training black employees and taking an active part in the betterment of the black community—and communicating this to the black community.

One of Doyle Dane Bernbach's ongoing media studies summarized black-oriented media as follows:

TELEVISION

Black people's TV viewing is generally average—daytime and weekend children's programs above-average; prime and sports somewhat below.

Programs featuring black entertainers almost always do better in the black community than other programs.

There are some local black-oriented programs, most of which have had limited success.

RADIO

Every market with significant black population has one or more stations primarily featuring music and/or religious programming. Reaching the black segment of any market will generally require the use of one or more black stations.

A relatively recent development is the organization of networks of black radio stations—the National Black Network and the Mutual Black Network. The use of black network radio involves the usual clearance and rapidly changing affiliation problems connected with network radio generally.

NEWSPAPERS

Black people's reading of newspapers varies in direct relationship with income/education. It is the oldest medium dedicated and directed to black people. Black newspapers number about two hundred, almost all weeklies. Their editorial scope and audience size show very great variation.

MAGAZINES

Magazines are currently the fastest growing medium aimed at the black consumer market.

In almost all cases, general (white-oriented) market magazines are considerably weaker among black people than among the population as a whole. This and a number of other social, political, and economic factors have led to the establishment of many new national black magazines. (Eleven were born in the 1970s.)

Examination of the various communications channels to the black consumer market provides no single "best" strategy. Direction must be decided by individual advertisers, and is dependent upon marketing objectives, black media availability, budgets, and so forth.

White-oriented messages in white-oriented media will not effectively reach the black consumer market. "Tailored" messages challenge the creative function: the message must demonstrate effective selectivity without alienation. "Tailored" messages in black-oriented media alone are unlikely to provide the required marketing thrust, but in combination with white-oriented media and support activity, as discussed, could provide an efficient media mix, and reach targeted marketing goals.

CHAPTER 14

Integrated Advertising

IN RECENT YEARS there has been an increased use of minorities in advertising, in white-oriented print media and television commercials, that has come to be called "integrated" advertising.

Integrated advertising was not part of a natural evolution in advertising. It was a forced change, intended to alter the image of the nonwhite in America—primarily in the minds of white Americans. Today integrated advertising is almost commonplace, although the issues surrounding it are far from resolved.

To understand the issues today, it is helpful to review what happened since the beginning of racially integrated advertising in the mid-1960s, and what some of the fears were about it.

In the early to mid-1960s the use of minorities in mass-media advertising was almost nonexistent. Such groups as Mayor Robert F. Wagner's Committee on Job Advancement in New York, the Congress of Racial Equality (CORE), and later the National Association for the Advancement of Colored People (NAACP), played varied roles in promoting the use of blacks and other minorities in mass-media print and television advertising.

Mayor Wagner's committee wrote to five hundred companies that had headquarters or major offices in New York and their advertising agencies, requesting that they use identifiable minority-group members in their advertising, to secure "a more realistic portrayal of the role of minority groups in our national life." By 1964, some fifty companies had placed integrated advertising in print media and on television.

CORE threatened to use a more direct approach—boycotts—if the "whites only" practice continued in the advertising industry. The

NAACP's approach was to obtain more employment in the advertising industry for minorities.

A 1967 study on minorities in TV advertising reflected that instead of progressively increasing each year, integrated advertising had actually fallen behind. The study "Report of the Frequency of Negroes on Televised Commercials," prepared for the NAACP Legal Defense Fund, Inc. by Dr. Lawrence Plotkin, monitored sports programs in the New York City area. It concluded that "the appearance of Negro athletes [as product spokespersons] on the TV screen is primarily the result of their skills and abilities and not dependent upon decisions by sponsors and television executives." The NAACP Legal Defense Fund, which is an independently incorporated organization and not a subsidiary of the NAACP, contended that there was an "under utilization of talent," with the rate of black commercial appearances at 5 percent, or one in twenty, despite the increasing numbers of blacks in the athletic arena.

Today there is little argument that blacks and other minority-group persons are increasingly visible in white-oriented advertising. Just how representative they are, in terms of prominence and realism, is more widely debated.

Spokesmen for the major networks and advertising associations feel there has been considerable progress. Both the Association of National Advertisers and the American Association of Advertising Agencies have issued statements applauding the increased use of minorities, and both have some monitoring of this activity.

The major networks, ABC, CBS, NBC, and Group W, concur that appearances of blacks and other minorities in commercials have increased and they are continuing to encourage additional improvement in quantity and quality. Corporations and advertising agencies, the networks point out, largely determine the content of such commercials.

In contrast, black leadership and black marketing and advertising consultants, although pleased with the increased use of minorities in mass-media advertising, generally feel that there is room for improvement. They say that many advertisers and agencies are still unconvinced that their selling messages should be racially integrated. And it is felt that most television commercials are still obviously structured to fit minorities into particular situations. Minorities tend to be seen in secondary roles unless the commercial is all-minority.

In addition, although more minority-group members are used, there is still considerable reluctance among advertisers and agencies to dramatically integrate blacks in more advertising scenes and commercials. Blacks still feel discriminated against, and many advertisers and agencies have nurtured a long-standing fear of white backlash. Their fear is that the use of blacks or other minorities may negatively affect the majority consumer, who is white. In a national advertisement or commercial, the optimum message is usually aimed at the masses, or roughly 85 percent of the population, with the hope that blacks or other minorities will be influenced as well.

There has been considerable effort in some areas to prove that the use of minorities has a negative effect on the sales goals of advertisers. Some advisers have strongly urged a cutback on black appearances, suggesting they have a deteriorating effect on a company's brands and products. Research, however, has not supported this claim.

The bureau of advertising of the American Newspaper Publications Association published a study on "Blacks in Newspaper Ads." The study concluded that the use of black models did *not* adversely affect the attitudes of whites. The overall objectives of the study were:

(1) To determine the extent to which white and black respondents are aware of black models in retail newspaper ads;

(2) To determine the differences among black and white respondents between the effects of ads with black models and those without, in terms of (a) holding attention and (b) attitude toward buying advertised products in the advertised store;

(3) To determine the perceptions of black and white respondents to ads with blacks and to the different kinds of ads with black models.

The study's findings are summarized below:

- The most important variables which seemed to affect the test measures were the merchandise and the ad itself. Considerably further down the line was the influence of black versus white models for both white and black respondents.

- A relatively small portion of whites (11 percent) and a relatively large portion of blacks (36 percent) spontaneously mentioned black models.

- Very few whites were negative toward the presence of black models in ads. A very large proportion of white and black respondents were positive or neutral.

- Use of black versus white models seemed to have little effect on attitudes toward buying the items in the advertised stores.

- Ads of clearly identifiable black models seemed to gain more favorable response from blacks than ads with black models only marginally different from white models.

- Ads placing blacks in subservient positions received more negative responses from blacks; white responses were more neutral.

Another study, "The Effects of Black Models in Television Advertising on Product Choice," by Dr. Paul J. Solomon of Virginia Commonwealth University, Richmond, Virginia, and Dr. Ronald F. Bush of the University of Mississippi, Oxford, Mississippi, focused not on the use of models but on whether the use of a particular model influenced actual (simulated) product selection.

The laboratory experiment, conducted among 293 college students (179 white, 114 black) in the Richmond, Virginia, area, concluded that "the behavioral process of selecting products from a simulated store shelf was not affected by the race of the model." "It seems," concluded the authors, "that neither the positive, neutral, and negative attitudes found in previous studies on black models, manifest themselves into corresponding behavior patterns (that is, product choice)."

The researchers looked at product choice behavior for bath soap and "pop" wine, and found that neither white nor black subjects selected the products any differently, per se. But what the study did find was that for a "socially conspicuous product like 'pop' wine a model similar in racial characteristics to the subject's (in this case black) was more influential with respect to product choice than a model of a different race (white)."

The authors observed that the findings were not entirely consistent with the literature dealing with black consumer responses to black models in promotional materials. Basically, it has been assumed that black consumers respond positively to all advertisements that contain black models. This research indicates that black consumer responses, like white consumer responses, may be *product* and *situation* specific.

The study concluded that black consumers responded in a different manner to white and black models, depending on the product advertised. An analysis was also made among the subjects based on demographic variables, indicating that neither the sex nor the age of the subject was significant in determining response.

The highlight of the study, of course, is that consumer response to black models may be *product specific*.

Additional research is needed in the use of integrated advertising, but it seems to have satisfied the goal for which it was intended: to raise the consciousness of white Americans to the minority presence.

Television and the mass print media are exhibiting the average minority person as well as sports and entertainment personalities. The quality of advertisements and commercials has improved in recent years.

The vignette technique, using blacks and other races indescriminately for product testimonials, continues to be popular in television commercials, and will probably continue to be.

The continuing practice of substituting a black model for a white model in a television commercial, with the same lines, still rings hollow, and should be avoided.

One segment that has been particularly effective is the use of both integrated and black consumer specific advertising for branches of the military. Their aggressiveness and creativity in print and television commercials will be an important factor in recruiting more minority-group members.

The advertising created by W. B. Doner and Company, Advertising, for the National Guard is credited with helping to overcome negative attitudes, and to raise black Guard membership from 5,000 in the early 1970s to over 50,000 by 1976.

At DPGI we try to determine with our clients where, when, how, and why integrated advertising should be used. Sometimes the work is routine, sometimes fraught with problems; yet overall we believe we have helped contribute to an improved picture—and no client has had a program backfire.

We are concerned with the needs and demands of minorities in relation to integrated advertising, yet also keenly aware of our clients' frequent need to have an advertisement reach maximum numbers of prospects at the lowest possible cost, and have equal appeal in all areas of the United States.

We do not equate integrated advertising with minority-oriented marketing and public relations goals. They are two separate functions. Too many companies confuse the two and then wonder why their programs are not as successful among black consumers.

The drive for integrating advertising should not be so strong as to stifle the creative juices. If, as often happens, a campaign is conceived that would not lend itself to such usage, would not be believable, integrated advertising should not be used. Thoughtful consideration must be given to the ad's reception in a dual society.

CHAPTER 15

Advertising Strategy and Black Consumers

ADVERTISING prepared for black consumers, with black identification, and placed in media oriented primarily to those consumers, is considered "black-oriented" advertising. This is to differentiate it from advertising that includes minorities but is placed in media oriented primarily to white consumers.

Advertising to the black consumer has taken many forms, and has often been misconceived, causing campaigns to fall flat.

An early technique, still used today, was to take the campaign prepared for white-oriented media, simply change the models, and put the campaign in black-oriented media. In the past, we occasionally recommended this technique to clients, but today it would not reflect the target audience or have the maximum effectiveness we believe can be achieved.

For some products, especially personal-care items, it simply makes sense to create nonwhite advertising. And perhaps no company has better demonstrated this than Clairol Inc., division of Bristol-Myers Company, through its use of targeted advertising to expand share of market for its hair-coloring products. As "Is it true blondes have more fun?" was to become a famous theme among whites, so was "If you want to . . . why not?" among nonwhites. Both Clairol themes represent the company's desire to have more women coloring their hair.

At one time, Clairol sold only two coloring shades in the black consumer market—black velvet and sable brown. Sales to black hairdressers accounted for less than 0.4 percent of the salon division's total sales in the New York market. In a few short years, however, Clairol was beginning to sell over half of its colors to the black consumer market, and sales to black hairdressers accounted for over 5½ percent of Clairol's total dealer-purchase sales in New York.

Although Clairol had been aware of the potential of the market for hair care and preparations, it originally lacked sufficient knowledge of how to realize that potential fully. The value of its products to black hairdressers was obvious. As one business publication pointed out, the average white woman spent $40 per year in beauty salons, while the average black woman spent $72.

While Clairol faced problems of getting hair tinting accepted generally and overcoming the idea that "good women" did not get their hair tinted (the South and Midwest lagged behind other areas in the acceptance of hair coloring), the company also had to face the sensitive issue of getting nonwhite women to accept the idea that hair coloring could be natural for their complexions.

Clairol management asked itself many questions when considering the black consumer market. Finally, a committee that had studied the market concluded that, with the natural range of complexions and skin tones among blacks, it would be hard to say that a nonwhite woman with blond hair is not natural. With most of its questions answered, Clairol set to work to develop the market.

The company's trade advertising and consumer advertising departments and its agency, Foote, Cone & Belding, decided that the advertisements would not differ from Clairol's standard educational-copy approach, and that the only difference made would be the use of black models instead of white in targeted media.

The campaign was to be backed with a strong sales-technician force, including blacks. In New York Clairol had seventy white distributors calling on 16,000 white beauty salons and ten black distributors calling on 2,500 black beauty salons.

In order to condition black hairdressers to the use of hair coloring, Clairol prepared a series of advertisements, "devoted entirely to hair coloring education," using five attractive nonwhite models with different shades of Clairol hair coloring.

The company centered its trade advertising in *Beauty Trade*, a black-oriented publication distributed to hairdressers throughout the United States. (Today *Beauty Trade* supplements this with two big shows attended by beauticians and suppliers.)

For its consumer advertising, Clairol selected *Ebony* magazine. Its copy was designed to explain to black women that a hair coloring is another cosmetic, and as such, was nothing unnatural. The copy headline was, "If You Want To . . . Why Not?" and the black models pictured had hair-coloring shades from brunette to blond.

While Clairol was to change one of its themes, it was to keep another, even though the artwork was to be different. After the initial ad, Clairol ran advertisements using its famous "Does She . . . or Doesn't She?"; but the attractive woman and child pictured were black.

Ebony distributed some 25,000 full-color posters from the "If You Want to . . . Why Not?" campaign to black beauty salons throughout the nation.

Clairol's distribution of posters to beauty salons also included 440 life-size posters of the five attractive black models and their hair colors. Questionnaires were distributed, and the results along with other market research helped Clairol to determine future activity.

Clairol knew that for the nonwhite market campaign to be successful, it had to carry out each program for black hairdressers as it had for whites. Clairol leans heavily on education, and following calls on these hairdressers by technicians, free educational programs were offered to them. In addition to five black sales technicians in New York, Clairol had an additional ten in the field who distributed literature and worked with salon operators in the use of Clairol hair colors.

To back its advertising, Clairol participated in numerous trade shows held by trade associations, and was the first company to sponsor an interracial show in New York, whose winners included a black hair stylist and a hair colorist.

Clairol effectively put the success formula for black consumer market development to work. It *recognized* the market, *identified* with it, and *invited* it to buy its products.

Clairol learned that black women were beginning to try new and different cosmetic ideas, and that the source of some of the new ideas was the hairdresser—the person Clairol was already geared to reach, influence, and sell.

Once having recognized the market, Clairol set about to provide the necessary *identification*, through targeted advertising and a competent sales force to capitalize upon the campaign. Clairol identified with the black hairdresser by understanding her needs and the sensitivities of her customers.

With the market recognized and identified, Clairol then invited the market—the hairdresser to purchase its products, and the consumer to understand why hair coloring is natural. The use of black-oriented media, with models (which in Clairol's case helped immeasurably to identify a wide range of skin tones with various hair colors) provided an unmistakable invitation to the hairdresser and to the consumer.

With the effective use of targeted advertising, Clairol developed an entirely new growth market for its products. With sensitive executives as the client, with understanding and creative talent at its advertising agency, Clairol helped shape an entirely new concept of what black-oriented advertising in personal care could do.

Another case of black-oriented advertising effectiveness was the campaign Pillsbury undertook for its Hungry Jack biscuits, through Vanguard Advertising Agency. (Vanguard has both the majority and minority markets for the product.)

Hungry Jack biscuits are the profit leader of the Pillsbury Refrigerated Food Division, and its situation was a stable share of the approximately 80 percent of the refrigerated-dough business. According to the Marketing Research Corporation of America, Pillsbury, and Vanguard research, it was determined that the Hungry Jack business was approximately 46 percent black and 54 percent white.

These consumer groups live in two different worlds. White consumers are concentrated in suburban and B, C, and D counties, while the black consumers in the North and West are located in A and central cities. In the South blacks are also found in rural settings.

Facing Pillsbury was the fact that the category of refrigerated biscuits and all biscuits was on the decline, as shown in a major study by National Analysts. Subsequent studies supported these findings, attributing the decline to a fundamental change in the American life-style—with less emphasis placed upon traditional big breakfasts.

Servings of biscuits were found declining at a rate of 10 percent per year. The South, traditionally the stronghold of biscuit consumption, is becoming increasingly urbanized. The Pillsbury Company has the only nationally advertised brands in the category. This lack of competition was defined as a problem; educational benefits of competitive advertising could possibly have prolonged the life of the biscuit business in addition to expanding the market.

Although blacks accounted for approximately 46 percent of Hungry Jack biscuit volume, there was only 11 percent penetration of black households. The heavy consumption patterns of black consumers showed the worth of a new black customer.

The other major opportunity area Vanguard found was a smaller-size Hungry Jack can. Over the eleven-to-twelve-year life of the product principal advertising emphasis had been on the ten-ounce, ten-biscuit can. However, analysis of Census data showed that 63 percent of all U.S. households have three members or fewer, and 40 percent two or fewer; in the thirty districts where 70 percent of the Hungry Jack business is located, black households average 3.2 members.

A strategy was devised to gain additional trials by the consumer of the small-size Hungry Jack, and to gain new authorizations with the trade. The tactic used to reach both objectives was a free offer.

A nine-hundred-line ad was placed in majority and black-oriented newspapers. Redemption was projected at 6 to 7 percent, and at one time ran as high as 10.3 percent.

The overall media strategy was a dual one. Marketing objectives coupled with budget considerations (the total budget was $1.5 million) dictated a maintenance strategy against the white consumer while making a direct attempt at bringing in new black users.

Vanguard's creative for Hungry Jack biscuits carried the message, "big tastin' " biscuits. A vignette-type TV commercial was produced, targeted to whites and blacks, and a black-oriented radio commercial used the hearty endorsement of a black mother. *Ebony* and *Essence* magazines were used to illustrate the "big tastin' " theme.

Pre- and postresearch showed the effectiveness of the black-oriented campaign. Overall, there was an increase in sales in 13 markets using radio of 9.6 percent, compared to a .6 percent increase in the 54 markets not using radio. At the end of 1975, sales of the product had increased dramatically.

Pillsbury and Vanguard proved that the black consumer weighed very heavily in the profit potential of Hungry Jack biscuits. Sales and deliveries were to be up by 56 percent. It also showed that every purchasing decision by the black consumer is not logical and objectively analyzable.

As marketing counsel, we are often called in by advertising agencies or by clients to help determine what the company's strategy should be on black-oriented advertising.

We have regularly reviewed advertising prepared by Ted Bates & Co. for Brown & Williamson Tobacco Corporation's Kool brand of cigarettes. At B. F. Goodrich we helped initiate integrated and black-oriented advertising policies, and worked with their advertising agencies in their execution.

On several occasions we provided counsel to McCann-Erickson, Coca-Cola's advertising agency, in the "Things Go Better with Coke" campaign.

Coca-Cola, which had been executing the campaign in radio commercials with white musical groups, appeared not to be having the desired success with these commercials on black-oriented radio. McCann asked us to come in and talk about the campaign.

After hearing the white musical-group commercials, we listened to a black singing group, the Shirrelles, a popular trio who had recorded the commercial in their style.

We felt that the campaign would go very well on black-oriented radio, but that some bottlers might not use the commercials. To build support we needed documentation of their effectiveness and what it could mean to Coke. So we played the commercials for black disk jockeys on twelve stations in New York, Chicago, Philadelphia, Washington, D.C., and Pittsburgh. Almost without exception each air personality who heard the Shirrelles' version of the Coke commercials liked it and asked if it could be substituted for the one currently being aired. All were impressed that Coca-Cola had seen fit to record a black group.

We learned that each time the white-group Coke commercial was played—in antithesis to the station's format—the station would insert a station identification with a soul sound following it, reflecting the station's predominant music; sometimes it was even played before the Coke commercial was aired.

Following our detailed report to McCann-Erickson and Coca-Cola, the shift was made to using black music groups on black stations.

Later Coca-Cola used the famous Supremes and singer Ray Charles in its commercials, not only on black-oriented radio, but on white-oriented stations as well. (The Charles commercial even got fan mail and consumer requests of stations for its play.)

In print advertising, several considerations are open, including whether or not to use models in the advertisements.

We operate pretty much by a standard rule that if people are used in the advertisements, then they should be black in target media. If an advertiser does not picture people, choosing instead to stress product or impersonal artwork, the results tend to be satisfactory, but not as effective.

In radio commercials, particularly musical ones, we recommend that black talent be used. Black talent is recognizable and believable. At one time we recommended that copy be read live by air personalities but today, with advertising's increasing sophistication, that does not seem to be as effective.

We are often asked about the advisability of using black celebrities in advertising. We recommend it when it is appropriate to the campaign. Black athletes and entertainers have been used more in campaigns for black-oriented, integrated, and white-oriented campaigns in recent years. With the popularity of blacks in athletics and entertainment, which whites pay to see, their use can be made without fear in either white-oriented or black-oriented campaigns. More positive results can be expected from the latter, however.

Johnson & Johnson uses singer Nancy Wilson for its Disposable Diapers, in its "To Your Baby's Health" campaign, in radio and in print. This campaign, which has been particularly effective, was developed by Central City Marketing for Johnson & Johnson.

Most blacks used in primarily white-oriented campaigns and media have been in the "superstar" category, including O. J. Simpson for Hertz; Pearl Bailey for Greyhound, White-Westinghouse, and Paramount Chickens; Muhammad Ali for Brut; Deacon Jones and Wilt Chamberlin for Miller Lite beer; and Lou Rawls for Budweiser.

Greyhound developed Pearl Bailey's campaign primarily as a television commercial on network, but adapted a black-oriented print ad as well.

Black athletes and entertainers have also been effectively used in public service campaigns.

On the other hand, few black businessmen have been used in advertising. An exception was *Black Enterprise* publisher Earl S. Graves, who appeared in a Chase Manhattan Bank advertisement. Another was Henry G. Parks, Jr., chairman of H. G. Parks, Inc., manufacturer of Parks' Sausage, who appeared in a U.S. Steel institutional ad.

Some guidelines have been established for the use of celebrities in black-oriented programming:

(1) Determine the objectives in the market, and how a celebrity could help achieve them as part of the campaign thrust.

(2) If the campaign lends itself to a type of public-service activity in which the celebrity can participate, in addition to the primary purpose of selling, by all means develop it.

(3) Successful sports and entertainment personalities are not always acceptable for the same reasons by whites and blacks. If there is any question on how an individual will be accepted that an agency or client wants to use, get some advice.

(4) Keep in mind that black sports stars and entertainers can be, and have been, effectively used in black- and white-oriented media without problems, but again be sure of the planned objectives.

(5) Personal appearances of the celebrity need to be planned well in advance, and publicity surrounding such activity also needs to be carefully planned and executed.

(6) Celebrity use at sales meetings and conventions is particularly effective. This activity should be publicized in the national black press, and business and trade publications as well.

(7) If a celebrity is to be used, be sure to back the marketing and advertising campaigns with good publicity, quality point-of-sale material, and good merchandising.

Targeted correctly, advertising to the black consumer can be a crucial ingredient in a company's campaign to increase this growth market.

The advertising campaign should be handled with understanding, care, and sensitivity. A sizeable investment can be as good as lost if the creative is not in keeping with the target audience, if the media mix is not a good one, or if no overall strategy has been developed.

In our work with clients and their agencies, we have prepared twelve specific guidelines for black-oriented print and broadcast advertising. In the hope that more effective advertising can be directed to nonwhite consumers, I would like to pass them on here:

(1) In print advertising we recommend that words and phrases be simplified, that copy be kept to a minimum and be easy to remember.

(2) Bear in mind that the market uses certain phrases and expressions easily understood there, but often not having meaning among other groups. An example is the tendency to shorten otherwise long brand names. It is best, however, to get a brand name established in full before any attempt is made to shorten it. But remember that if it can be shortened, the short form should be somewhere in the copy.

(3) Research facts or statements that generally have particular meaning for whites, may not have the same meaning for blacks. If these copy points are going to be used, beware: they could produce a negative reaction. Some advertisers have actually used, in nonwhite campaigns, such phrases as "leaves your hands lily-white," "flesh-colored," "won't show on your face," and other phrases that can be offensive to blacks. Also, be extremely careful in using what are believed to be "in" sayings among blacks, because often by the time whites hear them, they are in disuse among blacks.

(4) Use themes and creative approaches that reflect believable situations for black consumers, reflecting their life-styles.

(5) Avoid controversial and offensive themes that can become issues in the market.

(6) Seek to use subjects that enhance the image of the consumer. Avoid stereotyping of subjects.

(7) Do use attractive and easily identifiable models in print ads wherever possible, reflecting the *recognition* of, *identification* with, and *invitation* to the market.

(8) If integrated advertisements are used in black-oriented media, they too should reflect realistic situations that the majority of non-whites might experience.

(9) In broadcast advertising oriented to blacks, we recommend that air personalities read copy live only in special situations. The music should conform to the sound usually heard on the station.

(10) Care should be given not to make the music sound too exaggerated or stereotyped; this could be insulting to listeners.

(11) In dealing with multiple stations, individual station personalities should be used as determined by the campaign, as many have their own followings but no "crossing" of personalities or shows should be made.

(12) Too much copy should be avoided, but stress quality: appeal to brand consciousness, and avoid hard sell. Music is still the most effective format.

CHAPTER 16
Sales Promotion and Merchandising Techniques

FROM THE TIME a black-oriented customer program is conceived, through all of its development, there is only one place where the efforts can be measured, and that is *at the point of sale*.

The "total concept" in black-oriented marketing programs is growing. No advertiser should just put an ad in black-oriented media and let it go at that. Opportunities for sales-promotion and merchandising programs exist in support of the overall marketing mission.

A case in point is the Kool cigarette involvement with the Kool Jazz Festivals, presented by noted impresario George Wein, and produced by Festival Productions.

The Brown & Williamson Tobacco Corporation of Louisville, Kentucky, manufacturer of cigarettes and other tobacco products, has been an active developer of the black consumer market, particularly for the Kool brand. Black-oriented newspapers and magazines are utilized in the brand's advertising campaigns, and the results show it.

Kool is estimated to account for over 7 percent of the total U.S. cigarette market. Black smokers made up over 30 percent of the share of market for the brand.

B & W seeks to protect this share of market and even to increase it. As did other tobacco companies, when the ban on broadcast advertising took effect, the company sought other avenues of consumer motivation. It decided to consider a proposal to tie in with the jazz festival promotions that were held periodically in some cities, and give it national exposure. This led to Kool's sponsorship, now in its third year.

The format extends beyond jazz. George Wein's explanation of

95

it could apply as well to the use of music as a commercial approach in radio and TV:

> Many times we are questioned as to why we call our festivals "Jazz Festivals" when we present so many soul artists. The formula for presenting soul artists on a Jazz Festival has emerged in a very natural way. We find that people in each community where we work respond more directly to the great soul artists we present. Perhaps it has upset the balance of jazz artists to soul artists, but at the same time it has not affected the musical quality of our festival.

> Soul music and jazz come from basic roots—the gospel and blues music of Black America. However, those that like soul music also like jazz and vice versa. We will continue to present the great soul artists as long as the public wants to hear them. We still use the word jazz in respect to the tradition in which the festivals have been established. We have now, in a sense, given a meaning to the word jazz as a connotation to excellence in Afro-American music.

In 1976 the Kool Jazz Festivals played to primarily black audiences in fourteen U.S. cities. You can't escape the name *Kool;* it is everywhere.

Brown & Williamson Tobacco's president Charles I. McCarty issued support statements on B & W letterhead; and all other Festival letterhead and support materials, including point-of-sale material, brochures, and tickets, carry the Kool logo, and are, generally, in the Kool colors of white and green.

Audiences at the Festivals are also exposed to Kool advertising. In the first year alone, the Festivals attracted over 480,000 people in only six markets.

Two giant TV screens at the Festivals provide close-up pictures of the artists performing and, periodically, the Kool message, which consists of dancers performing in silhouette with the old, but updated, Kool radio jingle, "come up to Kool," and occasionally these words flashed on the screen. A Kool advertisement is in the Festivals' souvenir programs, and product samples are provided in each star's dressing room.

The Kool brand is also promoted in Festival newspaper and magazine advertisements in black-oriented media. The Kool Jazz Festivals' ad carries a coupon that allows readers to write in for a free brochure giving dates of the Festivals and cities.

One feature of the program is to provide a share of the profits to local groups, mainly nonprofit organizations, concerned with the arts, education, and community services. In the second year, about $40,000 in grants was provided.

The Kool Jazz Festivals allow a major cigarette brand to achieve in-depth exposure to persons in its target market; identifies with a music culture; gives exposure to top-name talent and those on the rise; and shows how a black-oriented program can support the over-all marketing mission.

Merchandising and personal-appearance programs can produce results when keyed to target markets. One such campaign was carried out by WEBB Radio in Baltimore, Maryland in behalf of Fab detergent.

For several months a familiar sight in Baltimore's black neighborhoods was a Chrysler station wagon driven by an attractive young woman, decorated with Fab signs and two huge simulated boxes of the product taped on the roof. The station employed a "Fab Girl" (who drove the station wagon), an attractive black schoolteacher who was capable of talking convincingly to prospective customers. Letters were sent to the owners of all the laundromats in Baltimore, advising them of demonstrations to be held over a two-month period. The letter explained that the Fab Girl would talk about the proper use of top-loading automatic washers and how the product "gets clothes clean clear through"; if the laundromat owner desired, she would hold a demonstration there.

Thirty-four requests for demonstrations were received by WEBB from laundromats, by phone and by mail. On the appointed day, the Fab Girl started making her visits, telling the laundromat's customers of the many advantages of using Fab.

She carried boxes of the product with her and actually did laundry for those who would let her. Meanwhile, her Fab station wagon was parked outside, in itself stirring consumer interest; the curious were given a product pitch.

The laundromats' owners and managers, pleased with the results of the demonstrations, asked the station if they could be rescheduled.

In addition to the laundromat demonstrations, the Fab Girl visited nineteen large independent supermarkets in the black sections of Baltimore. These visits were made during peak shopping hours so that the greatest number of prospective customers could hear the explanation of Fab's cleaning ability, and the reasons why they should buy it.

The final report indicated the success of the program. It also reported the number of women who were already using the product, and, surprisingly, the large number of men using it. Sales increased.

Another example of involving black-oriented media in a merchandising campaign took place in Chicago. There *Ebony* magazine cooperated in solving a problem General Mills was having with its Gold Medal Flour.

Gold Medal was being outsold by a competitive flour, three to one. General Mills and *Ebony* set up a plan to develop the Chicago black consumer market through a hard-sell campaign.

Once the plan was set up, assistance was given to divisional sales personnel for planning and the needed cooperation for successful implementation.

The program basically consisted of getting major chains and large independent supermarkets in predominantly black neighborhoods to have in-store demonstrations. Although it was against A & P's policy, that company cooperated with the program, along with Kroger, Jewel Food Stores, and other chains.

In all, sixty supermarkets participated. Nonwhite demonstrators distributed free cookies and *Betty Crocker's Pie Parade Cookbook*. A coupon worth fifteen cents toward the purchase of any sack of Gold Medal Flour was inserted in each issue of *Ebony* distributed in Chicago.

During the month-long, hard-sell campaign, some 36,000 black families participated, in one form or another. Some 15,000 families bought Gold Medal Flour, and thousands of cookies were distributed to customers.

Jewel Food Stores, a Chicago-based chain, has changed some of its practices in its inner-city stores, and this may well portend how other multistore retailers may concern themselves with minority consumers.

For several years, Jewel has had an ethnic merchandiser who works across all department lines in developing product sources for the chain and putting together weekly feature programs for each ethnic group. The goal is to provide all the flexibility needed to have whatever Jewel needs in each store while maintaining central pricing control and buying standards.

To determine ethnic preferences, Jewel has developed a procedure for tracking shipments to stores identified as black, Puerto Rican, Mexican, and Jewish. Shipments by item are then compared with shipments to a group of its stores representing the average white, suburban consumers. The significant differences are reported on an ongoing basis, so the stores can adjust shelf allocations, the merchandisers can select the right mix for sales programs, and customers can find what they want as they shop in Jewel stores.

Recently, Jewel has started considering the inner city in its review of private-label programs, and has changed its thinking on items in its warehouses. In the past, an item was not even considered for a warehouse slot if it was not going to be carried in all of its stores. Now Jewel evaluates:

- Potential case volume (disregarding number of locations);

- The retail price impression it could make if Jewel were to "trim case costs" by eliminating direct charges; and

- Providing stores with a more reliable source of supply (e.g., Jewel warehouse versus a street peddler whose service is erratic).

In addition to major suppliers, Jewel has worked with over 130 minority businesses to help build their product lines and service levels as successful suppliers of the greater retailing community.

There are ways manufacturers can improve marketing in the inner city, according to Jewel's Ronald D. Peterson, executive vice-president of marketing:

One of the things we really need from manufacturers (or their brokers) is increased store coverage for our inner-city stores. The problem is clearly illustrated every time we compare "sign-in books" (logs Jewel asks suppliers to sign each time they visit a store). Some inner-city stores don't collect fifty signatures a year! Some white suburban stores collect one hundred signatures a week.

We need your ideas, suggestions, knowledge, and constructive criticisms. We need you to train your people so they understand that each store can be a different market. We need your understanding of our role as the customer's buying agent as opposed to the manufacturers' sales arm.

We also need your help in getting more Spanish-language point-of-purchase material, and black P.O.P. material. Most manufacturers continue to offer promotional material that is all white, and all in English. Our attitudes and marketing plans are going to have to change, because the need for localized promotional material is going to continue to increase— it isn't going to disappear. This message isn't startling or new. What is startling is the continued lack of response—or worse, an inadequate token response.

For the alert marketing executive, advertising in black-oriented media can add supporting services right down to the point of sale, which can extend reach, potential, and conviction to increasing sales in minority communities.

Good planning and programming, coupled with the enthusiasm of the sales force, particularly in areas of urban minority concentrations, and the enthusiasm that can be generated among distributors and retailers, should improve the competition sales position.

This kind of activity should not be overlooked in considering nonwhites as consumers.

CHAPTER 17

How Public Relations
Is Practiced

HUNDREDS of millions of dollars are spent to influence the American public through public relations or public affairs, and institutional advertising. Yet all this does not do a full job: 11 percent of the population virtually ignores it, simply because for the most part *they* are ignored.

We have often pointed out the information vacuum existing between business and industry, and nonprofit organizations and the nonwhite community, and observed that it is costing business both goodwill and income, and an opportunity to precondition attitudes and opinions.

Public relations has long been part of the conditioning of minorities, more often to "include them out," and thus contribute to their feelings of being unwanted. James Baldwin has said that the most difficult and bewildering thing about the white world is that it acts as if blacks were not there. Public relations efforts directed to the majority American population reflect this.

Only when public relations activities have been directed at the national black community do they become believable. Through proven techniques of public relations, public opinion from this audience can be built favorably.

At one time, the nonwhite could be led via white-oriented leadership, white-oriented media, and the spill-off of some public relations effort. It is doubtful if this would work today.

Over the years we have carefully structured black-oriented public relations efforts, changing these practices as the company itself has changed. This process will continue as the community itself undergoes change.

There are three basic areas where public relations is practiced in this community—*press relations, community relations,* and *publicity.*

Almost all of the successful public relations efforts have made effective use of explicit, direct lines of communication to the desired audiences.

We have made several studies of the needs of the black-oriented media and, on behalf of our clients, have tried to meet their needs. These studies have been supplemented by personal visits to media executives and the working press. (We almost always visit media in a city, whether we have business to discuss at the moment or not.)

Minority-oriented media serve a wide audience, and will continue to grow in importance, especially in the nonwhite English- and Spanish-speaking communities in America.

Communications to white-oriented media should also be provided to nonwhite media, for the *interpretation* necessary for these minority groups that such media provide, to *insure* that they understand that the messages mean them, too.

To reach and effectively inform 25 million black Americans, there are an estimated: 21 national magazines, 178 newspapers, 250 radio stations, and 350 movie theaters. In addition, there are a large number of trade publications for tavern and bar owners, for women in the beauty trade field, for those interested in black travel in agencies; local and regional publications; newsletters and organs for scores of black-interest organizations; and supplements to black-oriented newspapers, such as *Dawn, National Black Monitor,* and *National Scene,* as well as an entertainment-oriented supplement, *The Happenings.*

Public relations people, in working for clients and organizations, need to understand that all media should be serviced, and how to service them. This should include media geared to the interests of 25 million black people.

The theory is that in order to achieve maximum identification, communications should be oriented as closely as possible to the interests of the intended audience. Thus it follows logically that information of a particular interest to nonwhites—as nonwhites, as consumers, as voters, as opinion molders—should be communicated through media geared to their interests.

Rather than being "reverse segregation," it is simply good public relations practice to serve black-oriented media with information of particular interest to their audiences.

Pan Am makes effective inclusion of black father and daughters in its multi-racial appeal to Americans to "claim your heritage." Their Heritage Brochure benefited from Alex Haley's *Roots*, as well as from the desires of all Americans to learn about their family histories.

Pan Am
invites you to
claim your
heritage

This is an exceptional technique, the silhouettes reflecting modified Afro hairstyles. It carries out the Miller theme, "If you've got the time. . . .", and suggests these men are heading for a beer.

Miller time

Time to head for the best tasting beer you can find.
America's quality beer since 1855.

Anheuser-Busch commissioned black artists to develop original art portraying black kings of African history. This project then grew into an advertising campaign, booth exhibits at black conventions, and public showings in key cities.

Great Kings of Africa

Hannibal – Ruler of Carthage. (247-183 B.C.)

Regarded as one of the greatest generals of all time, Hannibal and his overpowering African armies conquered major portions of Spain and Italy and came close to defeating the mighty Roman Empire.

Born in the North African country of Carthage, Hannibal became general of the army at age twenty-five. His audacious moves —such as marching his army with African war elephants through the treacherous Alps to surprise and conquer Northern Italy —and his tactical genius, as illustrated by the Battle of Cannae where his seemingly trapped army cleverly surrounded and destroyed a much larger Roman force, won him recognition which has spanned more than 2000 years. His tactics have been studied and successfully imitated by generals as recently as World War II.

The genius of Hannibal extended beyond the battlefield, however. After the Punic Wars, his leadership and administrative abilities brought Carthage great prosperity and prestige.

Discover home in a place you've never bee

It's somewhere far. Yet very close to home.
It's an island where Black is the majority. Where proud Black men and women govern the politics, and shape the culture of their land.
It's Jamaica, the Bahamas, Virgin Islands.
It's home. With warm beaches and clear tropical waters. It's Caribbean styled restaurants that serve everything from steaks to delicious island dishes.
It's rum drinks you've never heard of. And steel drums at an all-night, costumed carnival in the streets. And it's available 12 months a year.
So come on home, to a place you've never been.
Get into the music. And the people. Get into *your* people. And you may get into yourself. On an Eastern-planned vacation.
Call your travel agent or Eastern.

EASTERN The Wings of Man.

"We took a boat that cruised around Hamilton harbor. It was so lovely and relaxing the baby slept the entire trip."

Bevin and Jeanette Spence on their first visit to Bermuda.

"Bermuda really is a storybook place. It's like being on an enchanted island."

"Our daughter is just learning to swim and she practically lived in the water all the time we were here."

"This is the first vacation where we enjoyed ourselves as much as the children did."

Bermuda

Unspoiled. Unhurried. Uncommon.

See your travel agent or write Bermuda, Dept. 122.
610 Fifth Avenue, N.Y., N.Y., 10020 or 711 Statler Office Bldg., Boston, Mass. 02116

At one time this black family vacationing in Bermuda appeared only in black-oriented magazines, but now Bermuda uses them on a rotating basis in majority publications as well. This ad is effective both as part of a prestige campaign and as encouragement to black vacationers.

One of the most effective travel advertisements aimed at blacks, this speaks directly to them, and, long before *Roots*, encouraged black travelers to "discover home in a place you've never been."

This kind of advertising, with its emphasis on the word "cool" as well as the product's name, helps Kool remain the leading menthol cigarette in the U.S., and the dominant brand of black consumers.

This ad positions North Carolina Mutual as having stability, the ability to compete, and, particularly significant since NCM is the largest black insurance company in the U.S., bigness.

We've become a 3-billion-dollar company. Because our biggest investment is in the people we serve.

People are our business. We help care for their financial futures through life insurance. We help them progress through life insurance. We protect their families through life insurance.

And we can do the same for you.

With a life insurance plan from North Carolina Mutual, we can help you make definite plans for your family's future. Today.

Plans for college. Plans for a new home. Plans for a safe, financially secure future for your family--even if something should happen to you.

This has been our job since 1898. And because we've been doing it pretty well, we're America's largest black-managed life insurance company.

So invest in peace of mind for yourself, and security for your family.

Call your North Carolina Mutual agent today.

NORTH CAROLINA MUTUAL
LIFE INSURANCE COMPANY

Your family needs you. And life insurance.

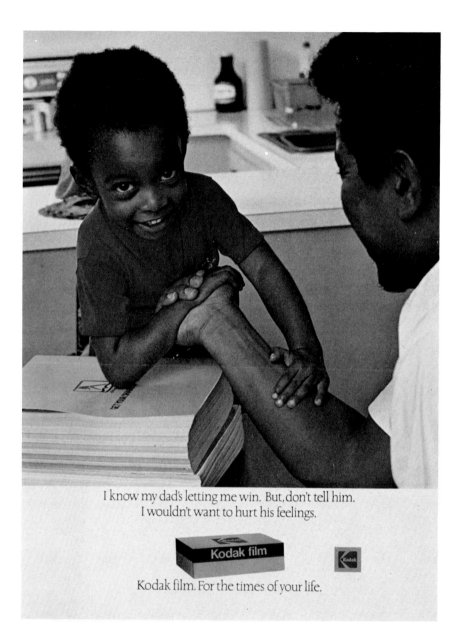

I know my dad's letting me win. But, don't tell him.
I wouldn't want to hurt his feelings.

Kodak film

Kodak film. For the times of your life.

The father figure is an important consideration in black-oriented advertising. This ad makes effective use of an appealing black child with his father to communicate Eastman Kodak's "memorable moments on film" campaign to black consumers.

In this Young & Rubicam ad for Johnson & Johnson baby oil, the multipurpose use of baby oil is dramatically presented. This bleed page ad was selected by magazines as the highest in terms of believability, credibility, and product usage. Other advertisers should explore multiple uses for their products in this market.

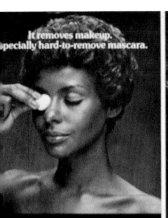

'I leave you love.'

Mary McLeod Bethune wrote these words in the "legacy"— a credo for living and serving others—that she left to the National Council of Negro Women.

To Ella Wynn of IBM, they are particularly important words.

Last year, the NCNW had them inscribed on a plaque and presented to her in appreciation for her work.

Ella Wynn, on a year's paid leave from IBM, worked with the NCNW to help streamline the operation of its Women's Center for Education and Career Advancement in New York.

IBM also contributes funds to help the center in its work.

But it's Ella Wynn and dedicated people like her who are keeping alive Mary McLeod Bethune's "legacy" of helping others.

IBM

This ad positions IBM as a caring company; gives exposure to a loaned executive; and effectively ties in the National Council of Negro Women. The "I Leave You Love" is from the "legacy" to blacks by NCNW's founder, Dr. Mary McLeod Bethune. This is an excellent example of the tie-in possibilities available with America's black organizations.

Created by W. B. Doner for the Army National Guard, this ad portraying the Army Officer's Club called attention to the leadership opportunities for blacks in the Guard. Ads like this helped the Army National Guard to raise its black membership from 7,000 to 49,000 in about five years and demonstrated how advertising can translate institutional objectives into black objectives.

There are 49,000 black people in the Army National Guard. We'd like to see more of them in the Officer's Corps.

The Army National Guard has about 400,000 people. There are about 34,000 officers. But only 750 are black officers.

We're looking for black officers. Black leaders. Men and women who can get out front.

It's tough. But you get a lot of satisfaction. And the chance to serve your country, and your community.

You also get good pay, insurance and retirement benefits. Even special PX and commissary privileges. Plus the opportunity to develop leadership skills that'll help you in business management, or any other career.

If you've had prior service experience as an officer, you can probably get right in. If not, and you qualify, you can get a commission through the Officer Candidate Programs.

Or you may be eligible to receive a direct commission based on your unique civilian experience.

Contact your nearest Army National Guard unit. Or call us, toll free, 800-638-7600 (except in Hawaii, Alaska, Puerto Rico and the Virgin Islands). In Maryland, call 301-728-3388.

The most important part-time job in America.

The Guard belongs.

Black Entrepreneurs.

Then...and now.

Black men and women have played major roles in the shaping of America. One was Alvin Coffey...a man of skill and sound business instincts.

Alvin Coffey was one of many talented Black artisans who went West during the Gold Rush. He panned for gold and worked as a cobbler for the other miners. He earned enough to buy his enslaved family's freedom and a farm, and eventually became a wealthy man.

Today, this creative business spirit is thriving within the Black community. Men like

William McKnight of New York City are finding success by meeting the needs of companies like RCA. McKnight's firm, Uni-World Electrical Distributors, sells light bulbs, outlets and switches, conduit, wire, cable, and other electrical supplies.

RCA recognizes the importance of talented people like Alvin Coffey and William McKnight who help keep America growing.

If you are a business person who wants to contribute to that growth, maybe we can help. Write for our free booklet, **"Doing Business With RCA":** Director, Materials—Minority and Small Business Programs, RCA Corporation, Building 204-2, Cherry Hill, New Jersey 08101.

RCA

RCA, through UniWorld Group, created a series of ads showing blacks in history as weavers and craftsmen of all types, and then related that history to RCA's program to encourage black entrepreneurial development, and its commitment to minority vendors.

A particularly effective ad for Seagram's Gin, representative of its black-oriented campaign. It was supported by strong point-of-sale material, including exhibits at black national conventions.

If you're going to do it...

do it with taste.

And taste means Seagram's Extra Dry Gin. Whatever you're drinking just naturally tastes better when you start with Seagram's, the fastest-growing gin in America.

Seagram's.
The Perfect Martini Gin.
Perfect all ways.

Consistent with the overall Avon image, and reflective of Avon's packaging and themes, this ad effectively positions its "Shades of Beauty" line as a complete group of products for the black consumer. The campaign is backed up with the "You Never Looked So Good" theme on radio and television.

THE LOOK: GLOWING COLOR.

It all starts with Shades of Beauty by Avon, the makeup created just for you.

Liquid Foundation in sheer, earthy colors that never turn chalky. And beautiful Creamy Blush...for anywhere you want an extra glow of dewy color.

Finish up with Avon eye shadow and lip color to complement your outfit and you've got a total fashion look.

When it comes to making faces beautiful, Avon has everything you need. And you can get it all from your Avon Representative.

SHADES OF BEAUTY
by AVON

How do kids love Kool-Aid?

Brand Soft Drink Mix

Preferably in their own glass. But anyone else's, or a paper cup, will do. Kids love Kool-Aid after school. After jumping rope. After cleaning their room. After almost anything. Kids love Kool-Aid when it's raining. When they're watching TV. Playing cards. And playing games. When they're good. And when they're sorry for being bad. Kids love Kool-Aid anytime. Anyplace.

Moms love unsweetened Kool-Aid because it's economical. About 12¢ a quart. Because it's easy to prepare. Just add sugar and water. Because it has 15% U.S. RDA of Vitamin C. That's good. And because kids love it. Get some Kool-Aid Brand Soft Drink Mix. It's pretty terrific.

Westinghouse accomplishes several objectives with this advertisement depicting a black nuclear engineer: 1) it indicates that Westinghouse has blacks among its engineers; 2) it portrays the engineer as concerned about youngsters and their careers and willing to volunteer his time; and 3) it shows Westinghouse actively supporting efforts to get more minorities into engineering and technology.

Ken Jones is a nuclear engineer. But Friday mornings at 11:00, you'll find him teaching math or science at Schenley High.

Meet Ken Jones, B.S., Nuclear Engineering, University of Michigan; M.S., Nuclear Engineering, Carnegie-Mellon University; past president of the Pittsburgh Chapter of the National Technical Association. In addition to his job as a Manager of Functional Analysis with Westinghouse, Ken is working on a master's degree in Business Administration at the University of Pittsburgh. He's a busy, busy man.

But Ken also makes time in his schedule to encourage young black men and women toward careers in engineering and technology. He teaches weekly seminars in math and biology to Schenley High School students and tutors black engineering students at the University of Pittsburgh. He also serves in the university's Black Engineer Council and

Engineering Impact Program and in the Westinghouse "Campus America" Program, visiting college campuses to discuss nuclear power and its role in our nation's energy mix.

At Westinghouse, we underwrite several enrichment programs to interest minority youngsters in careers in engineering and technology, but we also understand and appreciate the unique contribution that Ken Jones and many of our other black employees are making in their person-to-person work with high school and college students.

We hope that someday these young people will, in turn, continue this important work in the black community.

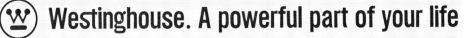

Westinghouse. A powerful part of your life

An equal opportunity employer

Good memories are only an instant away.
Maxwell House® Instant Coffee.

Why is it that some things that have been around a long time always bring back good memories. Like mama's old wedding dress and Maxwell House® Instant Coffee.

Maybe folks love Maxwell House Instant Coffee because its smooth fresh coffee taste reminds them of good times they've had. Or, it could be that they just know they're going to get a delicious, satisfying cup of coffee every time.

Maxwell House® Instant Coffee. Great tasting coffee, every time.

The nostalgia theme is one that has been underutilized in the black consumer market, but this unusual ad for Maxwell House Coffee makes effective use of it. Although the nostalgia theme offers some problem areas, its potential appeal for black consumers should not be ignored.

General Foods is aware of the high consumption of Kool-Aid among black consumers, and backs it with advertisements like this, showing youngsters working up thirst for the product.

At DPGI, we've taken many soundings of how minority editors, publishers, and broadcast executives feel toward corporate and government public relations practices. We have found that most feel that P.R. departments and firms still do not understand the need for and continuing existence of the black press in America. Most editors said that they usually get cordial attention from corporate public relations executives, although some feel they still do not. More minority editors are being invited to press functions, but the usual practice is to exclude them from the corporate function, unless it has some direct bearing on minorities.

The majority of editors feel that specially tailored material gets first preference over general-interest releases. Over two-thirds of the editors indicated they would not use, or would have extreme reluctance to use photographs without nonwhites. Nearly all editors indicate they run articles on nonwhites in responsible positions in business and industry, and government (with the comment that such material indicates blacks can achieve).

Their responses indicate why there is usually lack of identification with broad-based industry programs, issues, and even less-than-average identification with individual company programs. Obviously, there is a critical need to program communications directly to the national nonwhite audience.

For some clients, we have merely extended the efforts of the company, government agency, or other organization to communicate generally into the black community. For others, we have developed and executed specific public relations efforts. In almost all cases, we have found the black-oriented press to be the most effective approach. It offers circulation and listeners in the millions, and exerts a tremendous influence on the thinking in the community.

The second route to building goodwill, in addition to press relations, has been through community-relations activities, particularly with national leadership organizations. In recognizing the duality of the American society, observe a characteristic of certain organizations' names: many of those organizations with "American" in the title are white, and many with "National" in the title are black. For example, there is an American Medical Association and a National Medical Association, the latter comprised primarily of black doctors; an American Bar Association, and a National Bar Association; an American Dental Association, and a National Dental Association.

The American Medical Association's stand on many issues, especially where race is concerned, has differed from that of the National

Medical Association. Part of the success of public relations in this community is knowing what message to get to whom—and when.

National black organizations have been created by the social, political, economic, and educational horizons open to blacks in the United States during the twentieth century. Although many barriers in racial communication have been breached over the years, it is still necessary for blacks to foster closer ties among themselves—partly in recognition of the realities of a divided American society.

There are about 120 predominantly black national organizations in the United States today. (We list these in the annual *American Airlines Guide to Black Conventions and Conferences*, which we research and compile for the airline.)

The background of such organizations suggests that they are likely to continue. Thirty-seven out of one hundred major black organizations now in existence are over fifty years old, with the Prince Hall Masons, the oldest organization, at 192 years old. The national organizations have an outreach to between 13 and 15 million members, who are also consumers and influencers.

There are numerous opportunities for public relations efforts among these organizations, from having executives appear before audiences at national conventions, to exhibits and displays at convention sites, other extensions of courtesy, and undertaking special projects with these groups.

Many opportunities also exist at the local level, using chapters of national organizations as a springboard for local communication and program activity.

The third channel to the national nonwhite population—publicity—encompasses the first two. We have made a practice of tailoring material to the black press, and then calling the attention of opinion makers to this publicity through reprints and other means.

Publicity is a most important tool in the effort to let blacks know and understand they are being "included in." The manner in which it is shaped, and the plan to get it into the right hands becomes vitally important.

In addition to the three main channels to the minority community, a fourth avenue is always hoped for: word of mouth. We are happy when our clients are talked about favorably in the nonwhite community because of some activity or act. There is no substitute for getting on this grapevine.

Blacks have been so conditioned to responding, thinking, and acting as blacks, that there is an almost automatic unidentifiable channel of communications among this group.

Of course, bad news travels the fastest. This is particularly true of bad racial news. But, conversely, good racial news can also have immediate transmission. Almost all black "firsts" of any type still are considered "hard news" in the community.

We have, over the years, used a good many techniques to help spread information to the widest possible circles in the nonwhite community.

Following are some case studies in which public relations has been used effectively.

Case Study 1

As have many public relations firms, we have often been called upon to "put out a fire."

These fires may have been started with a spark of misunderstanding, or after evaluation and consideration, or in the belief that the right thing was being done.

The spark of misunderstanding was to be the case with "Expo '67," the Canadian World Exhibition.

Harry Carlson, president of Wolcott, Carlson & Company, public relations firm, telephoned one day and asked if I would lunch with him.

At lunch he told me that a possible explosion was coming concerning the charge of racial discrimination against Expo '67, which his firm was handling.

In the nonwhite community, fewer charges against a company are communicated faster than charges of racial discrimination—and so it would be with the charge against Expo '67.

We agreed to provide counsel to Wolcott, Carlson and Expo '67 should the need arise. It did.

During a press conference called by a leading and responsible black organization, the New York Urban League, the charges were leveled. They were to receive broad news coverage and editorials in both white- and black-oriented media. The organization called upon President Lyndon B. Johnson to withdraw the United States from Expo '67.

Specifically, the main charge was that:

Negroes and other nonwhites are being barred from employment solely because of their race, and they are being barred from suitable housing facilities in Canada for the same reason. The Negro press is being practically ignored in the advertising being placed in furtherance of Expo officials' desire not to encourage them to visit the Fair.

Further, it was charged that:

For many years the Canadian Government has been noted for its discriminatory practices toward the nonwhite peoples of the world and particularly the American Negro.

We set out to evaluate how bad the situation was following the initial publicity, and at the same time to find out how the climate had developed in which such charges could be made.

It turned out that what had been intended as a policy *not* to segregate or segment P.R. efforts for Expo had backfired. The decision had been made, instead, to appeal to *all* Americans to attend, assuming that nonwhites were automatically included. This was a wrong premise.

As we were to point out, such a policy, particularly in the field of travel, because of past experience has to *exclude* blacks. Mass, white-oriented, communications traditionally do not "speak" to the nonwhite.

This was a public relations policy decision. Advertising, using the same basic copy appeal for Expo '67, had already been scheduled for black-oriented media, but with only a change in models from a white family to a black family, which was an acceptable technique.

We pointed out the need to issue a blanket news release, from a Canadian official, in which should be included some pertinent facts about blacks and travel to Canada. We also advised that the black press immediately be sent all material received by white-oriented media. The objective was not to establish a "special" category, but rather to include them in the distribution of all news and features being disseminated.

One of our associates made an immediate visit to Montreal to talk with Expo '67 officials, public relations executives, and some key people in the Montreal nonwhite community.

At the same time, we moved to find out what effect the charges were having in travel plans of some key black organizations, churches, and individuals.

We recommended expansion of the list of black-oriented newspapers that were receiving advertising. The advertising department had also been making plans in this direction, so this was effected. The primary marketing area for Expo '67 advertising was along an imaginary line running from Chicago to Washington, D.C., and this was where the expanded newspapers were to be used. *Ebony* and *Tuesday* received the standard magazine ads, with a change of models.

Our efforts uncovered the following: there was an anti-discrimination law applying to hotels, restaurants, and camping grounds throughout Quebec Province, and officials were willing to prosecute under it. The term *hotel*, of course, did not apply to private homes, so this remained a questionable area.

We determined that nonwhites had been employed, including the man who set up the communications for Expo '67. West Indians, Africans, and other nonwhites were also employed in various job classifications. There were also guides (including an attractive Haitian woman who was to visit New York for personal appearances and publicity before the Fair opened).

We learned that while there had been discrimination reported, on the whole blacks had no problems in getting acceptance in public places, and could rent an apartment or buy a house in any part of Montreal where they could afford to live. (Montreal has made advances in race relations: there is a tendency for the nonwhite population to be divided more along the lines of income than along racial lines, and they are woven into the city's fabric. There are no ghettos per se.)

We also learned that, according to a national study made in major U.S. cities, 48 percent of blacks who visited a foreign country within a twelve-month period visited Canada. The second favorite vacation area was the Caribbean. We reasoned that if this were the case, nonwhites would hardly be visiting there if they felt discrimination and segregation were such serious problems.

We evaluated all the facts we had gathered, and recommended their incorporation into a release that had been prepared following a press conference by then Quebec Premier Daniel Johnson. In that press conference he gave his assurance that "American Negro visitors to Expo '67 would not be victims of discrimination in housing."

The facts, with Premier Johnson's remarks, were given fairly wide distribution through communications channels in the target community.

We met with executives of the organization that had charged Expo '67 with discrimination, and while they were not satisfied that all the requests they made had been met, they did feel that steps had been taken, and they would adopt a wait-and-see attitude.

Ebony magazine was to have a story on Expo '67 in its vacation issue, and many representatives of the black press (who had been invited on press junkets *before* the charges were leveled) wrote glowing articles about the fair.

Reprints of ads, and other materials, were distributed to a key list of opinion makers concerning Expo '67 and the black visitor.

Expo '67 was a highly successful world exhibition. Nonwhite visitors were welcomed, and few, if any, problems developed. No further charges were ever filed.

It has generally been agreed that if public relations efforts initially had been followed to *truly* include all people, the charges and resultant embarrassment might not have developed.

Case Study 2

We had been working on a number of assignments in behalf of *The Reader's Digest*—primarily in-depth publicity in the black national community on articles of particular interest to this audience—when Sterling Fisher, then vice-president of public relations and executive director of the Reader's Digest Foundation, asked if we would give some thought to an idea he had.

Reader's Digest Condensed Books was going to reprint Booker T. Washington's *Up From Slavery*. Since it was in the public domain and *Reader's Digest* was not required to pay the $5,000 fee for the right to reprint to anyone, the company wanted to know how this money might be used in the black community.

After some discussion in our shop, we decided that instead of a scholarship, it might better be used to encourage creative writing talent among black youth.

What evolved became an annual creative writing competition sponsored by the Reader's Digest Foundation and the United Negro College Fund.

In determining how best to encourage creative writing, we considered and recommended the United Negro College Fund, which is primarily a fund-raising arm for thirty-three predominantly black colleges. We felt in this way greater control could be exerted, and publicity and promotional efforts could be concentrated.

Both the Reader's Digest Foundation and the United Negro College Fund agreed, and the program was launched in 1960.

Entries were to be judged in three categories—short story, essay, and poetry.

A letter and materials were sent to each of the member colleges and universities, and acceptance of the idea was excellent.

In addition to cash prizes, the three top winners in each category would receive an expense-paid trip to New York, where they would receive their prizes.

As I looked on the smiling faces of the three youngsters who were to receive the first year's prizes in New York, I could not help but feel that Booker T. Washington would have been proud to know that even at this date, his biography was indirectly helping to encourage some talented black youngsters.

The publicity on the contest idea, and on the contest itself, got wide publicity in black-oriented newspapers, college newspapers, and radio news.

The program continues to fill a need in the community, which in itself has helped to guarantee its annual success.

Case Study 3

One of the most successful public relations efforts, with marketing implications, was the "Miss Rheingold" contest.

The winner would appear as Miss Rheingold in advertisements, personal appearances, and publicity efforts, and was to personify the typical American girl.

Since black women do not fit the profile of the "typical American girl," a nonwhite did not really have an opportunity to win, or, for that matter, a Spanish-speaking girl.

Liebmann Breweries (later sold to become Rheingold Breweries, under new management) sponsored the contest annually. Black and Puerto Rican young women did enter the preliminaries. But when the final six were selected to compete for the title, no black or Latin faces ever made it.

To describe the one-time popularity of the "Miss Rheingold" contest, consider that with 22 million votes cast in one election, it was second only to U.S. presidential balloting.

Yet, because a vital public relations area could not be satisfied, the contest was destined to be withdrawn. The contest neglected nearly 25 percent of the population in its primary marketing area.

In the 1950s while Rheingold was promoting its "Miss Rheingold" contest, primarily in New York, the F. & M. Schaefer Brewing Company was promoting its "Miss Beaux Arts" contest, also in New York.

The difference was that while Miss Rheingold was white-oriented, Miss Beaux Arts was black-oriented.

In the black community, instead of pictures of Miss Rheingold contestants, the lovely brown-skin models competing for Miss Beaux Arts appeared. They appeared in target newspapers and over radio. It was clear: a girl of color had to win.

Thus, even while a highly successful white-oriented effort was being made, a countereffort was successfully accomplished in the nonwhite community. It clearly arose out of an absence of opportunity for the blacks in the white-oriented effort. The "Miss Rheingold" contest was discontinued as it lost popularity, caused in part by this countereffort.

Case Study 4

One of the areas in which we have been most successful in using all of the elements of good public relations with the black community has been in our assignments for motion-picture companies.

From our first motion-picture assignment with Universal Pictures, through every major and several smaller companies, we have worked on getting more blacks to attend movies.

Most gratifying was our long relationship with Columbia Pictures Corporation. From the day Robert S. Ferguson, then Columbia's vice-president for advertising and publicity, told us he wanted to have us work on all Columbia products, regardless of racial interest, we did just that.

Although we worked on a wide range of motion pictures, those pictures that do have particular minority interest give us a wider range in which to work, because we have added advantages going for us with these motion pictures.

I would like to describe one campaign in particular.

There was little doubt that Columbia Pictures' *To Sir, With Love*, starring Sidney Poitier as a teacher in a London slum school, was one of 1967's biggest hits. The motion picture broke more house records than any other film in Columbia Pictures' history, and became one of its highest-grossing films.

For example, it grossed a record $3,625,000 in ten showcase weeks (where a selected number of theaters are used) in the metropolitan New York–New Jersey area. This figure represented the gross from twenty-eight theaters and was the biggest tally ever to be recorded for a film playing the New York area in one group of theaters.

Black moviegoers' response to the motion picture was unprecedented, and made up a significant share of the total audience for the motion picture. There is little doubt that Poitier, the most successful and popular actor of color in Hollywood's history, was the prime factor in moving Negroes to theaters, and moving audiences in general.

Columbia Pictures probably established the best rapport with black-oriented media representatives and opinion-making groups in the black community of any major studio in the United States. Based on our recommendations, all of Columbia's publicity material is distributed to nonwhite-oriented media as well as to "regular" channels.

Material we distribute is "tailored" supplementary material, keyed to the direct interests of the minority editor.

In addition, we built up a list of opinion-making group leadership in key cities; these persons were invited to screenings, to preview selected motion pictures before release to the general public. It has been a most effective way of developing favorable word-of-mouth support.

Critics and moviegoers alike had acclaimed *To Sir, With Love.* It had an Academy Award winner in Poitier; a talented writer-producer-director in James Clavell; a book that had won a number of awards and extremely wide readership, whose author, E. R. Braithwaite, was Ambassador of Guyana to the United Nations; a catchy title song; and bright young faces in English actors with the mod look. The strategy was to put all of these opportunities and personalities to work in the campaign—including our efforts in the black movie market.

Long before the release of the motion picture, a screening program for opinion makers was embarked upon. Black press and groups were effectively included in these programs.

Poitier hosted several screenings in New York to which high school students and youngsters in drama groups were invited, along with leaders of antipoverty programs. Poitier also appeared at screenings in Los Angeles.

"Previews and Pepsi" screenings of the film were held in several key cities, with the cooperation of the Manager of Special Projects at Pepsi-Cola. Pepsi's special-markets men worked with local bottlers in holding screenings for high school drama students, class presidents, and editors of high school publications of both predominantly white and predominantly nonwhite schools. (In the final scene of the graduating class dance, where Pepsi is served, Poitier is shown pouring a glassful for a fellow teacher.)

National and local black-oriented organizations were included in the screening program. These organizations gave publicity to the motion picture in their house organs circulated to their national memberships.

In the motion picture, Poitier portrays a teacher who faces the difficult and insubordinate group of youngsters in a problem school in London's East End. The teacher, who put his experiences into a book, was E. R. Braithwaite. The author, at the time of the film's release Ambassador of the Permanent Mission of Guyana to the United Nations, made himself available for public relations efforts in behalf of the film.

Screenings were held for delegates to the United Nations, and for the Premier of Guyana when he visited the United States. It was also arranged for those attending the annual summer convention of the National Newspaper Publishers Association—the trade association of publishers of black-oriented newspapers—to hear Ambassador Braithwaite at a luncheon, and to have a private screening of the motion picture. Both groups gave their enthusiastic support to the film.

At its biennial convention, the Delta Sigma Theta Sorority, a major black women's service organization, presented Columbia Pictures with an award for the film. At the award presentation, Ambassador Braithwaite received a thunderous standing ovation. During his visit, he also received extensive publicity, and appeared on three television shows.

Two other stars of the film in addition to Poitier, actress Judy Geeson and singer "Lulu," visited New York and helped promote the film. Lulu, a British recording and TV star, visited black-oriented media, appeared on a radio talk show, and visited a predominantly black and Puerto Rican high school, where she talked with drama students about her career and the movie.

The publicity *To Sir, With Love* received from the black press was probably greater than that received by any other motion picture.

Ebony, Jet, and *Sepia* magazines all carried features on the motion picture. Newspapers carried features on the actors, the author, and on the film itself.

Copies of the paperback movie version of the book were distributed to key editors and columnists, and radio commentators at target media.

Clearly, the black-oriented campaign for *To Sir, With Love* paid off for Columbia Pictures. This was evident in the quantity of exposure it received, the amount of money it made, and the nonwhite attendance figures quoted by managers. The campaign proved the point that the full use of available channels in the black community can help build both goodwill and sales.

CHAPTER 18

Getting Distributor
Cooperation

Coca-Cola USA, through its special market executives Kelvin A. Wall and Harold Hamilton, called us in in 1967 to determine if several efforts under consideration could be developed into programs that would be of interest to Coca-Cola Bottlers. This led us into two major projects with Coca-Cola.

The first involved what had originally been a training film, for bottlers, and which we expanded into a community-relations project. The film, *Special Men in Special Markets*, had been designed to point up the importance of black consumers and to encourage the hiring of special market men.

The film, which was well done, used as role models two actual salesmen, one from a northern bottler (Cleveland) and one from a southern bottler (Columbia, South Carolina). It proved, overall, why it made good business sense to hire men to work in special markets. Specifically, it showed how sales had improved; pointed out the number of coolers sold; described the point-of-sale advertising Coke put behind its black consumer market development; demonstrated that blacks often could get better shelf allocation for Coke; and showed how crew work could be beneficial.

The film had had good usage among bottlers, and rather than retire it to the shelf, its life was to be extended as part of a community relations project by bottlers in black communities. We were asked to develop this direction.

It was decided that most of the film could be used as a motivational film to encourage young blacks to enter the field of selling. So a portion of the film's narration was rewritten to promote selling as a career in general.

113

Support materials were developed to promote the program, named "Careers in Selling," which also became the new title of the film. News releases for the community-interest program were prepared, and a press kit developed on minorities in selling, opportunities in selling, and other facts.

To test community acceptance, three markets were selected to host community leadership, show the film, and distribute material: Cleveland, Atlanta, and Detroit. The first showing was held in Cleveland, as one of the "stars" of the film was there, and the bottler readily agreed to support the activity.

Heads of local organizations, especially those we felt would use the film and support materials, were invited to a film showing and reception. The effort was launched with good response and support from business editors and the black press.

The second reception, in Atlanta, was held in cooperation with the National Association of Market Developers, black professionals in marketing, sales, advertising, and public relations. Here, too, audience reception was enthusiastic for the program.

And so it went in Detroit as well. All of the bottlers involved felt the program was worthwhile, and through Coca-Cola USA, it was promoted in other markets as well.

Coca-Cola's Wall and Hamilton were also exploring the use of a black history program, for which we were called in. We were to implement the program and help develop a program to interest bottlers.

The black history effort included a slide film, supporting materials produced by the Jam Handy Organization, and Golden Legacy comic books, developed by Bertram Fitzgerald, a black businessman who originated the idea of stories of black heroes and heroines in comic-book form.

We recommend that, in ten cities, we (1) help sell the bottler on the idea; (2) get organizational support for the program; and (3) determine feasibility for school, library, media, and other usage nationwide.

The joint effort got underway. Three markets were visited immediately to establish personal contact with the bottlers and sell the program. Each bottler agreed to cooperate, and enthusiasm was strong. Gradually we moved into the remaining seven markets to achieve a base on which bottlers nationwide could build.

An immediate benefit was the agreement of most school districts to use Coca-Cola's black history material not only in predominantly black schools, but also to some extent in *all* schools. (This proved particularly convincing for bottlers who were reluctant to try the program even in black schools.)

The main library in each city was also visited, and almost all agreed to erect a Black History Week display, including the Coca-Cola material.

The results achieved within a year's time were gratifying:

SLIDE FILM ON BLACK HISTORY	
Number of participating bottlers	173
Number of kits distributed	10,200
Estimated film audience 9,200 kits × 300 viewers	2,760,000
Estimated number of schools in distribution	8,000
Estimated number of cities where kit distributed (including distribution by Association for the Study of Afro-American Life and History)	1,000
School-board approval in a number of cities, including Chicago, New York, Atlanta, Miami, San Francisco, and Oakland	
COMIC BOOKS ON BLACK HISTORY	
Number of participating bottlers	130
Number of books distributed	800,000
Number of responses to magazine ad	7,479
Number of magazines sold through ad	36,000
Distributed to offices of 750 black dentists	
PUBLICITY RESULTS	
Number of newspaper mentions in 1½-month period	106
Estimated total exposure (including Wall on the "Today Show," *Jet*, *Ebony*, black-oriented newspapers, bottler activities, and film audiences	45,000,000
Number of consumer impressions from free black history tape uses (33 markets × average audience of 25,000 × 7 days @ minimum 4 times per day	25,000,000

So, the major effort to develop an involvement in black history was begun with ten bottlers of Coca-Cola and ended with 173 participating in the program. *Black Treasures*, a color sound slide film on the importance of black history, and *Golden Legacy* comic book were the principal vehicles for its implementation.

Both we and the client had theorized that if the distributors, or bottlers in this case, could be offered a sound program, shown the need it would fill, and asked for their cooperation, we would get it. And we did.

CHAPTER 19

Corporate Social Responsibility as an Economic Support System

AN ACKNOWLEDGED NEED in our society is to build economic foundations in minority communities. An encouraging development in this area has been the extra effort put forth by a growing number of American corporations to facilitate the entrance of minority businesses, black and Hispanic, into important factors in the community, and into the mainstream of American life.

I have selected an effort put forth by Avon Products, Inc., the world's largest manufacturer of cosmetics and toiletries, as an example that extends beyond minority enterprise into the wide concerns of minorities, illustrating how the company sought to meet such need.

A unique program developed by Avon, a New York-based multinational company, showed dramatic results—both in terms of dollars spent by the company with minority suppliers, and the ripple effect the program generated in the marketplace.

At the end of 1975, Avon reported that goods and services purchased from minority companies totaled more than $3.5 million, an increase of ten times the dollar value of contracts awarded in 1972.

Equally noteworthy was the number of minority businesses the firm had under contract. Beginning with a nucleus of 30 companies in 1972, when the program was formally set in motion, by 1976 Avon called on more than 300 minority-owned suppliers and advertising media to help satisfy its needs in services or supplies.

Avon's needs encompassed a broad variety of outside goods and services, ranging from plastic parts and product ingredients, to such services as cleaning supplies and maintenance, as well as the utilization of advertising and sales promotion services.

Avon effectively explored opportunities to contribute to minority economic development. As part of its minority vendor program, the company offered the technical assistance of its skilled personnel to enable small minority establishments to meet Avon's particular standards. Banks and other sources of financial aid were also encouraged to assist new Avon suppliers to obtain adequate capital.

Corporate investment relationships also exist with minority-owned banks, insurance companies, and brokers. Avon had more than $10 million in tax deposits placed in minority financial institutions in nine states.

The company purchased $1 million in Certificates of Deposit from twenty-five minority banks in fifteen states. Additionally, $25 million in life insurance coverage has been reinsured through three black-owned insurance companies, and an insurance brokerage firm now places and administers group insurance for Avon's mail-order subsidiary, Family Fashions.

Banks handling Avon's corporate pension trust fund have been encouraged to use the services of minority investment brokers.

Avon's Minority Purchasing Program embraces an "outreach" operation, with a resultant ripple effect in the economic arena. The company encourages other corporations to set up similar programs of minority economic development.

In charting the course of the program, Avon president (now chairman) David W. Mitchell sent letters to twenty-nine high corporate executives of various companies, telling of Avon's unique program and offering to share Avon's expertise in this effort. Eleven companies responded, and Avon gave nine of them referrals to minority vendors. Requests for information were followed up with visits by members of Avon's staff.

In communicating its program to other corporation executives, Avon was a peer corporation saying, "We have tried this and it has worked for us. Why don't you try it?"

The outreach program's approach has had a significant impact on efforts to bring minority businesses into the economic mainstream. One corporation that responded to Mr. Mitchell's letter pointed out that Avon's leadership role has been extremely helpful. Additional inquiries came from corporations not contacted by Avon's president, but who had heard of the company's program from other sources.

Several corporations have since started programs based on Avon's experiences, as a result of Mr. Mitchell's efforts and personal visits by Glenn Clarke, Avon's purchasing manager for Minority Business

Development, and Margaret Richardson, executive director of the Development Council.

In addition to using a broad range of products and services from minority vendors, Avon also offers:

- Assessment of a minority vendor's bid, with counseling for suppliers whose bids are not competitive;

- Suggested sources for acquiring materials needed to fulfill contracts;

- Advance capital and facilitating the obtaining of supplies needed for contact completion; and

- Evaluation of the minority business on a regular basis to assist in quality-control management and other areas to aid in building expertise and productivity.

Speaking of the program, Avon's Clarke said, "You have to have insight into a minority businessman's problems and be able to find a way to help solve these problems, which in actuality are no different from those of majority suppliers. All business problems have a solution and Avon is in a unique position to do something for the minority businessman by virtue of the quantity of business we do."

Clarke added that all business placed with Avon by minority vendors is done on the philosophy of being "mutually beneficial to both Avon and the minority entrepreneur." The program is based on the same criteria used for all suppliers—quality service at a fair price. Standards are not lowered. Suppliers who meet these standards can do business with anyone.

Avon has put vendors in touch with such groups as the Development Council and the Volunteer Urban Consultants group and made referrals to other corporations.

Avon participates in organizations that promote minority enterprise, such as the Minority Purchasing Council, which has placed more than $100 million with minority vendors.

Much of the success in Avon's Minority Purchasing Program can be linked to the volunteer approach the company takes and a willingness to put forth extra effort to achieve mutual goals. Voluntarism at Avon in recent years has contributed greatly to the implementation of corporate commitment goals, and opened avenues of opportunity for minority business pursuits.

A most productive effort has come in cooperation with the Volunteer Urban Consulting Group, in which Avon Task Forces of from two to six persons respond to calls for help from minority businesses and nonprofit organizations.

Drawn from representative departments in the company, the technical- and management-assistance teams bring expertise into areas of accounting, marketing, personnel procedures, and other problems. Challenges have been as varied as clients.

In some cases, Task Force members have helped businesses that were facing bankruptcies to become viable. One team successfully aided a group in obtaining a $100,000 grant from the U.S. Department of Health, Education, and Welfare.

Avon's technical-assistance teams work with businesses or other agencies, which are usually referred by such organizations as the Greater New York Fund or the Volunteer Urban Consulting Group. The problem is identified and the Task Force is tailored to meet the problem. Work with client organizations may occur during regular business hours, on the employee's time, or a combination of both. Assignments are usually for an indefinite period, depending upon the needs of the particular organization.

A unique feature of the program is the racially integrated composition of the Task Forces, with at least one minority employee participating on each. The visible involvement of minorities from the corporate sector is reassuring to the client and aids in establishing confidence and trust.

The assistance teams have operated from a "people bank" resource, built up by Avon volunteers from management and technical levels who are committed to promote the program. The bank has grown to impressive figures, with the program extending beyond New York City, particularly in areas where Avon has installations. The teams are managed by members of Avon's Corporate Responsibility Committee, which includes thirteen representatives of various departments.

The Committee develops, implements, and monitors the various programs designed to fulfill company social commitment goals.

Avon has undertaken several other projects geared to establish long-range advantages for minorities in the economic mainstream.

In the Living Witness Program, black Avon employees go into predominantly black junior and senior high schools as "living witnesses" to instill hope, confidence, and a sense of self-worth into the discouraged students of inner-city schools. A key word in this program is "credibility." Youngsters want to believe, but the role models to whom they have been exposed in the past do not fit the mold of witnesses. The witnesses must bridge that gap between community and corporation.

In 1972 Avon became a part of the Project LIVE (Learning through Industry and Volunteer Educators) tutoring program for junior high school students. While the emphasis in the Living Witness Program is on motivation, emphasis in the Project LIVE is on learning.

Avon volunteers spend two hours per week with students in a one-to-one teaching experience, concentrating on math and reading skills, and stressing that proficiency in those subjects can help lead to future careers in industry.

The company's commitment to social responsibility begins with its corporate structure, as an equal opportunity employer in hiring and promotion. Avon's 1975 level of more than 15 percent minority employees was comparable to that of other large socially conscious companies. The company had over 10 percent minority management personnel, including a vice-president (of personnel worldwide) and 60 percent women in management, including district sales managers. Avon has undertaken projects in the affirmative-action hiring of minorities, women, the handicapped, and ex-offenders.

Avon's Job Opportunity Program, originated in 1970, provides a way for employees to request higher-level job openings as they occur. Its Tuition Refund Program offers reimbursement to employees who undertake work-related courses.

Avon and other corporations with similar commitments have found that real opportunities are effective tools for minority economic progress, both within the company structure and in the community at large. The outreach concept for minority business enterprise development strikes an impressive note of promise for all segments of the population.

CHAPTER 20
Travel and Leisure— Growing Potential

ONE-FOURTH to one-half of all blacks are now considered to be members of the middle class. Thus, it is not surprising that travel has become a status symbol among black Americans.

Transportation of all types comprised 11 percent of black expenditures, amounting to $7.1 billion, and recreation expenditures at 6 percent, amounting to $3.9 billion in 1973.

Comparison of air travel reflects the growth of the black travel market. A 1958 study of urban black Americans showed expenditures for air travel of $12,694,611. By 1976, this had grown to an estimated $305 million, of which approximately $40 million was spent on foreign air travel.

Ship travel was the lowest category of transportation influenced by minority spending (0.5 percent), and other spending included, according to a U.S. Department of Commerce study, 15 percent of minority income for bus service, and 10 percent of such income for rail transportation.

Blacks account for over 5 percent of the total airline industry revenue.

Interesting findings came out of a BASICO study, funded by Eastern, Pan American, Trans World, and United Airlines for the purpose of analyzing travel motivations. The study, based on a random sample of 1,400 black people with a median income of $13,000, found that:

- 61 percent had flown during their lifetime.

- 62 percent had taken pleasure trips of at least 800 miles during the past three years.

- 90 percent of black people who had flown had taken pleasure trips by air within the last three years.

- only 23 percent had used a travel agent; 77 percent had not.

- 53 percent of those interviewed preferred a mixed travel group, only 5 percent wanted all-black tours, and 42 percent said it made no difference whether a travel group was mixed or not.

- 27 percent stated they were definitely oriented toward the use of a black travel agent.

The study showed that the black travel market is an excellent market for future development, and both general and specific programs will increase the probability of that happening. People's interest and sense of self-discovery warrant promotional emphasis. Pleasure travel should include quality service, and black travel agents will be important in developing it.

The growth and potential in the black travel market is supported by other attitudinal studies as well.

According to "New Markets for Air Travel" (Negro Market Extract), conducted by the Behavior Science Corporation, "Negroes have almost universal recognition and appreciation of the airlines industry for the way Negroes are accepted and treated on trips. Apparently there is the feeling among Negroes that the airlines have done more than competing travel industries to reduce discrimination and to treat Negro customers in a courteous and hospitable manner."

According to that study, when blacks travel for pleasure more tend to go by air (23 percent versus 17 percent for whites), and a slightly higher percentage would select air travel if the cost for a trip by air and auto were approximately the same (given such a choice, 48 percent of blacks and 40 percent of whites would select air travel).

The *Black Consumer Index* study of the black travel market found that black and white priorities in vacation travel are different. According to the study, blacks preferred to:

- meet new people;

- visit friends/relatives;

- receive luxury service; and

- see/do new things.

While whites chose to:

- "recharge batteries";

- see/do new things; and

- broaden children's education.

Further differences were shown within the black group itself. The more affluent, the educated, and the young black segments of the sample traveled more frequently than other individuals interviewed.

Blacks with personal incomes of $15,000 and over were ten times more likely to take three or more trips during one year than the average black male household head.

In the travel industry, the saying goes: "It takes three things to travel: *time, means,* and *desire*."

Time is becoming less of a problem in the black community as many are now engaged in professional work, there is a developing entrepreneurial class, and upgrading has occurred in certain job classifications where summer vacations were not always the norm.

Means are rising as well, in the emerging black middle class. Travel is one of the new minority benefits.

Desire, or motivation, is a prime factor in the cultivation of travel among blacks. Generally, blacks have not formed a pattern of travel for its own rewards—personal enrichment, change of scenery, cultural enlightenment, personal pleasure. Instead, because of racial and other barriers to complete and free mobility, the black American historically has tended to restrict his travels to his immediate environment, or to places where he had personal friends or relatives. The idea of travel for its own inherent rewards has not been a basic consideration in the black's personal pattern of life.

A concentrated area of black travel is to conventions and conferences of national black organizations (see Chapter 17). National black conventions represent solid business for host cities, hotels, car rental agencies, and carriers serving convention sites.

The 1976 convention of a major black organization had approximately 8,000 delegates and guests, used 33 hotels and 3,200 rooms. By conservative estimate, those 8,000 delegates at $30 per day for five days, represented $1,200,000 to hotels and motels. Include air fare or other modes of travel, and the total amount is enormous.

A boon to the hotels was the fact that this, like most major conventions of black groups, was held in the summer—traditionally off-season for these properties.

The growth of the black convention market business has been significant. In 1960, 73,195 delegates, representing 9,203,308 members, attended national black conventions in 52 cities. By 1976, this had grown to 400,000 delegates, representing 13 million members, meeting in 43 cities.

At one time most conventions were held in major Northern cities, which had large black populations, and so presented less likelihood of discriminatory treatment. By 1976, however, over 25 percent of the cities selected as convention sites were Southern cities.

While not all members attend conventions, the nation's national black organizations have an outreach to some 13 to 15 million members, consumers, and influencers.

There are an estimated two hundred accredited black travel agents in the United States, as well as a considerable number of blacks selling in predominantly white agencies.

Development of efforts can include the InterAmerican Travel Agents Society (ITAS) which is the professional and trade association of black agencies. ITAS was formed nineteen years ago to unite all minority-owned travel agencies operating in the United States and other countries, engaged in the sale of travel and related services.

A newsletter, *Inside Travel News*, is keyed to agents interested in this growth market. The newsletter is published in Los Angeles and disseminated worldwide.

Those who would learn where some of the new black middle-class will be spending its money can look to the travel and leisure market that exists for a wide range of products and services.

Minorities spend 6.1 percent of expenditures for recreation, and comprised 7.5 percent of the total U.S. recreation market. In the mid-seventies, minorities were spending $3.9 billion on books, magazines and newspapers, toys and sport supplies, television, radio, and musical instruments, spectator admissions, and club dues.

The growth continues.

PART IV

How Some Companies Developed Black-Oriented Campaigns

CHAPTER 21

Black History in Corporate Campaigns

WHAT does a company do when its sales are not as high as desired in the black market? When it has little to show by way of endeavor in this area? When nearly every other company in the industry is conducting hard-sell programs? How does a late starter get talked about favorably?

These were some of the problems we faced as public relations counsel to P. Lorillard Company some years ago. The company was doing limited advertising in black-oriented media, and its sales force had blacks in major cities; yet we felt there was latitude to make the company better known and improve its competitive sales position.

My associate Brad Laws and I decided that one possible direction was through a public relations program that would include the entire industry, yet for which Lorillard would get the major share of credit. Only such a massive effort, we reasoned, could compensate for the deficiencies the company then had in comparison to other tobacco companies. It turned out we were right.

We proposed to Lorillard that we research and plan a public relations project concerned with the Negro's contribution to the entire tobacco industry, and tying in Lorillard's desire to make these facts known, and describing what it as a company was doing.

After consideration, Herbert Temple, Lorillard's brand development manager (later its president), to whom we reported, and Sidney J. Wain, Lorillard's majority public relations counsel, agreed. Lorillard management backed them.

We initiated our research, determining that Negroes were involved in the tobacco industry from its beginnings. Among other sources, we found an old print showing blacks at work in a primitive 1615 tobacco factory.

We learned that in the nineteenth century, black inventors and manufacturers played a part in the tobacco industry's growth. One of these was Elijah McCoy, a Negro inventor who in 1872 developed a lubricating device that led directly to the mass production of cigarettes. McCoy's device allowed cigarette-making machines to run continuously for the first time. We learned about Lunsord Lane, an early tobacco manufacturer who marketed a superior brand of smoking tobacco, and Stephen Slade, who in 1839 created the flue-curing process still used today for the curing of bright tobacco.

Our research indicated, too, that a Blackamoor preceded the Indian as a symbol of tobacco advertising in the industry.

We named our project "Brown Skin and Bright Leaf," which at the time seemed a bold step in identifying the Negro. We subtitled the project, "The American Negro's Role in the Tobacco Industry," and we kept as our objective the desire to create a favorable image among blacks for Lorillard and its brands, by showing the utilization and contributions of blacks throughout the years.

Our research, which investigated all of the specialized programming of all the major tobacco companies, revealed that despite all of the specialized efforts to win black smokers, including sampling programs at black affairs, student representatives on college campuses, films using black personalities, scholarships, training programs, black salesmen, advertising in black-oriented media, and other efforts, none of the companies had ever thought to research or execute a program on what blacks had contributed to the industry. Other companies were to take similar steps in later years; Lorillard was the pioneer.

We recommended that the public relations effort include a convention exhibit, a series of newspaper features, magazine articles, radio discussion features, reprints to black opinion makers, and possibly a booklet.

Since some felt that the name "Brown Skin and Bright Leaf" might be abrasive to black executives, despite our assurances that it would not, we did a survey of black leadership to get their thinking. The consensus was that the name "Brown Skin and Bright Leaf" would not be offensive, since the program and its purposes were of particular interest to blacks themselves.

We wrote the story of the Negro's contribution to the tobacco industry, beginning with the early contributions, and climaxing with the contributions—through Lorillard—that blacks were making in advertising, sales, and sales promotion.

The story, in eight chapters, with photographs, was released to the black press throughout the United States, and the response was highly favorable. Newspapers especially supported the series, conducting essay contests among black schoolchildren on what they had learned from *Brown Skin and Bright Leaf*. The newspapers then published the winning students' names, grades, and often the winning essays. Editorials appeared in some newspapers as well, commending Lorillard on its highly effective use of black history.

We constantly hammered home to black media, interest organizations throughout the United States, and colleges and universities that this was a public-service project to make known the Negro's contribution to the tobacco industry. In addition, of course, we gave exposure to Lorillard's brands of cigarettes and other tobacco products. We felt that we were on safe ground in the public service concept, and we were proved right.

Based on our recommendations, Lorillard had a portable convention exhibit prepared, featuring blown-up pictures of outstanding figures in the history of the tobacco industry. Lorillard sponsorship was tied in with a picture of the company's products, and the words "presented as a public service."

"The Brown Skin and Bright Leaf" convention exhibit began its rounds of leading black conventions, and the exhibit drew praise and much favorable comment from conventioneers. Many of those attending the conventions took pictures of the exhibit. The highest praise we felt the exhibit received was picture taking by competitive firms who wanted a record for the home office of an exhibit that drew such crowds.

When the convention season ended, the exhibit was sent on a tour of black colleges and universities throughout the South. It drew faculty and student praise alike wherever it was shown. The hardest job was to keep the scheduling of showings intact, as almost each institution wanted to keep it beyond the allowed date.

The *Negro History Bulletin*, published by the Association for the Study of Negro Life and History, requested and was granted rights to reprint the eight newspaper feature articles that had also been disseminated to the black press.

The thousands of lines of publicity, the favorable written comment by not only leadership, but a wide cross section of the black community, proved that the program was successful. It did not hurt, either, that the sales picture for Lorillard brands showed improvement in the black market.

Within a reasonable period of time the two primary objectives of the program were accomplished: (1) Lorillard and its brands of tobacco were brought to the forefront in the black community; and (2) the company was being talked about in a favorable manner.

The way the program was presented afforded no pressure group, in either the white or the black community, an opportunity to malign, criticize, or produce any unpleasant results.

"Brown Skin and Bright Leaf" proved that a specialized approach to the black market can achieve desired results if properly handled.

The "Brown Skin and Bright Leaf" program also was an early demonstration of the effective use of black history in corporate public relations and advertising efforts directed at black consumers. This overlooked subject in the nation's history books has become an important area of communications for some corporations with the black community.

Other significant campaigns have since been developed using black history, including American Oil Company's "American Travelers Guide to Negro History"; National Distillers Company's "Ingenious Americans"; Pepsi-Cola Company's "Adventures in Negro History"; and Scott Paper Company's "Distaff to History."

"Finding a need and filling it" is the key to success. The use of events, people, and historical facts in black history as themes in corporate advertising and public relations fills a long existing need among the nation's black population. Black contributions to American life in business and industry have too long been unknown except to scholars, intellectuals, and those with a special interest in history.

An important advertising campaign using black history is the "Ingenious Americans" campaign for National Distillers' Old Taylor Distillery. National's advertising agency, Batten Barton Durstine & Osborn (BBDO), developed the campaign and prepared the advertisements. BBDO's Clarence L. Holte, Ethnic Markets, conceived the campaign for Old Taylor.

Holte felt that liquor advertising, though quite heavy in the black market, contained too much "me-tooism," and that no company was using a theme to identify with the well-being of these consumers. He felt that Old Taylor could easily do a new type of campaign. Old Taylor, currently using black models, photographed at the distillery, in its four-color magazine and black-and-white newspaper print ads, scrapped that campaign in favor of "Ingenious Americans."

As an extension to the print advertising campaign, a booklet was prepared to reach those who were not regular readers of newspapers and magazines, but who did buy liquor. Liquor stores, serving a wide cross section of people, were the primary distributors of the booklet.

At the beginning, there was little to indicate to National Distillers and BBDO the demand for the booklet that would be created through the advertisements, nor the eventual success of the program.

Booklet availability was not mentioned in the first two ads placed in black-oriented media. When the booklets were mentioned, numerous requests were received by the client from a wide section of the black community. More than 3,085 booklets were mailed within an early period of the campaign to 154 cities in twenty-six states, the District of Columbia, and two provinces in Canada. Requests were received from schools, churches, prisons, and other sources.

Judging from the language and handwriting of the thousands of pieces of mail that were received, the "Ingenious Americans" campaign reached a wide cross section of the black community, with the vast majority apparently working-class people. Responses were enthusiatic, often expressing gratitude. One mother wrote to say she was keeping a scrapbook of Negro history for her children, and that the "Ingenious Americans" would definitely become a part of it.

Sales gains from a black-history-oriented program are hard to gauge. But one letter writer commented: "May I say that this ["Ingenious Americans" campaign] is a very great deed and respect shown to our people. From now on we will have Old Taylor on hand."

This campaign, and others of its type, have been successful because they related to blacks (and to whites) the proud history of black people. Companies that use the technique perform a service and earn a response that may never be measured in numbers of new customers.

The BBDO-created ads had a crispness and sharpness that made them standout advertisements. With sketches by Detroit's Carl Owens, a talented black artist, and copy by BBDO's Charles Clio, who is white, the ads were impressive. Each told a capsule story of a black who had made a significant contribution.

An unusual benefit accrued to Old Taylor for its "Ingenious Americans" campaign that allowed it to be viewed by millions of Americans, at no cost to the distiller. The Traveller's Times, producer of transit cards, selected and showed the series as educational material for transit cards in buses, subways, and elevated systems—to 12 million riders daily in sixteen cities. A credit line was given to

Old Taylor. White communities also received the series favorably. The success of its first series led to the development of a second "Ingenious Americans" series.

American Oil Company had great success with its *American Traveler's Guides to Negro History*. Some 500,000 copies have been distributed since the first edition in 1963, the centennial of the Emancipation Proclamation.

American Oil Company employees wrote and produced the guide, which included descriptions and photographs of notable monuments and landmarks in Negro history in twenty-eight states and the District of Columbia.

Scores of black organizations requested copies for their memberships. Boards of education in most major cities have included the book on lists for supplemental reading in history classes. Public and school libraries have increased the continuing demand for the guide.

The American Traveler's Guide to Negro History has been mailed to every state in the Union, to Canada, Asia, Europe, Africa, and Mexico. It has been serialized in black newspapers. It is in the overseas libraries of the U.S. Information Agency, and the Catholic Interracial Council uses it in its Chicago school programs.

While at one time companies' activities in the black consumer market were kept virtually top secret, recently this has changed, and efforts in that area are mentioned in annual reports, employee publications, and the like. American Oil's pride in its *Traveler's Guide* was communicated to its employees through *Torch and Oval*, the company's internal magazine.

The Pepsi-Cola Company had running accounts of its "Adventures in Negro History" program in *Pepsi-Cola World*, which was distributed to its executives, employees, and bottlers. In its "Adventures in Negro History" program, Pepsi-Cola Company primarily used an audio approach, through long-playing records. Volume I, released in February 1964, describes the contributions of forty blacks to American life during the period 1400–1950, and brings to light some little-known facts. Volume II, *The Frederick Douglass Years, 1817–1895*, intertwined highlights of Douglass's life with the momentous events that occurred in this country during the nineteenth century, especially around the issue of civil rights. Pepsi used black consultants, Dr. Broadus Butler, Professor of Social Studies, Wayne State University, and Dr. John Hope Franklin, Senior Professor of History, University of Chicago, as technical advisers to insure accuracy.

Twenty-six Pepsi-Cola bottlers held formal introductory ceremonies at which the record and a filmstrip were presented before community leaders. More than 250,000 copies of the "Adventures" volumes, including the filmstrips, have been distributed. Over five hundred school systems throughout the United States have adopted them as educational materials, and they have proved popular among both white and black groups.

Scott Paper Company sponsored a booklet entitled, "Distaff to History," which told of the contributions of a number of Negro women. Scott held a series of luncheons for black women's groups and obtained cooperation from the National Council of Negro Women (with its outreach to four million women) in the distribution of its booklets.

The Scott booklet also produced a wide demand for copies. It was serialized on women's pages of black-oriented newspapers, and received excellent usage among women's groups and historical interest groups.

Black-history advertising and public relations programs, as well as those reflecting contemporary black life, can be important vehicles for selling more products and services to this segment of the consumer market.

They can be an effective means of establishing identification, instilling racial pride, and encouraging initiative by providing concrete examples of accomplishment.

Here are some guidelines for use of black history or contemporary black life in corporate advertising and public relations programs:

(1) Get technical help to avoid inaccuracies or misuse of material.

(2) If good, clear pictures are not available, use sketches or artists' concepts.

(3) If the title of the campaign is thought to be at all insensitive to blacks, research it in the black community before too much investment is made.

(4) Design a plan for execution of the campaign, including use at black conventions, colleges and universities, libraries, and determine what materials will be needed.

(5) Alert dealers and distributors to the campaign, and seek their support to make it effective.

(6) Do not seek to attach a hard sell to this campaign; the soft sell will gain a much higher degree of acceptance.

CHAPTER 22

Pepsi-Cola: Forty Years of Special Marketing

EPSI-COLA COMPANY'S appointment in January 1962 of Harvey C. Russell as vice-president in charge of special markets made him the highest-ranking black executive of an international business firm. Events since that time have proved the soundness of the decision.

Although Russell's appointment received wide attention in white- and black-oriented media, his appointment was part of a long-existing policy, which had begun in 1937 with the establishment of the first special-markets department at Pepsi-Cola. In 1977 the company marked its fortieth year in special-markets activity and celebrated its historic position of leadership in recognition of the minority consumer.

Russell, who later became vice-president of corporate planning at Pepsi-Cola and then vice-president of community relations at PepsiCo, the parent corporation, helped to direct the company into successful paths in marketing to blacks.

Pepsi-Cola is a massive marketing specialist whose relations with its franchised bottlers have improved over the years. When Russell was appointed, only 16 bottlers had well-rounded black market programs; three years later, 53 bottlers—in both the North and the South—had such programs. This change attests to the success of the segmented marketing approach at Pepsi-Cola.

From its marketing efforts Pepsi-Cola was to reflect sales gains that included this black-oriented effort, which saw Pepsi-Cola's sales rise from $157.6 million in 1960 to some $250 million four years later.

Black Americans represent a large, attractive market for soft drinks in general and for Pepsi-Cola in particular. Here are some reasons why:

(1) Blacks are heavier consumers of soft drinks than the general market. Studies have shown that blacks consume nearly 10 percent more soft drinks than the population as a whole.

(2) Blacks are important consumers of the cola flavor segment. Within the all-important heavy-using household (where 20 percent of homes do about 62 percent of the soft drinking), the black home consumes at least as much cola as other heavy-using homes. There is also evidence that black heavy-using homes buy cola more frequently than white heavy-using homes.

(3) More black heavy-user households (57 percent) purchase Pepsi-Cola than purchase Coca-Cola (52 percent) as compared to white heavy-using households, where only 43 percent buy Pepsi.

(4) Greater black heavy-user loyalty to Pepsi partially explains this high purchase incidence favoring Pepsi. After five purchases, 6 out of 10 black heavy-user households are still exclusive Pepsi buyers, compared to only 4 out of 10 white households.

(5) A black Pepsi-loyal user has a higher consumption rate than white and Coke-loyal counterparts—almost one-third more glasses drunk weekly.

(6) Pepsi black advertising and brand awareness declined significantly in 1974 (compared to 1973) in spite of relatively stable black Pepsi consumption. The next year, 1975, showed a slight increase in advertising awareness. However, "top of mind" brand awareness continued to drop and could eventually turn into consumption losses.

(7) The central nonmarketing reason for special black programs is the need to create positive opinions and attitudes within the local black community that can not only preserve bottler sales volume but also aid Pepsi-Cola growth. The recommended 1977 marketing program was targeted at two subsegments: black opinion leaders and black youth. These two segments of the black community must be reached to successfully impact this market.

Pepsi-Cola's decision to name its first—and American business's first—black vice-president in a marketing capacity had its roots in a changing market picture. It was part of a larger decision the company had made on new strategy for selling to blacks.

In the early 1950s, Pepsi-Cola was the preferred soft drink among blacks throughout the United States. Blacks were a prime market for many Pepsi-Cola bottlers, who were often able to expand their sales on a franchise-wide basis because of what the market had become to them.

But during the 1950s the product lost ground among blacks to other soft drinks. Because of the downward sales trend among black consumers, Pepsi-Cola gave serious thought to where the company stood in the black market for its product. Company-wide thinking on the market was reshaped, and a new marketing plan resulted.

In 1961 Pepsi-Cola thoroughly researched the black market. Concurrently, many Pepsi-Cola bottlers had become aware of the soft drink's decline in their marketing territories and were searching for ways to reverse the downward trend.

In its study Pepsi-Cola learned that in the prior ten-year period: black population had increased by more than 25 percent, compared with 17 percent for the total population; while black per capita consumption for Pepsi-Cola had been standing still, per capita consumption for other soft drinks had more than doubled; and black preference for its product had increased at only one-third of the rate of white acceptance.

New marketing and media strategy were needed, for the company to recapture the market it once had.

Pepsi-Cola's loss of market share showed that unless black-oriented programming is executed to protect it, there is no reason to expect blacks to be any more loyal than other customers. When a company has a significant share of market, but elects not to protect it, the share becomes endangered.

In early 1961, therefore, Pepsi-Cola had a national consumer survey conducted to determine the exact position and preference rating for Pepsi-Cola versus competition in the total domestic market. That survey, conducted by Elmo Roper & Associates, contained a special breakout of black consumer preferences and attitudes, and gave Pepsi-Cola its first overall picture of black consumer trends.

In 1961, according to the study, the 19 million blacks in the United States constituted 11 percent of the total population. They accounted for 17 percent of soft drink case sales. The above-average case buying meant that they were above-average per capita users. Black usage per capita was one hundred drinks more than the average white usage.

In the preference for flavors, colas, and mixers, the survey pointed out that blacks were strongly flavor-conscious, and that they consumed nearly half of the grape soda yearly, and well over a third of the orange flavors. In all, they were buying some 300 million cases of soft drinks each year.

Although blacks made up 17 percent of the soft drink market, and only 15 percent of the cola consumption, it did not mean that they were not a strong cola potential, because in fact, their cola consumption was definitely higher than average. On a per capita basis, blacks consumed 163 bottles of cola, as compared to 120 bottles among whites.

In the 1950s, Pepsi-Cola had a 43 percent preference share among blacks versus a 25 percent overall market share, and Pepsi-Cola usage was three times higher among blacks than among white consumers.

Yet in 1961 Pepsi-Cola consumption among blacks was almost exactly where it had been ten years before, while it had tripled among whites. *This lack of sales growth among blacks meant a loss of 60 million cases per year to Pepsi-Cola.*

This did not mean that the black soft drink market had remained the same for ten years; it had gone in directions away from Pepsi-Cola.

Much of Pepsi-Cola's business had gone to Coca-Cola, regarded by many blacks as the higher-quality cola, especially after Coca-Cola's introduction of the twelve-ounce unit; to other colas, including Royal Crown; and to other regional products.

Following its study, Pepsi-Cola decided to solve some of the problems it faced in the black market, and to try to get the market back. It appealed directly to the market, as it had in earlier years, through planned strategy and execution.

Pepsi-Cola set guidelines for company and bottler activity in three areas—advertising, promotions, and community relations—and compiled them into a thirty-page manual.

The manual pointed out that consumption patterns and competitive activity were enough to justify special Pepsi-Cola programs for the black consumer market. Beyond this, there was the need for identification, and the opportunity to provide it in black-oriented advertising by Pepsi.

Pepsi pointed out to its bottlers that there were media and community promotional channels open in the black consumer market, and that Pepsi had advertisements keyed to this market.

Pepsi Cola and its agency, BBDO, had created a series of black media ads that pictured Pepsi-Cola usage in the best surroundings and showed situations which blacks of all ages and levels could identify with immediately.

Pepsi-Cola was aware at the time that blacks were a young market, averaging ten years younger than the national age median, and so it used the same theme in black media that it was using elsewhere: "Now It's Pepsi—For Those Who Think Young."

As a rule, Pepsi-Cola does not create any special themes for the black market, but hammers home its overall theme—with black orientation. It is one of the few companies that has never used product-oriented ads, but has always used black subjects in its advertising.

The company stressed the use of black-oriented print media as an effective voice in the community. In its guidelines to bottlers, it described fresh and imaginative ways to effectively use black-oriented newspapers. One example was a bottler who took space in his local black-oriented newspaper to sponsor a weekly social calendar. Organizations holding affairs were listed under the Pepsi-Cola imprint. As a result, the bottler had an entrée to black organizations and special events, and was often able to facilitate Pepsi-Cola participation in sampling activities at these affairs.

On a national level, the company stepped up its national advertising efforts. Beginning in January 1962, Pepsi-Cola ran twelve four-color pages in *Ebony* magazine, and black-and-white advertisements in two nationally circulated black-oriented newspapers.

Pepsi-Cola cautioned its bottlers, however, that this advertising could only support and add to the bottlers' local program of black market development.

Pepsi urged its bottlers to use their regular commercials on radio, but to use station personalities for live tags or lead-ins to the Pepsi spots. In addition, the company urged bottlers to tie in with local promotions of the stations, and to use its personalities for personal appearances, at teenage dances, and in other areas that would create community visibility for Pepsi-Cola.

Pepsi-Cola gave its bottlers three important suggestions in using black-oriented newspapers and broadcast media:

(1) When you schedule, let the media know what some of your plans and problems are. Then, let them work *with* you to extend the impact of your advertising. They know the community and their audience—use their knowledge.

(2) Use the media both for *hard Pepsi selling*, and for directed promotional or public relations effort.

(3) Continuing campaigns (instead of big but sporadic efforts) greatly multiply effectiveness.

Product sampling at black conventions, and other participation, continues as a prime activity of Pepsi-Cola. Convention participation by companies has grown over the years, and Pepsi's efforts with it.

With a budget in excess of $100,000 for conventions, not including manpower or product, Pepsi attends more than thirty national black conventions annually.

One example of how Pepsi involved itself was with the National Medical Association (comprising over 5,000 black physicians), where it has a medallion cast for each incoming president of the organization. The medallion is worn when the president is officiating, and at other activities.

Pepsi-Cola cosponsored the International Golf Tournament, attracting black golfers throughout the United States. The tournament has been held in Puerto Rico, the Bahamas, and Spain. It has become one of the top social and sports events in the black national community.

In recent years, the Pepsi-Cola *Adventures in Negro History* long-playing record, described in the previous chapter, has become one of the most successful programs ever launched by a company.

An article in a trade magazine in February 1963 appraised "The Negro Market." The *National Bottlers' Gazette* stated that "it would almost be impossible to conceive a successful consumer marketing campaign without the support of a significant portion of the black market."

It went on to point out that "Pepsi pursues the policy that the single mass market concept is fading and that the trend is now toward specialization. In recognizing this, the company has been particularly successful in its efforts to show that Pepsi wants the Negro as a customer."

Pepsi-Cola's efforts in the domestic black market are part of the company's one-world marketing concept. In discussing this, in an issue of *Pepsi-Cola World International*, a Pepsi executive wrote:

Facing up to reality, we know that we are confronted with language factors, different types of consumers, different package designs, different bottle sizes, different pricing and different economic conditions generally from country to country. To present the same image everywhere, despite different conditions, we must work together—we must share our experience and our information as one cohesive force.

In keeping with this philosophy, Pepsi reports events in nonwhite countries of the world as well as white countries. And in its domestic *Pepsi-Cola World*, Pepsi describes events that take place in black communities, and programs for this market.

Pepsi-Cola's approach to the black market holds the key to successful market development.

Problems many companies have long had to contend with—conditioning field forces, dealers, and distributors to the potentials of the black market—are being successfully handled by Pepsi-Cola Company. Although attitudes can't be changed overnight, waiting too long can be quite costly. The attitudes of middle men, between the company and the consumer, should constantly be reviewed and analyzed. Where it is possible to show by example the benefits of considering the black consumer, this should be done. A change in attitude is helped along by the promise of economic rewards.

Learn & Earn

The Pepsi-Cola/DECA Learn & Earn Project, a high-school-level educational program, has become one of the most viable community-relations efforts in recent years. The project, originated by Pepsi in 1968, and since 1973 a cooperative venture with the Distributive Education Clubs of America (DECA, Inc.), has now expanded to more than two thousand schools and four hundred cities. It seeks, "in an interesting and practical way, to help strengthen students' *broad understanding* of business as business—particularly its broad marketing and management aspects."

The project features *learning* exercises that point to *earning* experiences ("elementary, but comprehensive"). Basic high school marketing/management texts are used as well, plus a fifteen-minute audiovisual presentation highlighting and explaining project concepts.

The earning base suggested for participating chapters or clubs is the familiar operation of refreshment sales, including soft drinks, although the principles apply to the sales of other goods and services as well. Participating Pepsi bottlers help in this phase and in other learning aspects.

National prize-winning chapters develop competitive reports on: (1) what was learned; (2) what was earned; (3) how it was accomplished; and (4) how the project might be improved by the chapter and/or sponsor company. Chapters receive shares of PepsiCo stock at DECA's Annual Career Development Conference. One year's top prize was $1,000 in stock, with other stock awards of $750, $500, $400, and $250; two chapters received Honorable Mention.

Awards and honors are also presented to:

- Teacher-coordinators of national winners, who receive attractive plaques;
- State-level winners, who receive appropriate prizes provided by area bottlers;
- Officers of chapters or student clubs conducting Learn & Earn projects—whether or not they develop competitive reports for state or national review.

These chapter or club officers receive Achievement Certificates from their local bottlers and their respective principals at the schools' general assemblies.

Not all of the chapters are active in selling products. Some are serving as marketing and/or management consultants to other groups involved in fund raising. Aided by DECA's specialized service, the principal groups' earnings might be significantly increased. The group is encouraged to share the income with the DECA chapter.

There are situations in which product or services sales are not feasible. Then the Learn & Earn Project may still be used as an applied-learning vehicle. For instance, the chapter may plan a complete hypothetical operation, with cost figures obtained from real suppliers and customer-traffic estimates checked against actual counts at scheduled events.

"Money is not the sole object," says H. Naylor Fitzhugh, project consultant for PepsiCo and the Learn & Earn program. "The important thing is how well they plan . . . and understand the importance of planning."

When Fitzhugh, then president of special markets for Pepsi, wrote the program in 1968, his primary target was black students, whom he felt were less likely than whites to be exposed to the interactions of the business world.

The program now reaches a broader segment of minorities, and with the integration of school systems around the country and increasing interest in the project, whites now outnumber blacks.

Initially Pepsi took the program to schools alone, was encouraged by its results, and moved progressively toward broadening its outreach, to foster a new understanding of business basics that will be helpful to all participants in coping with present job opportunities, living responsibilities, and future career possibilities.

A plot venture was launched in 1973 with DECA, an organization that deals with groups of students who elect to join clubs to enhance their skills and get exposure to business through interaction in realistic situations.

More than fifty schools in fifty-one cities were involved in the Pepsi-Cola/DECA Pilot Program. Among the principal contributors were a special DECA Advisory Committee; DECA's Harry Applegate, Dale Clarke, Loris Lorenzi, Lynn Rhudy, and Cindy Saulness; National Association of State Supervisors of Distributive Education's (NASSDE) Gary Searle and Gail Trapnell; The National Association of Distributive Teachers' (NADET) Cal Farmer, Louis Giallanardo, and Manera Constantine; Frank W. Archer of General Electric Company; Lawrence E. McGourty, President of Thom McAn Shoe Company, and members of DECA's National Advisory Board.

The Pilot/Test phase also involved twenty state representatives of DECA; local teacher-coordinators and the NASSDE/NADET Committee of Judges.

The pilot venture also involved the cooperative efforts of several Pepsi-Cola Company departments, including Public Relations, Syrup Marketing, Bottler Liaison, Field Operations, Graphic Arts, Purchasing and Reproduction Services; and twenty local bottlers—cosponsors of the Pilot/Test Projects.

Concepts, materials, and coordination were developed by the company's Special Markets Department, under the direction of Mr. Fitzhugh. Fitzhugh also served as national cochairperson of the project with Pamela Powell of the Friends of DECA.

This was not a commercial promotion in the usual sense, project officials pointed out, noting that "the sponsoring company is mentioned only for the copyright purposes." However, it was further noted, "the Project does offer opportunities for direct commercial relationships as a practical learning—and earning experience. . . ."

More than two thousand DECA chapters have received the Learn & Earn Project Kit, provided by local Pepsi-Cola bottlers. The latter also lend audiovisual materials that explain such project highlights as objectives, content, and procedures to chapter members. The bottler may also offer the initial inventory of product on consignment, once the chapter has laid the necessary plans and is considered eligible for such credit arrangements.

The Project Kit spells out the objectives of the program to teachers and student managers; explains how to use the kit; and includes a set of Business Pointers, which combine compact discussions of elementary management basics with applications to a concrete marketing operation. Comments are sprinkled among these pointers to emphasize the practical utility of arithmetic and algebra, reading, writing, and general intellectual development. Materials are written to appeal specifically to young adults, "who have no exposure to the inner working of management."

Updated and revised editions of the project kits continue to alert students to possible accomplishment: "One Chapter earned $4,345 in seven months; another $3,226 in three months; and another $2,564 from sales at six football games."

The kit explains that everybody benefits from participation in the project:

(1) Customers benefit from the Service they receive;

(2) Your Chapter benefits from the profit it earns, and

(3) You and other Chapter Officers and members can benefit personally from this practical business experience.

The project has expanded since DECA's involvement. Learn & Earn now rings a familiar note to high schools in Alaska, Honolulu, and Guam, and the 1976 national competition winners came from high schools in many states.

"One of the most satisfying developments," says project originator Fitzhugh, "is that student interest in stock has been boosted. . . . Many now decide to invest in shares of stock rather than buy frivolous things."

The Pepsi consultant also feels the program has been a boon to teachers: "First, it helps teachers in their motivation of students, increasing their work potential; second, it increases the teachers' own comprehension of business . . . and transcends their textbooks."

While the community-service aspect of the Learn & Earn Project remains the primary concern of PepsiCo, the success of the program and the audiences to which it is directed suggest positive reactions in the marketplace.

The firsthand contact with Pepsi Bottlers products and the rewarding "learn and earn" experiences will not be easily forgotten.

Mobile Tennis

Another program targeted to black consumers, particularly young blacks, was launched by Pepsi-Cola Company in 1971. The program is called Pepsi-Coca Mobile Tennis. That year it was tested in three major markets: Boston, New York City, and Philadelphia.

Designed mainly for urban, inner-city areas, Pepsi-Cola Mobile Tennis is run in cooperation with local Pepsi-Cola bottlers and departments of recreation.

The concept of the program is to take free tennis instructions right into the inner-city neighborhoods. All tennis equipment, including specially designed mobile vans, portable tennis nets, and rackets and balls and other supplies, are paid for by local Pepsi bottlers and Pepsi-Cola Company.

Trained leadership in the program is provided by the local department of recreation, which also selects the sites and blocks off streets where the program is conducted.

Pepsi-Cola Mobile Tennis runs for ten weeks during the summer when youngsters are out of school and in need of wholesome recreation for their leisure time.

Most of the youngsters who participate in Mobile Tennis have never before picked up a tennis racket. But by the time the program is over, they have had at least twenty hours of tennis instruction. Incentive awards are given for reaching minimal achievement levels in the program.

In six years, Pepsi-Cola Mobile Tennis expanded from its three test markets to thirty-nine cities across the country, exposing some 40,000 urban youngsters to the game for the first time.

Hotshot

In 1976 Pepsi-Cola Company developed and implemented another young sports program targeted at this market. Tests had indicated urban youngsters would enjoy this new Pepsi-Cola program. But the indicators woefully underestimated the actual response.

The new program, called Pepsi-Cola/NBA Hotshot, is a basketball skills program. In it, youngsters run, dribble, and shoot to see how many points they can score in one minute, without committing infractions, from five "hotspots" on a half basketball court.

Hotshot is run in cooperation with the National Basketball Association, department of parks and recreation, and other youth service organizations.

In its first year, the game was conducted in areas surrounding the twenty-one NBA cities; about 1.4 million youngsters participated. Both girls and boys, ages nine through eighteen, were eligible—except high school and college varsity basketball players.

There were equal prizes for both boys and girls in each age category from playground level all the way to the National Championships.

Every youngster who took part in Hotshot received an award. Preliminary levels of competition ran from playground, district, citywide, area playoffs, to area semifinals and finals. At the area semifinals/finals, played at halftime on NBA courts, six contestants, three girls and three boys, emerged as winners. These six winners went on to represent their NBA team or city in further competition. These levels of competition included divisional, conference, and national championship playoffs. The Hotshot national finals were held during halftime of the NBA All-Star game.

NBA Commissioner Larry O'Brien and Pepsi-Cola Company's vice-president of public relations, Joe Block, presented trophies to winners and runners-up. Each of six top scorers, three girls and three boys, were also awarded $4,000 scholarships.

From the Divisional playoff rounds to the National Championships, all transportation for the youngsters and their chaperons to and from the various NBA cities, hotel accommodations, and meals are paid for by Pepsi-Cola Company. For the conference and championship levels of competition, Pepsi also pays all expenses for the youngsters' parents to travel and watch them play.

In 1977 the Hotshot Program went nationwide. Bona fide youth service organizations anywhere in the country can participate.

In its second year, were 2.7 million youngsters shared in the unique social and marketing phenomenon of Hotshot.

"Black Journal"

Positioned high on the list of audiences Pepsi-Cola Company is convinced it must relate to, in its marketing plans, is the black community thought-leader brigade. If sales and share of market are to flourish, then a respectable degree of accountability must be established and maintained with the decision makers in the national black community.

Out of such awareness grew the decision by Pepsi-Cola Company managements to underwrite the 1976 season of the "Black Journal" Public Broadcasting Service TV series. This sponsorship of "Black Journal" marked the first time that a major corporation had ever underwritten a national TV series dealing with black public affairs.

Now in second year of "Black Journal" sponsorship, Pepsi-Cola officials say response from consumers, black and white, has been overwhelmingly good. Despite the fact that "Black Journal" is deemed in some quarters to be highly provocative and controversial, Pepsi-Cola Company has never attempted any censorship over editorial content of the show.

"Black Presence" Poster Art Promotion

Early in 1977, the Pepsi-Cola Company created a new and exciting promotion that draws on black heritage and values. It is a collectors' series of six four-color posters depicting contributors to Afro-American culture. The eighteen-by-twenty-four-inch "Black Presence" posters represent blacks in the fields of art, literature, music, sports, history, and folklore. They are reprints of original paintings by famous black artist Charles Lilly, under commission by Pepsi-Cola. The people featured are: Paul Robeson, Jackie Robinson, Harriet Tubman, John Henry, Alexander Dumas, and Charlie Christian.

The posters were available through participating Pepsi-Cola bottlers. Pepsi-Cola Company also distributed complete sets of the posters, in limited quantities, at several national black conventions.

The favorable climate for idea creation that will successfully motivate blacks can only come about in an area of enlightened management that is trying to understand and sell black consumers.

Pepsi-Cola Company has shown how a company can expand its share of market among black consumers, through a planned, concerted effort. Its share of market has grown considerably from 1961, and of course, the company is continuing its black-oriented programming to reach black consumers.

CHAPTER 23

Hospitality and Publicker Distillers

OVER 90 PERCENT of all urban black households in the top fifteen markets regularly serve some type of alcoholic beverage, such as liquor, wine, or beer, or some combination of these basic types.

Studies have indicated that in proportion to population and income, blacks buy more liquor than whites in big cities; they buy it by brand, and they have a definite preference for quality.

The American black woman plays a matriarchal role, and utilizes her role as a homemaker to achieve a distinctive status in the household and in the community.

This was the climate and the backdrop against which Publicker Distillers moved to improve its image, establish positive identification for its brands, and through public relations activities pave the way for increased consumer demand for its products.

Publicker Distillers implemented a program for its subsidiaries— Continental Distilling Corporation, Old Hickory Distilling Corporation, and the W. A. Haller Corporation. The program was designed to:

(1) Establish a brand awareness of Publicker products within Pennsylvania's black community;

(2) Help increase the sale of Publicker products in the area, with emphasis on the half-pint package; and

(3) Establish a firm foundation for continued public relations and publicity activities.

To focus the campaign into a sharper light, and to get the products of the company known in the black community, the public

147

relations effort took form as the "Art of Gracious Hospitality" program.

Employment of blacks to implement programs almost always assures utilization of press releases about the program. Since two women were to be employed in the program, it was announced to the black press that two official "Publicker Hostesses" were being appointed. The utilization of the news release was enhanced by the fact that these were the "highest positions ever held by black women in the distilling industry."

Despite the fact that the effort was basically local, the publicity on the appointments was carried in most of the nation's black-oriented newspapers.

The Publicker Hostesses, assisted by black public relations counsel, sought out individuals, club groups, and organizations with special party-planning problems.

The Art of Gracious Hospitality (AOGH) program included a sampling activity, and women's groups were told how they might make their hostessing job easier yet more effective. The groups were shown how to mix drinks (with Publicker Products, of course), and provided with food recipes for any occasion.

Black-oriented sampling programs and activities that had no predetermined guidelines have often fallen flat. Therefore, an *AOGH Standard Operating Procedures* manual was prepared, outlining the program's implementation in local markets, and distributed to executives, hostesses, salesmen, and area supervisors.

A form letter went to local women's groups, telling them of the program and asking if they would like to have the Publicker Hostess give their group a demonstration.

A business reply card, returnable to the Publicker Hostess at the company's offices, was inserted in each mailing to accurately determine the number of groups requesting demonstrations, and for scheduling.

The program, begun in the Philadelphia area, was an almost automatic success among women's groups. Clearly it filled a need in the community that many other firms had overlooked.

Within a few months, the program had gained momentum, and was expanded to Baltimore, Washington, D.C., and Chicago.

An evaluation was made at the end of the first year to determine if the program objectives were being met. The sales department confirmed the effect in the improved sales position for company brands in Philadelphia.

In the Commonwealth of Pennsylvania, liquor is sold only through state-operated stores; this is the case in a number of states, which are referred to as "monopoly" states because the state government controls liquor sales. It is easier to check the records of such stores in black areas to determine the sales posture for the company's brands.

As a result of the program, the company had come to be regarded as "friendly," and as marketing top-quality products. Through the unique use of black women, the company had launched a much-needed, personalized, information service that was appreciated.

The year's evaluation revealed the following:

- *Scheduled Activity:* A cocktail party for the Philadelphia-area black-oriented media.
  Accomplishment: The introduction of Publicker executives and the Art of Gracious Hospitality program was successfully made to managing editors, women's editors, columnists, and broadcast executives.

- *Scheduled Activity:* A news story on the appointment of the two black women as Publicker Hostesses and on the AOGH program were given national release.
  Accomplishment: The story was prominently placed, usually on women's pages, in more than thirty key black-oriented newspapers and news magazines throughout the United States.

- *Scheduled Activity:* Letters announcing the consideration of a monthly column on the Art of Gracious Hospitality, along with an information copy of the Hostesses' appointment, were directed to 193 women's editors and columnists on black media staffs.
  Accomplishment: Sixty-four newspapers requested placement on the regular mailing list for the column. Thirty-four newspapers utilized releases during the year on a continuous basis.

- *Scheduled Activity:* Information copies of the Publicker Hostesses' appointments were disseminated to leading black opinion makers throughout the United States.
  Accomplishment: Acknowledgments and expressions of approval of the action were received from three black members of Congress, and from numerous leaders of organizations.

During a year's operation of the program, more than fifty demonstrations were given for black women's organizations, with 2,743 women in attendance. As a follow-up to the demonstration, newsletters were sent to approximately 2,400 women who requested that the information be sent regularly.

The Publicker Hostesses drew attention wherever they went, and were interviewed on black-oriented radio stations on a regular basis, where they described the Art of Gracious Hospitality Program. They also appeared on television.

The AOGH program, which gave black women their own Emily Post, easily identifiable with their own social group, also caught the eye of retailers in retail establishments other than liquor stores.

In markets outside Pennsylvania, the campaign helped to gain new product placement. It created a brand awareness and utilization on a scale that had not been previously achieved.

Publicker field sales personnel and distributors were receiving support in a developing segment of the consumer market, and a solid foundation was established for the continuing activities in sales and promotion for the company's black salesmen.

Product publicity kept both the products and the Art of Gracious Hospitality program before the black consumer.

"Art of Gracious Hospitality" columns, with beverage recipes using two or more Publicker products, were distributed periodically to sixty-four black weekly newspapers.

New innovations in marketing were tied in with the AOGH program. When Publicker decided to produce a matched set of decanters for its products, an article and still photos were distributed to black women's editors. The story made the women's pages of thirty-two publications, and the social page of a news magazine.

One black magazine did a feature on the program, inspiring many favorable comments and requests for information and further copies. A reprint of the piece was included in mailings to women's editors and black opinion makers nationally.

The successful Art of Gracious Hospitality program combined almost all of the techniques that can be applied in a public relations and sales promotion effort oriented to black consumers. It demonstrated that when objectives in black market programming are clear-cut, thoroughly understood, and properly implemented, success can be achieved.

The tailored program allowed the company to focus in a specific direction, and to reach market areas never before reached for the company's liquor subsidiaries. It helped to increase distribution and create consumer demand in weak and spotty areas.

The program increased public knowledge about the company, its management, and its products, with thought leaders, business people, consumers, and black-oriented media.

The company name was introduced and kept before the press and public through personal contact and regular news releases on the company's activities in the black community, Publicker's thinking, and the company's brands.

The Art of Gracious Hospitality program itself, as well as the appointments of black women as hostesses, commanded the attention of editorial writers, clubs, and organizations on a local and national basis. The company's industrial "firsts" in the appointments drew editorial praise, and Publicker received awards for its race-relations practices and many unsolicited comments from leading national figures.

Publicker came to be viewed by blacks as a leading producer of alcoholic beverages. Its products, particularly Old Hickory Bourbon, began to enjoy enviable sales positions throughout Pennsylvania and in other black markets.

The information-service approach in the black market has proved itself effective many times over, and it will continue to pay dividends when properly used.

CHAPTER 24

How Greyhound Develops
the Black Market

GREYHOUND LINES, INC., is the world's largest intercity transportation company today. Its parent company, the Greyhound Corporation, America's forty-first-largest firm, is a highly diversified, multinational holding company with over one hundred subsidiaries engaged in a wide range of business throughout the "Free World."

Its Special Markets Department, a corporate-level unit headed by a vice-president, has altered greatly over the last fifteen years, since it was begun. The department grew out of a similar organization within Greyhound Lines, Inc., the transportation subsidiary.

Back in 1962, Greyhound recognized the black consumer market segment as an integral part of its overall marketing programs, not as something to be considered after forming the basic marketing programs. The company's organizational manual described responsibilities, organizational relationships, and the function and duties of the director of Special Markets.

To head its Special Markets activities, Greyhound hired Joe Black. An alert, hardworking, and people-oriented individual, he had been a relief pitcher in the major leagues and subsequently a school teacher. From the beginning, Black has had top management support and the cooperation of his associates.

He first joined Greyhound in 1962, as its Special Markets representative, based in New York City. In September 1963, he was promoted to the national marketing staff, as director of Special Markets. And in May 1967, he was elected vice-president for Special Markets for Greyhound Lines, Inc., thus becoming the first national black vice-president in the transportation industry.

In March 1969, Black was advanced to his present position, vice-president for Special Markets, The Greyhound Corporation.

The Greyhound Corporation's black consumer-oriented programming has earned the reputation of being among the very best in American business. In 1972 the National Association of Market Developers, a national organization of black professional men and women dealing with urban marketing and management concerns, awarded Greyhound its coveted Plans for Progress award for outstanding performance in all areas of minority affairs.

Adverse public opinion, changing local customs, and years of segregation and discrimination all reflected negatively on Greyhound, even though it was not due to any action of its own. It was within this context that Greyhound Lines, Inc., initiated moves on its own to *recognize*, *identify*, and *invite* black passengers.

Greyhound has been pleased with the results of its Special Markets efforts to date; yet the corporation has not been content to rest on its laurels, because Greyhound recognizes that much more remains to be done.

The success of Greyhound's Special Markets endeavors has been due in large measure to a real commitment from the top, and to the respect that top executives have for Black. Since becoming an officer of the Greyhound Corporation, Black has always reported directly to the president—a departure from common practice in other companies, where the chief special-markets executive usually reports to another corporate vice-president.

Black, a weekend golfer, is often the partner of the chairman and chief executive officer, Gerald H. Trautman, in Phoenix area tournaments and plays regularly with other members of the top management team. It is a fact of life that often more business is transacted on the golf course or at the country club than in the confines of the office. So, at Greyhound, the vice-president for Special Markets is on the "inside" in more than a mere business sense, and thus senior executives are continually kept abreast of the department's programmatic thrust; also, he may try out ideas on them in informal settings, before developing them into formal proposals.

To say that Mr. Trautman is a highly perceptive, sensitive, and concerned individual in the area of race relations is an understatement. Perhaps the best insight into his character and his genuine concern in this area can be perceived in these excerpts from his article, "A Sensitive Approach to Black Relations," that appeared in the November, 1970, issue of *The Chief Executive:*

> If Greyhound has experienced a degree of success in communicating with the Black community, it is the result of a single, basic corporate concept: Those who carry the responsibility and the accountability must have the highest level of organizational authority and support.
>
> It will come as no surprise that Greyhound considers efforts to obtain a share of the $32 billion annual Negro market a worthy corporate goal, or that we feel it is good business to give some attention to the non-white community.
>
> It may, however, surprise some that the corporate units bearing these responsibilities have cabinet-level authority.
>
> Greyhound's Special Markets segment is headed by a Vice President who reports directly to the President. This peer relationship with traditionally accepted corporate development and the like is essential, it seems to me, if the policy statements of commitment are to be translated into positive programs.
>
> Involvement is getting to be one of those tired words, largely because it too often is used in fuzzy frustration.
>
> But a disciplined, planned, programmatic involvement in the Black community is entirely appropriate. And only people who know and relate to the Negro community can become really involved.
>
> We believe we are.

In June, 1975, Morgan State University, in Baltimore, one of the nation's foremost predominantly black institutions of higher learning, conferred upon Mr. Trautman an honorary Doctor of Laws degree because of "genuine concern for improvement of the quality of life of all citizens and for responding to their unmet needs." A year later, he was honored by Florida A & M University, which bestowed upon him its Meritorious Achievement Award "for setting high standards for the assimilation of minorities and women into American business and industry." Claflin College in Orangeburg, South Carolina, paid tribute to Mr. Trautman in May 1977, when it too awarded him an honorary degree.

Mr. Raymond F. Shaffer, Corporate President, was the recipient of an honorary Doctorate of Laws degree from Miles College in Birmingham, Alabama, in May 1974. He was also the commencement speaker. The Greyhound President had this to say to the graduates:

Without being presumptive, I thought perhaps I might pass on to you some thoughts or ideas I have learned that you might find helpful.

Many of you will be looking for a job. May I suggest you approach each application with the same self-assurance you approached in college. Some would call this a positive approach.

Take a job whether or not it was your major in school and please let me tell you why—the important thing is to get started and prove yourself.

In this day of advanced sciences you might easily have the idea that we are living in a world of technology and that employees are hired and maintain their jobs by card-fed computer profiles. Nothing could be further from the truth. Please remember this: there has never been a test, interview, or computer program invented which will tell whether a person will be loyal, lazy, or a liar. I call these the three "L's"—loyal, lazy, or liar. Having or avoiding those characteristics is 100 percent within your control.

These three characteristics will have more to do with happiness and success than anything else.

In his fifteen years at Greyhound, Mr. Black has earned a reputation as a highly creative, hard-working, and untiring executive. He is a graduate of Morgan State and has pursued graduate study at Seton Hall and Rutgers University. In 1974, Shaw College at Detroit conferred upon him an honorary Doctorate of Human Letters. And in February 1977, King Memorial College of Columbia, South Carolina, honored him with an honorary degree.

Greyhound's Special Markets approach is highly diversified and reflects the company's original concept: to work for and achieve the image of being a "good neighbor" within the national black community. Black is responsible for the development and recommendation of policies, practices, programs, and procedures of marketing for the black consumer market. The basic thrust of this work encompasses the Greyhound Corporation and its operating companies, including Greyhound Lines, Inc., Armour Food Company, and Armour-Dial, Inc. Each plan book is divided into sections on "The Market," "Review," "Programming," and "Budget." They are submitted to the chief executives/presidents of the respective three companies. Once plans have been approved, Black has full control, authority, and responsibility for the administration of the total Special Markets program.

Greyhound's policy over the years has been to give Black not only the organizational authority he requires, but also their wholehearted support to carry out his duties and responsibilities. Some people will occasionally test this support when they receive a negative response or reply to a request, ranging from advertising to a contribution. They may counter with, "I'll write or call the chairman and/or the president." To which Black's standard rejoinder is, "That's fine with me."

This top-level support clearly distinguishes Greyhound's Special Markets Department from similar operations in other major companies, where special-markets executives, though they may have approved budgets, must have their expenditures approved by their immediate superiors.

Greyhound's approach is based on its successful luncheon formats for Woman of the Year, Father of the Year, and Drug Abuse Seminar.

The Woman of the Year luncheons were started in 1964. They grew out of the sense that many black women in communities throughout America possess outstanding qualities, and have made substantial contributions to making their communities better places in which to live, but have not received public recognition.

Greyhound and a local black media facet cosponsor the luncheons on an every-other-year basis in various cities. In addition, the Special Markets department often utilizes the functions to sample products of Armour-Dial, Inc., and/or Armour Food Company.

Greyhound's Father of the Year luncheons, similar in format to the Woman of the Year programs, are fulfilling an important need in black communities.

Greyhound also cosponsors Drug Abuse Seminar luncheons. An average of eight to ten Drug Abuse Seminar luncheons have been held throughout the country every two years in cities such as Boston, Los Angeles, Miami, San Diego, New York, Jacksonville, Detroit, Birmingham, Chicago, New Orleans, Omaha, Houston, and Atlanta. Sponsorship of the program is an attempt to bring information on drug abuse to American youth.

Speakers at the luncheons have included ex-drug addicts, many still in the rehabilitation process, others already completely rehabilitated and engaged in occupational pursuits as productive members of society.

The Special Markets department has served as the coordinating unit for a "Back to School Shopping Spree" promotion for Armour-Dial, Inc. The concept has resulted in the awarding of thousands of dollars in gift certificates for clothing to encourage black youths to return to school.

Another key aspect of Greyhound's community relations programming is "By the Way" commentaries published in black newspapers and aired on black radio stations. A compilation of the media messages, in a pamphlet entitled "By the Way," is published annually.

Convention participation continues to be an integral part of Special Markets activities. Among the major conventions in which Greyhound participates are NAACP, National Urban League, Elks, and *The Louisville Defender*'s Home Show and Exposition.

Greyhound's Special Markets staff make guest appearances on television and radio, discussing anything from sports to contemporary issues, with an occasional mention of Greyhound products and services. Total media exposure over the past several years has exceeded 130 hours; if a price tag were placed on this free time, it would easily exceed $5 million. The staff is also frequently asked to speak or serve as guest lecturers before a variety of national organizations, colleges, and universities.

Greyhound print advertising appears in *Ebony*, *Black Enterprise*, *Essence*, and *Jet* magazines, and in many local black weeklies. Black-owned and -oriented radio stations are also utilized for markets.

Through the recommendation of Joe Black, Armour-Dial and Armour Food Company have retained a black advertising firm, Vanguard Associates, Inc., Minneapolis, to handle black consumer-oriented advertising.

An important segment of Special Markets' programs is scholarships for minority students. Scholarship monies are provided annually to forty-four predominantly black institutions of higher learning; and Spanish-speaking students on the West Coast are aided through Spanish-language radio stations. Greyhound also contributes annually to the United Negro College Fund.

John H. Johnson, head of America's largest black-owned publishing company, Johnson Publishing Company, Chicago, and several other major businesses, is a member of Greyhound's board of directors. He is also a member of the board's executive committee.

Greyhound is very active in the vital areas of equal employment and upward mobility. As part of its commitment to minorities, Greyhound purchases from minority vendors and suppliers, goods and services used by its various companies. Another phase of this economic thrust is the deposit of several millions of dollars in the nation's black-owned and -operated banks.

Greyhound contributes financially to national organizations such as the National Association for the Advancement of Colored People, Opportunities Industrialization Centers of America, National Association of Market Developers, Southern Christian Leadership Conference, Operation PUSH (People United to Save Humanity), and the Martin Luther King Memorial Center for Social Change. Local involvement and support is restricted to Greyhound's headquarters city of Phoenix, Arizona.

Staff members hold or have held key posts in several national organizations, and have served in advisory capacities to national organizations such as the National Urban League, NAACP, Office of Minority Business Enterprise, National Alliance of Businessmen, American Revolution Bicentennial Administration, U.S. Census Bureau, and National Association of Market Developers.

Today Greyhound is respected in the national black community as a company that cares about and is in touch with the black consumer. The Greyhound story reflects what can be accomplished with careful planning, good leadership, and high corporate commitment.

CHAPTER 25

How Teacher's Scotch Markets a Community-Oriented Project

HOW DOES a company parlay a community-relations-oriented vehicle into an effective marketing tool? It helps if the vehicle is a timely, relevant, identifiable symbol such as the black athlete. *The Black Athlete*, in fact, is the title of a film produced by Wm. Teachers and Sons, Ltd., makers of Teacher's Highland Cream Scotch Whisky. Schieffelin & Co., New York City, sole U.S. distributor for Teacher's, involved both its public relations and sales forces in delivering this vehicle to a growing audience, while greatly enhancing the image of Teacher's Scotch in the black community.

The Black Athlete, an excellent collection of historical sports footage in baseball, football, basketball, boxing, tennis, and track and field, could well serve as a model for future community relations projects designed to improve a company's image in the black community. According to Schieffelin & Co., the thirty-eight-minute film, which world-premiered in New York City on April 13, 1971, has since been used by scores of groups and seen by millions of people throughout the United States. It has won several awards. In the summer of 1972, the Bottle and Cork Club of New York City cited Wm. Teacher & Sons for the most outstanding contribution to the black community by a wine and spirits concern. The B & C Club members are black beverage salesmen in the New York metropolitan area.

Narrated by legendary track-and-field great Jesse Owens, the film begins with his spectacular performance in Berlin in the 1936 Olympic Games, traces the feats of such famous black stars as Joe Louis, Sugar Ray Robinson, Bill Russell, Jim Brown, Gale Sayers, and Willie Mays, among others, and presents both sides of debate over black press in sports. "An honest attempt is made to accurately portray the course black men have followed in the amateur and professional sports world," wrote a sports columnist, "a world in which they excel and, in many cases, have come to dominate." Critics have labeled the film entertaining. There is a touch of nostalgia for people who remember seeing famous events and great athletes of the past: fighting machines such as Louis, Robinson, and Henry Armstrong in their primes; a twenty-four-year-old Willie Mays; or a Jackie Robinson breaking into the major leagues. For those too young to have seen these great athletes at their best, it is new and informative.

The film has been a tremendous success, according to Herbert P. Douglas, Jr., vice-president of special markets for Schieffelin, drawing "outstanding news coverage in the broadcast and print media. The black and white press has given it first-class treatment wherever it has premiered."

Mr. Douglas added: "It has been a good vehicle for bringing people together . . . but the aim of it is to sell Teacher's Scotch. There is no secret about that."

Actually, *The Black Athlete* was on the drawing board about two years. Douglas, himself a bronze-medal winner in the long jump (another Owens specialty) in the 1948 London Olympic Games, recommended that Schieffelin undertake this project and lay a stronger foundation for future sales in the black community. (Despite the fact that blacks make up only 11 percent of the U.S. population, Census reports say that blacks consume as much as 50 percent of all Scotch sold in America.)

At the time, the 1972 Olympic Games in Munich, Germany, were approaching and interest would be high. The narrator would be Jesse Owens, who dominated the 1936 Games in Germany. The film would not be a race relations message as such, but an attempt to illustrate how sports in the United States had been changed for all time by the presence and performance of the black athlete.

The Black Athlete was set for completion by March 15, 1971. At that time arrangements were made for a special screening for Schieffelin & Co. executives. The live sequence—epilogue and prologue by Owens—was filmed January 29 in his home. The following day Mr. Owens flew to New York where the balance of his narration was recorded. The producer then put the finishing touches on what turned out to be a masterpiece.

In his opening paragraph of the prologue, Jesse Owens states that the film was made possible by a grant from Wm. Teacher &

Sons, Ltd., Glasgow, Scotland. At the close of the film, following credits to the narrator and producer, a superimposed slide states "Production sponsored by Wm. Teacher & Sons, Ltd., Glasgow, Scotland."

Schieffelin & Co., introduced *The Black Athlete* in major U.S. markets with a Hollywood-style premiere. Engraved invitations went to civic, business, government, educational, sports, and organizational leaders. High-powered publicity strategy assured excellent press coverage, with host Owens a major interview personality.

A typical premiere opened with a Teacher's Scotch cocktail party. This segment would last from thirty to ninety minutes. A Schieffelin special representative would welcome the guests and explain Teacher's role as sponsor of the film. The film would then be shown, followed by a subtle reminder of Teacher's role. Herb Douglas would then be introduced to discuss the purpose of the film and introduce some of the outstanding guests and, finally, Jesse Owens.

Premieres were held in all cities with significant black populations. New York was the site of the world premiere, which received an enthusiastic reception and extensive press coverage.

Meanwhile, a broad general distribution program was effected through Modern Talking Picture Service, whose own publication, featuring the film's availability, was sent to several thousand U.S. firms. Prints of the film were sold to Schieffelin distributors who wanted them for continuing use in their markets, as well as to public libraries and other institutions.

A special four-page supplement on the program was produced and included in the summer 1971 issue of *The Schieffelin Reporter*, distributed to about five thousand wine and spirit distributor executives and salesmen.

Schieffelin people were quick to follow up on the premieres in their markets. According to Douglas, black salesmen in St. Louis began booking the film in bars. The first week after the screening, about thirty bars were booked. A special representative returned to Detroit and started a Teacher's cap-saving consumer program with 105 members of the Detroit NAACP's Women's Auxiliary. Sales programs were immediately established with the Baltimore salesmen, and the film was shown in former Baltimore Colts football star Lenny Moore's bar one week later to a leading sports group.

Douglas himself developed a Teacher's Scotch Sports Night program of screenings in selected bars and taverns in New York, Chicago, Detroit, Los Angeles, Cleveland, Washington, and Baltimore.

He also arranged with the U.S. Olympic Committee (USOC) for proceeds raised at these screenings to be turned over to the USOC. The latter's decals and lapel buttons were sold at these events. A special Teacher's bar display piece was produced for this program. Association with the U.S. Olympic fund-raising effort was another plus for Teacher's image.

The film captured the interests and enthusiasm of a broad range of age and class groups, from youth to traditionally elder groups and individuals, and including both whites and blacks.

The film offered some moments of touching discussion among black sports figures. Bill Yancy, all-time great in athletic circles, died on the same day the film was released. Kenny Washington, former UCLA football teammate of Jackie Robinson, died shortly after appearing at the Los Angeles premiere. Similarly, death overtook former Olympian Lorenzo Wright of Detroit. Washington and Wright appeared in photos taken at their local premieres. Additionally, the premieres and screenings served as happy reunions for many blacks in sportsdom.

It is not often that a company community-oriented project makes such a hit with its target audiences and maintains a level of high interest and demand. In the development of such programs, it is important to remember:

(1) *The Black Athlete* offered positive contributions to the black and general communities with its informative and entertaining documentary.

(2) The film identified with a broad range of audiences, from youth to the elderly, all working classes, various interest groups.

(3) Wm. Teacher & Sons, Ltd., and Schieffelin & Co. went to great lengths not to overcommercialize the film with their involvement (though many black newspapers carried Schieffelin and Teacher's in their story headlines).

(4) The film sponsors also saw to it that their public relations and sales forces worked closely together. Key personnel at Wm. Teacher & Sons, Ltd., and Schieffelin were well informed on the goals and potential of the film.

(5) *The Black Athlete* is the product of expert effort: Schieffelin's Herb Douglas is black, a former great track star at the University of Pittsburgh, and an Olympian. Jesse is a symbol of athletic achievement. Both speak effectively about their experiences. Bud Greenspan, who wrote, directed, and produced the film, is a well-known sports producer.

CHAPTER 26

How Carnation's Program
Won PRSA's Silver Anvil

ARNATION COMPANY, with a history of corporate involvement and marketing activity in the black and Hispanic communities, selected "Pride Through Education" as its theme of an institutional public relations program. It won the 1975 Public Relations Society of America (PRSA) Silver Anvil.

Projects were aimed at developing greater goodwill with both communities and establishing clearer public identity of Carnation during its seventy-fifth-anniversary year.

Carnation's Edward J. Atkinson, then assistant director of public relations (promoted to manager, urban relations in 1975), spearheaded a multifaceted program including:

- Creation, publication, and distribution of *Rising Voices/Voces Que Surgen*, a 212-page paperback (in Spanish and in English) containing biographies of fifty-two outstanding Spanish-speaking Americans;

- Communication of Carnation's urban-relations program to opinion makers via an audiovisual presentation;

- Enlargement of corporate participation in United Negro College Fund;

- Continuance of the Carnation Teaching Incentive Awards;

- Distribution of three English/Spanish educational pamphlets on employment; and

- Extending participation within more than 100 ethnic organizations.

While Atkinson's broad range of activities harvested an impressive number of accomplishments in the areas of corporate involvement and community relations, the selection committee of the PRSA —the national organization for public relations—was particularly impressed with *Rising Voices/Voces Que Surgen.*

Thus, Eddie Atkinson was honored with the Silver Anvil, the "Oscar" of the seven thousand-member society for his institutional program on behalf of Carnation. His program was named the best in the United States for greater goodwill and a clearer public identity for a business organization. PRSA reported that there were nearly 350 entries for the 1975 awards competition.

Carnation's purpose in creating the book was to reaffirm our company's continuing social responsibility and dramatically communicate our very real commitment to the progress of Spanish-speaking Americans. . . ."

The fifty-two biographies selected, it was hoped, would approximate the ratio percentage of the groups comprising the Latin American population.

Alfred Martinz, *Los Angeles Times* feature writer, was selected to author the bilingual books, with New American Library as publishers. A researcher would contact the persons chosen by a special selection committee. Selection criteria consisted of the following:

(1) Subjects would be men and women who had achieved success in education, business, arts and sciences, government, engineering, medicine, sports, religion, performing arts, and other appropriate disciplines and areas.

(2) Subjects would be selected from all age groups.

(3) Subjects would be representative of the various Latin national groups in the United States.

It was decided that the chosen individuals would not have to be active in Latin-American community affairs, and that membership on the selection committee did not preclude inclusion in the book. (In the planning stages, Atkinson had emphasized that Carnation was not qualified to determine who was to be written about and had called for a meeting with Spanish-speaking leaders to organize a "qualified" selection committee.)

Initial plans were for a 4½-by-7-inch paperback, to be published in a quantity of 100,000 to 200,000. Carnation would purchase 100,000 copies of the book from New American Library and distribute them free to high schools, colleges, state teachers' associations,

Latin-American study groups, U.S. embassies, and other interested groups.

Carnation's share of royalties from public sale of the books would be used to buy additional books for free distribution or for other cultural propects in the concerned areas. Other promotional opportunities—such as syndication by major newspaper service and adaptation for use on television, radio, and in motion pictures—were discussed.

Rising Voices/Voces Que Surgen was published in 1974, and before the year's end, Carnation had distributed 22,732 of English editions, 21,569 of the Spanish.

Free distribution was made to school districts around the country, to all identified Spanish-speaking Americans influential in politics and education, and to 670 daily newspaper book review editors, with news releases, plus long and short book reviews. Releases in mat form also were distributed nationally. Carnation, via its sales force, made distributions in plant cities and set up in-store displays.

Atkinson described publication of *Rising Voices* as a "public relations accomplishment . . . and . . . a very real PR challenge."

The challenge involved Carnation's imagination and aggressiveness in exploring print and broadcast media, the use of audiovisual aids, and overall community outreach.

The book was introduced to the "influential community" with four major receptions for Mexican-American, Puerto-Rican, and Cuban-American influentials, including editors, senators, religious leaders, actors, athletes, musicians, corporate executives, and others.

All Spanish-speaking radio stations in the country received copies of the books. Kickoff releases and features, with photos, were distributed to print media, with "considerable fallout from both the free distributions and receptions." The company was flooded with clippings from all parts of the country and from Spanish-speaking countries.

Further, Carnation produced a fifteen-minute film featuring some of the biographees. A filmstrip of more than fifty frames was prepared for museums, art schools, airports, and libraries throughout the United States.

Also on the drawing boards was the use of audiovisual materials tying in with the National Bicentennial Celebration.

Edward Atkinson describes *Rising Voices* as a "book of pride, telling inspiring stories of fifty-two outstanding Spanish-speaking

Americans who have contributed in a special manner to our nation." Some of the biographees may be familiar to many Americans: Congressmen Herman Badillo and Edward Roybal, Senator Joseph Montoya, athletes Roberto Clemente and Jim Plunkett, actor Anthony Quinn and entertainer Vikki Carr, Ambassadors Horacio Rivero and Phillip Sanchez, U.S. Treasurer Roman Banuelos, Met opera star Martina Arroyo, singer Jose Feliciano, concert pianist Horacio Gutierrez, and ophthalmologist Dr. Antonio Gasset, among others.

Despite the acclaim that the program has received, Atkinson suggests its overall objectives merely "scratched the surface," that "publication of *Rising Voices* was a beginning."

Atkinson's institutional contributions also included introduction of a national radio program, "The Sounds of Black Music"; promotion of a tour by "Mrs. America"/"Mr. USA"; arrangements for a California–Washington tour by a Mexican governor; regular personnel releases on company minority employees; counsel for the company's advertising program; and support of Los Angeles's Watts Summer Games.

He also provided assistance to Carnation's Equal Employment Opportunity Department; recipe distribution to minority media; development of a radio "Children's Workshop"; personnel counseling; support of the Miss Black America Pageant; sponsorship of a summer work program; and extended distribution and publicity for the book *Black Dimensions in Contemporary Art*, which he authored.

Atkinson, who joined Carnation in 1965, served as public relations supervisor, senior public relations supervisor, and assistant director of public relations, prior to assuming the post of urban relations manager in 1975. Earlier, he owned and operated two restaurants in the Los Angeles area, and, although unsuccessful in a 1958 campaign for City Council, was the first black to reach the election's finals.

He has been honored a number of times for his P.R. and community involvement contributions, including the L.A. PRSA Chapter's award for his attainments in these areas.

It is important to remember that the Spanish-speaking and black consumer markets are the fast-growing markets in America. The best initial sales pitch, however, may carry "goodwill" and "image" objectives. Atkinson's Silver Anvil Award serves as a reminder that effective community relations and P.R. projects contribute greatly to overall marketing and sales objectives.

CHAPTER 27

How American Airlines
Develops the Black Travel
Market

IN THE EARLY 1960s, American Airlines determined that airlines generally were ignoring a real growth potential among blacks. Consequently, the carrier commissioned a black research firm to study the market; its study became a benchmark for the active program the airline continues.

George E. Jackson, American Airlines' director of sales development, is the individual who has guided American's black travel market development through the years. In 1966, in a speech in Mexico to the Interamerican Travel Agents Society, the professional association of minority travel agents, he pointed out what American had done and was doing to expand the market for air travel, and to presell in behalf of black travel agents. The results have benefited not only American but other U.S. and foreign flag carriers as well.

American's objectives included the identification of the black travel potential in major on-line cities; interests in travel by "thought leaders"; organized group contact for travel; education on air travel; creation of the desire on the part of blacks to travel; and preselling in behalf of black travel agents. (American pioneered many of these same efforts among all travel agents as well.)

American Airlines has had a number of firsts in the black travel market and human relations. It was the first company (not only the first airline) to use a four-color, twelve-page supplement in black-oriented media; the first to hire black pilots, ticket agents, sales representatives in major cities; and the first to employ a black female sales representative.

American was the first airline to "integrate" brochures (showing black and white travelers) used in promoting travel to vacation destinations.

Through fashions and *Ebony* magazine, American provided editorial support, tying in the glamour of travel.

In 1972 George Jackson developed a "Green Side of Black" program that pointed up American's development programs in the black travel market and the airline's market opportunity for air travel among blacks, and how it could develop this potential. The program was communicated throughout the system and included an internal bulletin to managers of passenger sales and advertising from the vice-president of passenger sales, in support of the program.

To promote ticket sales, American provided black-oriented sales promotional materials, including flight attendant die cuts (life-size and desk-size); folders (picturing a destination) with inside pages keyed to the target market; direct-mail brochures; visual aids; and a "Traveler's Guide to Black History," later incorporated into "Fly/Drive Into Black History."

Travel columns were provided to black newspapers nationally, and press releases on various topics.

Black travel agents, as well as travelers, supported the American effort with favorable word-of-mouth publicity.

In 1975 Jackson made a presentation to American's marketing management that showed the need to concentrate on the burgeoning black travel market, and black conventions and conferences in particular.

Although American had been assisting in preconvention planning, the opportunity existed for even closer organizational contract. It was agreed that with the number of conventions in American's on-line cities, and charter possibilities, Jackson should pursue promotional opportunities.

Jackson asked me to have my firm develop a proposal on how American Airlines could have a greater impact on national black organizations and their travel plans.

It was agreed and proposed that a booklet be developed listing dates and sites of each national black convention, background information on the organization, a photograph of the national president, nature of the meeting, expected attendance, and travel tips.

Thus was born the *American Airlines 1975 Travel Guide to Black Conventions and Conferences*, and the guide has been published annually since.

The 1977 edition carried, in addition to the previous information, many pages of useful travel tips.

The guide is available free at American Airlines sales offices, and is distributed to national black organizations listed, and to those who request it. Thousands of requests have been received from government, industry, public, and private organizations who have an interest in the meetings of national black organizations. The guide clearly filled a void.

It has supported other American marketing efforts, including the rental and manning of convention information and reservations booths at national black conventions; convention receptions; and promotion of tours.

American Airlines promotes tennis tournaments with the National Association of Tennis Clubs; participates in *Ebony* Fashion Fair presentations (a national program of *Ebony* magazine in some 178 cities), including the placement of an attractive American Airlines flight attendant as a model; and the Congressional Black Caucus Tennis Tournament and reception in Washington, D.C.

American's may be the largest advertising program among carriers. It supports activities of minority travel agents, including participation in meetings of agents.

To further improve its relations with presidents of national black organizations, and to familiarize them with convention services of American Airlines, Jackson presented to management a proposal that he and I had put together, for a "Presidents' Weekend." He received approval, and working together with my firm, we began contacting and inviting the presidents to the 1976 Weekend.

With sponsorship by American Airlines, Americana Hotels, and the New York Convention and Visitors Bureau, presidents of national black organizations were brought together, for the first time in history, for the first Presidents' Weekend in New York City.

The presidents were hosted at Gracie Mansion in New York by Mayor Abraham D. Beame and sipped wine and tasted cheese with Governor Hugh L. Carey at the State Office Building in Harlem. Their three-day "familiarization" visit received wide attention, including press and television coverage.

The occasion also gave American Airlines an opportunity to introduce the new edition of its Travel Guide. At a welcoming reception numerous New York City officials and American Airlines and Americana Hotels management executives were joined by local presidents.

ITT Continental Baking baked a cake. William Toles, an ITT executive, arranged for a special cake—a four-foot-high apple creation that used seventy-five pounds of flour and forty-nine dozen eggs.

Schenley Distillers' vice-president Chuck Williams created a "Big Apple" cocktail to celebrate the presidents' visit.

The weekend was packed with enthusiastic receptions, seminars, screenings, sightseeing, a Broadway show, and a visit to the Bedford-Stuyvesant Restoration Corporation to allow the national black leaders an opportunity to see how community and corporate concern can rebuild an inner city.

In 1977 the event was repeated, with presidents of national black organizations invited to Washington, D.C. Some eighty-five presidents, most of them with their spouses, were hosted by the Washington Area Convention and Visitors Association, American Airlines, and the Shoreham Americana Hotel, where they stayed and where many of the official functions were held.

The visit gave the presidents an opportunity to learn more about the nation's capital as a convention site. A highlight of the weekend was a White House briefing for the national presidents. Mayor Walter Washington of the District of Columbia was keynote speaker at a Saturday luncheon. That evening the presidents attended a dinner and reception hosted by the Washington, D.C., Hotel Association, and then went to Ford's Theatre, to see the latest production. The National Guard Association of the United States sponsored a closing reception at its Heritage Gallery, located in the national headquarters in Washington, D.C.

The goodwill—and the increased business—that has resulted from its closer relationships with national black organizations should make itself felt for years to come at American Airlines.

American has demonstrated, and continues to demonstrate, that when *recognition, identification,* and *invitation* are properly applied, successful outcomes can be achieved.

Many executives contemplating minority consumer market development will need to ask themselves some of the following questions:

(1) Is there a sufficient black travel market to warrant development?

(2) Are our majority marketing and advertising programs not reaching all segments of the travel market, including the minority?

(3) Is there a correlation between the employment of blacks and other minorities and the sale of products and services?

(4) Is the use of tailored programs, and advertising in black media important to programming?

(5) Are we at a competitive disadvantage in the black travel market?

(6) Are there unique opportunities existing in this market?

American Airlines took these questions into consideration as far back as the early 1960s, when it took steps to learn more about the potential by conducting its benchmark study. This foresight made the company a market factor early.

Obviously, majority advertising and marketing efforts were not having an equal effect on black travelers, and American demonstrated that tailored programs could produce business.

A significant aspect of successful public relations programs in the national black community has been the ability of a company to communicate its equal-opportunity efforts, as part of its marketing program.

The expansion of its travel agency services to include black travel agents, many of whom were and are developing businesses, gives American an extension of its offices directly into the black community through concerned agents who understand how American is preselling customers for them.

The extension of convention services to provide direct benefits to national black organizations, and to those who exhibit or observe at such conventions, has paid unlimited dividends. The presidents of these organizations, whose membership numbers about 13 million, cannot help but be aware that American Airlines is concerned about them and their organizations.

Moreover, involvement with the black press assures continuing consumer awareness of the services and programs of American, and American is cognizant of the role the black press can play in communicating the benefits and pleasures of travel.

American Airlines has proven that there are unique opportunities in the black travel market. Other carriers, as well as other forms of transportation, will increasingly be seeking the black travel dollar. Many have already followed the lead set by American Airlines, and will undoubtedly seek to challenge its leadership role in marketing to minority travelers.

It would appear, however, that American is "doing what it does best," and its course in the black travel market seems sure.

CHAPTER 28

Outlook for the Future

A RISE in minority-group incomes, brought about by occupational upgrading, is giving the minority population greater discretionary spending power and latitude for upgrading their way of life. Although the ebb and flow of the black labor force will depend upon the economy, this trend is expected to continue well into the 1980s.

Present saturation points for marketing various goods and services will become obsolete, and consumer socioeconomic characteristics will become important in setting new saturation points. As incomes rise, the strongest demand by minorities will be for products associated with an overall upgrading of their standard of living, such as education, housing and household operations, and medical and personal care—goods and services for which demand was previously elastic.

During the period through 1980, personal consumption expenditures by minorities are likely to increase. The impact of this increase on specific categories of goods and services could be significant in the years ahead.

It is unlikely that the black consumer market will disappear in the foreseeable future, because the reasons for its existence are not dissolving enough to decrease its recognition as a consumer market. It should remain a distinct market into the projectable future.

Blacks and other minorities have found new identification and pride in their ethnic origins, due in part to the *Roots* phenomenon, and in recognition of their accomplishments in American society, despite some of the barriers to full participation and years of discrimination.

This shifting mood, counter to the ideal of a "melting pot" for all Americans, still presents some problems for management and marketing executives who do not understand how to distinguish marketing opportunities from society-related problems.

The inclusion of minorities in the American mainstream reached its height during the years of the civil rights movement's greatest struggles and triumphs, and has abated since with the advent of other social problems. Some Americans even think minorities have gone too far in their demands for equal opportunity and treatment.

This has helped to solidify the duality in society that has existed, exists, and is expected to exist well into the future.

Today as never before, those who would sell goods and services to expanding markets must become familiar with the characteristics, behavior patterns in the marketplace, and socio-economic data on minority consumer markets.

The black consumer market and other minority markets will continue to be a prime marketing opportunity. Population and income will be influencing factors. The black population is expanding at an average annual rate of 1.7 percent—considerably faster than the United States as a whole—and the same average rate is projected for the next ten years. If this happens, blacks would number 26.7 million in 1980 and 29.1 million in 1985. They would account for 11.8 percent and 12.1 percent, respectively, of the total U.S. population, the same as today.

It should be noted that blacks are not the most rapidly growing segment of the population. Other racial minorities (including Americans of Japanese and Chinese descent, and American Indians) have much higher growth rates—averaging 4.9 percent in 1970–1975; and projected at 5.3 percent in 1976–1980 and 4.3 percent in 1980–1985. The Spanish-speaking population is also growing at above-average rates, 4.2 percent in 1970–1975.

In the United States, blacks, Hispanics, and undocumented minority aliens total more than 25 percent of the population. Therefore, one out of every four persons living in America has behavior patterns influenced by backgrounds considerably different from the mainstream, and their status is lower than most of American society.

As the largest minority group, black Americans have potential impact on a wide range of consumer goods and services and demand consideration for future marketing plans.

In his paper, "U.S. Long-Term Economic Outlook, Implications for the Black Consumer Market," Dr. Andrew Brimmer discussed prospective growth of black incomes. Dr. Brimmer is president of Brimmer & Company, Inc., a Washington, D.C.–based economic and financial consulting firm. From March 1966 through August 1974, he was a member of the Board of Governors of the Federal Reserve System. He pointed out that in 1975, when aggregate money income amounted to $1,008.4 billion, whites received $923.6 billion, blacks got $69.9 billion, and $14.9 billion went to other races. Black share represented 6.9 percent of the total. Brimmer estimated total money income of around $1,100.3 billion in 1976, with the black community's share at $77.1 billion—7.1 percent of the total.

For 1977, Brimmer predicted total money income of approximately $1,312 billion. Of this amount, blacks were expected to receive $87.3 billion—or 7.2 percent of the aggregate income.

In per capita terms, according to Brimmer, money income for the country as a whole amounted to $5,101 in 1976. For whites the figure was $5,372 and for blacks it was $3,084. Thus, the white-black income gap was around $2,288. The per capita income of blacks in 1976 was about 57.4 percent of that received by whites.

If blacks had received the same share of money income which they represented in the population (11 percent), they would have received $116.7 billion in 1976—or $39.6 billion more than they actually received. This shortfall, of course, reflects a legacy of discrimination and deprivation that has limited blacks' acquisition of marketable skills, says Brimmer.

By 1980, aggregate money income may expand to $1,644.0 billion. Of this amount, blacks may receive $123.3 billion—equal to 7.5 percent of the total. However, says Brimmer, in that year, blacks might constitute 11.8 percent of the population. Thus, if they got their proportionate share of total income, the black community would receive $194.0 billion, or $70.7 billion more than they seem likely to get.

By 1985, the total may have risen to $2,344.7 billion, and the money income received by blacks may amount to $185.2 billion. Again, however, blacks will represent 12.1 percent of the population in 1985; so a proportionate fraction would lift their receipts to $283.7 billion—or $98.5 billion more than the amount forecast.

So, according to Brimmer, blacks will continue to lag well behind whites in the proportion of income received in the next decade; however, they are likely to improve their relative position somewhat.

According to the U.S. Department of Commerce, the consumer section of the economy will see minority personal consumption expenditures growing at about the same rate as disposable income. Minority spending for nondurables and services will have a higher growth rate than durables. Overall outlays by minority consumers should rise from the 1973 level of $64 billion to about $119 billion in 1980—an increase of $55 billion over the seven-year period.

Looking into the eighties, expectations of slower population growth in the United States, scarcities of raw materials and fuels, and greater emphasis on environmental costs indicate a slower rise in the standard of living for all consumers, including minorities.

Increases in minority population and consumer income should generate a rising level of demand between 1989 and 1990, while the number⁣ of wage earners should also increase significantly as more young adults enter the work force. Age distribution of the population affects housing needs, education, medical, and personal services and supplies. In addition, an expected larger number of persons in the under-thirty-five and over-sixty-five groups could in the future bring about increases in very different consumer requirements. Married women in the labor force will continue to expand family income and generate further demands for products and services.

As incomes continue to rise, the strongest demand by minorities will be for products associated with an overall upgrading of their standard of living.

There will be social, cultural, and psychological influences continuing to affect minority consumers in the future, as well as the projected growth in population and income. More study will continue to be needed of these consumer market segments for efficient market development. Marketing efforts will continue to be needed that are target-oriented to these consumer segments.

Valuable consumer franchises could be lost if they are not protected now for the future. Those companies who would want to benefit from the future increasingly important minority market purchases will have to look extremely hard at their future market development projections.

Much of what has happened, and will happen to black and other minority races, will continue to be reflected in the individual's reactions in the marketplace. Part of this will be the need to establish a strong economic base in minority communities.

As long as the dual society exists in America, it will be necessary to program to dual markets. The ideal would be, of course, to be able to sell goods and services to all persons through a single effort in a total marketing approach that would give equal consideration to all consumers. But, as I have attempted to point out here, the climate still does not exist for the ideal to be the most effective manner.

The ideal is a desirable goal; yet today a market exists that can be effectively *recognized, identified* with, and *invited* to purchase goods and services.

These consumers happen to be blacks and other minority races.

APPENDIX
Tables on Minority Consumer Expenditures and Minority Income

Contents

177

TABLE 1   Minority Personal Consumption
Expenditures, 1973

	DISTRIBUTION OF DEMAND	
	PERCENT	$ BILLION
Food, alcohol, and tobacco	26	16.1
Housing[1]	16	10.5
Household operation	15	9.9
Clothing, accessories, and jewelry	12	8.1
Transportation	11	7.1
Medical care expenses	6	4.1
Recreation	6	3.9
Personal business	5	2.9
Personal care	2	1.3
Private education	1	.8
Total	100	64.7

[1] Demand Distribution is computed as follows: Minority expenditures for housing in 1973 were around 9% of the total market for housing, based on 1966 data. In 1973, expenditures for housing totaled $116 billion. Minority expenditures in this sector were 9% of $116 billion, or $10.5 billion. The sum of $10.5 billion represents 16% of all minority expenditures during 1973.

SOURCE: Computed from tables in *Market Profiles of Consumer Products*, prepared by The Conference Board based on the survey of consumer expenditures conducted by the U.S. Department of Labor, and the *Survey of Current Business*, July 1974, the U.S. Department of Commerce.

TABLE 2   Distribution of White and Nonwhite
Personal Consumption Expenditures,
1973

	WHITE (PERCENT)	NONWHITE (PERCENT)
Food, alcohol, and tobacco	22.4	25.8
Household operation	14.9	15.2
Housing	14.7	15.9
Transportation	14.1	10.8
Clothing, accessories, and jewelry	10.1	12.4
Medical care expenses	8.1	6.2
Recreation	6.7	6.0
Personal business	5.8	4.5
Private education	1.7	1.2
Personal care	1.5	2.0
Total	100.0	100.0

SOURCE: Computed from Bureau of Economic Analysis and The Conference Board, Inc., data.

TABLE 3   Historical Spending Patterns: Nonwhite
Personal Consumption Expenditures,
1966 and 1973

	1966 (PERCENT)	1973 (PERCENT)
Food, alcohol, and tobacco	28.3	25.8
Housing	15.8	15.9
Household operation	14.8	15.2
Clothing, accessories, and jewelry	12.6	12.4
Transportation	10.2	10.8
Recreation	5.6	6.0
Medical care expenses	5.3	6.2
Personal business	4.1	4.5
Personal care	2.2	2.0
Private education	1.1	1.2
Total	100.0	100.0

SOURCE: Computed from Bureau of Economic Analysis and The Conference Board, Inc., data.

TABLE 4   Overspending[1] and Underspending[1]—
Nonwhite More Than White, 1973

OVERSPENDING	PERCENT
Food, alcohol, and tobacco	3.4
Clothing, accessories, and jewelry	2.3
Housing	1.2
Personal	0.5
Household operation	0.3
Total	7.7

UNDERSPENDING	PERCENT
Transportation	−3.3
Medical care expenses	−1.9
Personal business	−1.3
Recreation	− .7
Private education	− .5
Total	−7.3

[1] The terms "overspend" and "underspend" are not intended as an evaluation, but are used for comparing nonwhite to white spending.

SOURCE: Computed from Table 2.

TABLE 5   Estimated Minority Expenditures,
Distribution of Expenditures, and Share
of the Market, 1973

	MINORITY PERSONAL CONSUMP-TION EXPENDI-TURES ($ MILLIONS)	DISTRI-BUTION OF MINORITY PERSONAL CONSUMP-TION EXPENDI-TURES (PERCENT)	MINORITY MARKET SHARE (PERCENT)[4]
Food, alcohol, and tobacco	16,080	25.8	9.5
Alcoholic beverages	2,150	3.3	10.0
Food, excluding alcoholic beverages	12,925	20.0	9.0
Tobacco products	1,289	2.0	9.5

	MINORITY PERSONAL CONSUMP-TION EXPENDI-TURES ($ MILLIONS)	DISTRI-BUTION OF MINORITY PERSONAL CONSUMP-TION EXPENDI-TURES (PERCENT)	MINORITY MARKET SHARE (PERCENT)[4]
Clothing, accessories, and jewelry[2]	8,127	12.4	10.0
Shoe cleaning and repair	46	0.1	10.5
Clothing and accessories, except footwear	4,776	7.4	8.0
Cleaning and laundering	654	1.0	14.5
Personal care[1]	1,293	2.0	10.5
Toilet articles and preparations	782	1.2	10.0
Barber shops, beauty parlors	517	0.8	11.5
Housing[2]	10,473	15.9	9.0
Owned, nonfarm dwelling-space-rental value	3,854	6.0	5.0
Rented nonfarm dwelling	4,590	7.1	14.5
Household operation[2]	9,988	15.2	8.5
Furniture	1,069	1.7	9.5
Kitchen and other appliances	1,130	1.7	9.0
China, glassware, table-ware, and utilities	592	0.9	11.0
Household utilities[2]	2,620	4.0	8.0
Electricity	1,033	1.6	7.5
Gas	531	0.8	8.5
Water and other sanitary services	193	0.3	6.0
Telephone and telegraph	1,239	1.9	9.0
Domestic service	259	0.4	5.0
Medical care expenses[2]	4,077	6.2	6.5
Drug preparations and sundries	558	0.9	6.5
Physicians	1,080	1.7	6.5
Dentists	220	0.3	4.5
Other professional services	159	0.2	5.5
Health insurance	356	0.6	7.5
Personal business[2]	2,937	4.5	6.5
Legal services	365	0.6	6.5
Funeral and burial expenses	260	0.4	10.5

	MINORITY PERSONAL CONSUMPTION EXPENDITURES ($ MILLIONS)	DISTRIBUTION OF MINORITY PERSONAL CONSUMPTION EXPENDITURES (PERCENT)	MINORITY MARKET SHARE (PERCENT)[4]
Transportation[1]	7,100	10.8	6.5
Automobile purchase	2,752	4.2	5.5
Gasoline and oil	1,982	3.1	7.0
Repairs and parts	1,699	2.6	9.0
Auto insurance	285	0.4	6.0
Local transportation	536	0.8	20.5
Intercity transportation[2]	279	0.4	7.0
a. Railway	16	_[5]	10.0
b. Bus	65	0.1	15.0
c. Airline	168	0.3	5.0
Recreation[2]	3,921	6.0	7.5
Books and maps	246	0.4	6.5
Magazines and newspapers	352	0.5	7.0
Toys and sport supplies	614	1.0	8.0
TV, radio, musical instruments	1,292	2.0	10.0
Spectator admissions	275	0.4	9.5
a. Motion pictures	129	0.2	10.0
b. Concerts, plays	50	0.1	5.0
c. Sports events	46	0.1	7.5
Club dues and membership	61	0.1	4.5
Private education[2]	794	1.2	6.0
Tuition and fees		1.1	7.0
Total	64,791	100.0	n.a.[3]

[1] Detail does not add to total due to rounding.
[2] Total includes data not shown separately.
[3] Not Applicable.
[4] Assumes same market shares as in 1966, the year of the latest available data.
[5] Less than 0.1 percent.

SOURCE: Computed from data from the *Survey of Current Business*, July 1974, the Bureau of Labor Statistics, and The Conference Board.

TABLE 6 Estimated Nonwhite Share of Market, 1966

	MARKET SHARE (PERCENT)
Distribution of nonwhite families	11.5
Expenditures for current consumption	8.5
Food, tobacco	9.0
Food prepared at home	9.0
Food away from home	8.5
Alcoholic beverages	10.0
Tobacco	9.5
Housing	8.5
Shelter	9.0
Fuel, light, refrigeration, water	8.0
Other household operations	8.5
House furnishings and equipment	9.0
Appliances	9.0
Furniture	9.5
Other house furnishings	8.5
Clothing and accessories	10.0
Men's and boys' clothing	10.0
Women's, girls', and infants' clothing	10.0
Materials and services	10.5
Transportation	6.5
Automobile	6.5
Other transportation	11.5
Medical care	6.5
Services	6.5
Supplies	6.5
Personal care	10.5
Services	11.5
Supplies	10.0
Recreation and equipment	7.5
Reading and education	6.5
Other expenditures	6.5

SOURCE: Percentages from The Conference Board, based on data from the Bureau of Labor Statistics, U.S. Department of Labor.

TABLE 7   Nonwhite Consumer Expenditures for Food, 1966[1]

	MARKET SHARE (PERCENT)
Food at home	10.5
Cereals and bakery products	11.0
Cereals	15.0
Flour	18.5
Biscuit, roll, muffin mix	9.5
Cake mix	6.0
Pancake and waffle mix	12.0
Pie mix and fillings	6.0
Other prepared mixes	5.5
Cornflakes	15.0
Wheat cereals, cold	5.0
Rice, other cold cereals	5.5
Cooked breakfast cereals	12.5
Macaroni, spaghetti, noodles	10.0
Rice	39.0
Cornmeal	38.0
Other cereal items	27.5
Bakery products	8.5
White bread	11.5
Other bread	4.5
Rolls, biscuits, muffins	9.0
Soda crackers	9.0
Other crackers	7.0
Cookies	6.0
Cakes, pies, pastries	8.0
Doughnuts, sweet rolls, coffee cake	7.0
Other bakery items	6.5
Meat, poultry, and fish	12.0
Meats and poultry	12.0
Beef steaks, fresh and frozen	7.0
Beef roasts, fresh and frozen	8.0
Ground beef, fresh and frozen	9.0
Pork, fresh and frozen	15.5
Other meat, fresh and frozen	12.0
Poultry, fresh and frozen	17.5
Bacon	14.0
Ham	11.5
Cold cuts	8.0
Frankfurters	13.0

[1] Estimated market share for expenditures by nonfarm families and single consumers. (Nonwhite consumers = 11.5 percent of population.)

	MARKET SHARE (PERCENT)
Meat, poultry, and fish (*cont'd*)	
Smoked sausage	21.0
Other meat	26.0
Canned ham	8.5
Other canned meat and poultry	11.0
Fish and seafood	14.0
Fresh, frozen, smoked, cured	16.5
Canned tuna	8.5
Canned salmon	15.0
Other fish and seafood	11.0
Milk, cream, and cheese	8.0
Milk, cream and ice cream	8.0
Fresh whole milk, retail	4.0
Fresh whole milk, delivered	8.5
Chocolate, other fresh milk	8.5
Evaporated and condensed milk	22.0
Dry milk items	6.5
Cream	4.0
Ice cream, sherbet, popsicles	9.0
Other milk and cream items	6.0
Cheese	6.5
American, other solid cheese	8.5
Cottage, other soft cheese	2.5
Cheese spreads	5.0
Fruits and vegetables	9.5
Fresh fruits	9.5
Apples	10.0
Bananas	7.5
Citrus fruits	11.0
Berries	4.5
Melons	9.0
Other fruits	9.0
Frozen fruits	4.5
Strawberries	4.5
Other fruits	4.0
Canned or bottled fruits	7.5
Peaches	12.0
Pineapple	4.5
Apples, applesauce	7.0
Other fruits	6.0
Dried fruits	6.5
Prunes	6.0
Raisins	7.0
Other fruits	6.5

	MARKET SHARE (PERCENT)
Fruits and vegetables (*cont'd*)	
Fresh and frozen fruit juices	6.5
Fresh juices	12.5
Frozen orange juice	4.0
Frozen lemonade	6.5
Other frozen juices	8.5
Canned, bottled fruit juices	10.5
Orange juice	13.5
Pineapple juice	13.5
Apple juice	10.0
Grape juice	10.0
Other fruit juices	8.5
Fresh vegetables	11.0
Potatoes	12.5
Tomatoes	6.0
Lettuce, other salad greens	7.0
Snap beans	29.0
Carrots	5.5
Celery	6.5
Onions, dry	14.0
Other vegetables	14.0
Frozen vegetables	10.0
Broccoli	6.5
Corn	7.0
Green beans	7.0
Lima beans	16.0
Peas	8.5
Spinach	11.5
Other vegetables	11.5
Canned or bottled vegetables	9.0
Peas	11.5
Tomatoes	8.0
Corn	11.5
Snap beans	6.0
Other vegetables	8.0
Dried vegetables	24.0
Canned, bottled vegetable juices	5.0
Tomato juice	4.5
Other vegetable juices	6.5
Other foods	9.5
Eggs	12.5
Fats and oils	11.0
Butter	8.5
Margarine	10.5
Lard	32.5
Other shortening	13.0

	MARKET SHARE (PERCENT)
Other foods (*cont'd*)	
Mayonnaise and cooked dressings	12.5
French, other salad dressings	7.5
Peanut butter	8.5
Salad and cooking oils	9.5
Other fats and oils	12.0
Soups	7.5
Canned chicken soup	9.0
Canned tomato soup	6.5
Canned vegetable soup	11.5
Other canned soups	5.5
Frozen soups	1.5
Dried soups	1.5
Frozen prepared dishes	3.5
Fish sticks	5.0
Meat, poultry or fish pies	3.0
Prepared dinners	3.5
Fruit, berry, cream pies	4.0
French fried potatoes, puffs, patties	4.0
Other frozen dishes	3.0
Other prepared dishes	6.5
Baked beans	9.5
Corned beef hash	13.0
Spaghetti	10.0
Potato chips	6.5
Other snacks	7.5
Other dishes	5.0
Sugar and other sweets	10.5
Candy	6.5
Chewing gum	10.0
Jellies, jams, preserves	9.0
Puddings and gelatin mixes	4.5
Sugar	15.0
Syrups, molasses, honey	14.5
Icings and fudge mixes	6.0
Other sweets	4.0
Beverages	9.0
Cocoa	8.0
Coffee, in bags	10.0
Coffee, in cans	7.0
Instant coffee	8.0
Coffee substitutes	4.5
Tea	6.0
Cola drinks	11.5
Gingerale	8.5
Other carbonated drinks	9.0
Noncarbonated drinks	13.0

	MARKET SHARE (PERCENT)
Other foods (*cont'd*)	
Baby and junior foods	8.0
Cereals	14.0
Meats	7.0
Fruits, vegetables, and other	7.5
Miscellaneous foods	10.0
Leavening agents, flavors	19.5
Olives	4.5
Pickles and relishes	6.0
Salt, other seasonings	17.0
Catsup, other sauces, gravies	10.5
Nuts	4.5
Other food items	4.5

SOURCE: Percentages prepared by the National Industrial Conference Board, based on data from the Bureau of Labor Statistics, U.S. Department of Labor.

TABLE 8   Alcoholic Beverages and Tobacco, 1966[1]

	MARKET SHARE (PERCENT)
Alcoholic beverages, packaged	10.0
Beer and ale	10.0
Blended whiskey	11.5
Bourbon, scotch, straight rye	11.0
Wines	5.5
Other alcoholic beverages	8.0
Tobacco	9.5
Cigarettes	9.0
Cigars	9.0
Other tobacco	16.5
Smokers' supplies	5.0

[1] Estimated nonwhite market share for expenditures by nonfarm families and single consumers. (Nonwhite consumers = 11.5 percent of population.)

SOURCE: Percentages prepared by the National Industrial Conference Board, based on data from the Bureau of Labor Statistics, U.S. Department of Labor.

TABLE 9   Housing, 1966[1]

	MARKET SHARE (PERCENT)
Shelter, other real estate	9.0
Rented dwelling	14.5
Rent	15.0
Repairs	7.0
Special fees, commissions	16.0
Owned dwelling	5.0
Interest on mortgages	5.0
Property taxes	3.5
Insurance, real property only	6.5
Homeowner insurance policy	3.0
Repairs by contractors	8.0
Repairs by homeowner	5.0
Other expenses	3.5
Owned vacation home or cabin	4.5
Interest on mortgages	2.5
Property taxes	3.0
Property insurance	1.5
Repairs and replacements	11.0
Other expenses	–
Lodging out of home city	2.5
Other real estate	8.0

[1] Estimated nonwhite market share for expenditures by nonfarm families and single consumers. (Nonwhite consumers = 11.5 percent of population.)

–: Less than .1 percent.

SOURCE: Percentages calculated by the National Industrial Conference Board, based on data from the Bureau of Labor Statistics, U.S. Department of Labor.

TABLE 10   House Furnishings and Equipment, 1966[1]

	MARKET SHARE (PERCENT)
House furnishings and equipment	9.0
Household textiles	11.0
Sheets	11.5
Pillowcases	12.5

[1] Estimated nonwhite market share for expenditures by nonfarm families and single consumers. (Nonwhite consumers = 11.5 percent of population.)

	MARKET SHARE (PERCENT)
Household furnishings and equipment (*cont'd*)	
Pillows	9.0
Bedspreads, comforters, quilts	17.0
Wool blankets	22.5
Electric blankets	3.0
Other blankets	12.0
Curtains	8.5
Draperies	11.0
Tablecloths, placemats, napkins	6.5
Slipcovers	11.5
Bath towels	10.0
Other towels	8.5
Other household textiles	6.5
Furniture	9.5
Living room suites	13.5
Other living room pieces	6.5
Dinette sets	10.5
Other dining room pieces	7.5
Bedroom suites	14.0
Other bedroom pieces	10.5
Mattresses and springs	8.0
Nursery furniture	11.5
Kitchen furniture	7.0
Porch and garden furniture	4.5
Other furniture	5.5
Floor coverings	5.0
Wall-to-wall carpets	2.0
Wool or wool blends	1.5
Other fibers	3.5
Room-size rugs	5.0
Wool or wool blends	5.5
Other fibers	4.5
Other soft surface rugs	7.0
Hard surface floor coverings	10.0
Tile	3.5
Other	12.0
All other floor coverings	2.5
Major appliances	8.5
Refrigerators	10.5
Home freezers	10.0
Dishwashers	1.0
Cooking stoves, gas	14.0
Cooking stoves, electric	5.0

	MARKET SHARE (PERCENT)
Major appliances (*cont'd*)	
Floor waxers, electric	3.0
Garbage disposal units	4.5
Vacuum cleaners	7.5
Washing machines, automatic	6.5
Washing machines, nonautomatic	19.5
Clothes dryers, gas	1.0
Clothes dryers, electric	1.0
Washer-dryer combinations	5.5
Air conditioners, demountable	3.5
Dehumidifiers	5.0
Sewing machines	12.0
Ironing machines	1.5
Other major appliances	21.5
Small appliances	15.0
Electric toasters	11.0
Electric irons	15.0
Electric fans	20.0
Other small appliances	13.0
Housewares	11.0
China, earthenware dish sets	6.5
Plastic dish sets	12.0
Other dishes	7.5
Knives, forks, spoons, etc.	14.0
Sterling silver	17.5
Silver plate	8.5
Stainless steel, other	13.0
Drinking glasses	8.5
Cooking utensils, nonelectric	15.5
Cleaning equipment	13.5
Laundry equipment	9.0
Kitchen wares	10.5
Other housewares	13.5
Miscellaneous items	7.5
Insurance on furnishings, apparel	9.0
Baby carriages, strollers	13.0

	MARKET SHARE (PERCENT)
Miscellaneous items (*con't*)	
Electric light bulbs	8.5
Typewriters	10.0
Clocks, pictures, vases, etc.	6.5
Lamps	10.0
Hand luggage	7.5
Lawn mowers	5.5
Tools (hand, power, garden)	4.5
General household hardware	5.5
Other items	8.0

SOURCE: Percentages calculated by the National Industrial Conference Board, based on data from the Bureau of Labor Statistics, U.S. Department of Labor.

TABLE 11   Housing—Fuel, Utilities, and Maintenance, 1966[1]

	MARKET SHARE (PERCENT)
Fuel, light, refrigeration, water	8.0
Coal and coke	17.0
Kerosene	10.5
Fuel oil	5.5
Other solid and petroleum fuels	19.0
Gas	8.5
Electricity	7.5
Gas and electricity, combined	10.5
Water, sewage, garbage	6.0
Food freezer rentals	2.5
Other expenses	20.5

[1] Estimated nonwhite market share for expenditures by nonfarm families and single consumers. (Nonwhite consumers = 11.5 percent of population.)

	MARKET SHARE (PERCENT)
Telephone and telegraph	9.0
Local telephone	9.5
Long distance telephone	8.0
Telegrams and cables	16.5
Laundry supplies	11.0
Cleaning supplies	9.5
Household paper supplies	9.0
Laundry and cleaning services	14.5
Laundry and cleaning sent out	13.0
Coin-operated washing machines	17.5
Domestic and child care services	5.0
Other household operations	6.0
Repairs, furniture and equipment	4.5
Moving, freight and storage	6.5
Writing supplies, cards, stationery	6.0
Special holiday decorations	7.0
Garden seeds, sprays, fertilizers	3.0
Other expenses	7.0
Household supplies	9.0
Liquid laundry detergents	6.0
Soap (bars, flakes, granules)	11.5
Synthetic detergents, dry	10.0
Bleaches, disinfectants	13.0
Starch	9.0
Bluing	8.0
Liquid household detergents	6.5
Scouring powder	9.0
Scouring pads, sponges	8.0
Floor waxes	10.0
Other household polishes	9.5
Insect sprays, powders	17.5
Air fresheners, deodorizers	13.5
Aluminum foil	9.5
Wax paper	12.5
Toilet tissue	10.5
Paper napkins	7.5
Paper towels	6.5
Paper plates, cups	2.0
Other supplies	5.0

SOURCE: Percentages calculated by the National Industrial Conference Board, based on data from the Bureau of Labor Statistics, U.S. Department of Labor.

TABLE 12   Clothing, Accessories, and Jewelry, 1966[1]

	MARKET SHARE (PERCENT)
Clothing, materials, and services	10.0
Clothing, men 18 years and over	9.5
Outerwear	9.5
Overcoats	14.5
Topcoats	12.5
Jackets, heavy	10.0
Jackets, lightweight	8.5
Sweaters	13.5
Raincoats	9.0
Suits, sport coats, trousers	8.5
Work trousers, overalls	10.5
Shirts, dress	9.0
Shirts, other	9.5
Other outerwear	5.0
Underwear	9.0
Nightwear	12.0
Hosiery	9.0
Footwear	10.0
Shoes	10.5
Special sports shoes	3.0
Other footwear	9.0
Hats, gloves, and accessories	11.5
Hats and caps	15.0
Gloves	8.5
Accessories	7.0
Jewelry	15.0
Other	1.0
Expenditures not allocated	7.5
Clothing, boys 16 and 17 years	8.5
Outerwear	8.5
Overcoats	12.0
Topcoats	14.5
Jackets, heavy	8.0
Jackets, lightweight	9.5
Sweaters	8.5
Raincoats	2.0
Suits, sport coats, trousers	9.0
Work trousers, overalls	8.0

[1] Estimated nonwhite market share for expenditures by nonfarm families and single consumers. (Nonwhite consumers = 11.5 percent of population.)
−: Less than .1 percent.

	MARKET SHARE (PERCENT)
Clothing, boys 16 and 17 years (*cont'd*)	
Shirts, dress	8.0
Shirts, other	7.5
Other outerwear	5.0
Underwear	7.5
Nightwear	4.0
Hosiery	6.5
Footwear	10.0
Shoes	10.5
Special sports shoes	6.0
Other footwear	3.5
Hats, gloves, and accessories	11.5
Hats and caps	28.5
Gloves	6.5
Accessories	7.0
Jewelry and watches	12.0
Other	–
Expenditures not allocated	10.0
Clothing, boys 2 to 15 years	10.5
Outerwear	11.5
Underwear	10.5
Nightwear	6.5
Hosiery	9.5
Footwear	10.0
Hats, gloves, and accessories	9.5
Jewelry and watches	5.0
Expenditures not allocated	13.5
Clothing, women 18 years and over	10.0
Outerwear	9.0
Winter coats, cloth	13.0
Lightweight coats, toppers	8.0
Fur coats, stoles, other furs	3.5
Raincoats	10.5
Jackets	9.0
Sweaters	10.5
Suits	11.0
Dresses	9.0
Skirts, jumpers, culottes	10.0
Blouses and shirts	7.5
Slacks, shorts, dungarees	6.0
Other outerwear	7.5
Underwear	10.0
Nightwear	9.5
Hosiery	14.0

	MARKET SHARE (PERCENT)
Clothing, women 18 years and over (*cont'd*)	
Footwear	10.0
Shoes	10.5
Special sports shoes	3.0
Other footwear	10.5
Hats, gloves, and accessories	9.5
Hats	9.0
Gloves	11.0
Handbags, purses	11.0
Jewelry and watches	7.5
Other	12.0
Expenditures not allocated	9.0
Clothing, girls 16 and 17 years	8.5
Outerwear	8.0
Underwear	9.0
Nightwear	8.5
Hosiery	13.5
Footwear	10.5
Hats, gloves, and accessories	8.0
Expenditures not allocated	3.5
Clothing, girls 2 to 15 years	10.5
Outerwear	10.5
Underwear	12.0
Nightwear	8.0
Hosiery	10.5
Footwear	10.5
Hats, gloves, and accessories	9.0
Jewelry and watches	4.0
Expenditures not allocated	16.0
Clothing, children under 2 years	15.0
Clothing materials	8.0
Clothing upkeep	12.0
Dry cleaning and pressing	12.0
Shoe repairs and services	10.5
Other clothing services	7.5

SOURCE: Percentages calculated by the National Industrial Conference Board, based on data from the Bureau of Labor Statistics, U.S. Department of Labor.

TABLE 13   Transportation, 1966[1]

	MARKET SHARE (PERCENT)
Transportation	6.5
Automobile purchases	5.5
Total purchase price	5.0
Allowance for trade-in	3.5
Auto operating expenses	7.0
Gasoline	7.0
Motor oil	7.0
Antifreeze	7.0
Lubrication, washing, oil filter	6.5
New tires and tubes	7.5
Other tires and tubes	9.5
Batteries	10.0
Spark plugs	7.5
Other operating expenses	5.5
Operating expenses, combined	5.5
Auto insurance	6.0
Comprehensive coverage	7.5
Collision coverage	9.5
Public liability coverage	8.5
Insurance premiums, combined	5.0
Refund on insurance	5.5
Repairs and parts	9.0
Other auto expenses	6.5
Local transportation	20.5
Intercity transportation	7.0
Train	10.0
Airplane	5.0
Bus	15.0
Shared or rented car	7.5
Steamship	.5
Other intercity transportation	10.0
Other transportation expenses	3.0
Car rental and operation	3.5
Motorcycles and scooters	4.0
Boats, outboard motors, trailers	1.0
Bicycles	8.0
Other transportation	5.5

[1] Estimated nonwhite market share for expenditures by nonfarm families and single consumers. (Nonwhite consumers = 11.5 percent of population.)

SOURCE: Percentages calculated by the National Industrial Conference Board, based on data from the Bureau of Labor Statistics, U.S. Department of Labor.

TABLE 14   Medical Care, 1966[1]

	MARKET SHARE (PERCENT)
Medical care	6.5
Group plans and insurance	7.5
Single or limited coverage	7.5
Health center care plan	9.5
General coverage	7.5
In-hospital care (uninsured)	6.5
Hospital services	6.5
Physicians' services	5.0
In-hospital care combined	10.5
Professional services	5.5
Medical services	6.5
Dental services	4.5
Eye care	5.5
Drugs and Medicine	6.5
Vitamins	6.0
Prescriptions	6.5
Nonprescription drug items	8.5
Medical appliances	2.0
Other medical supplies	6.5
Drugs and supplies combined	2.0
Other medical care	4.0

[1] Estimated nonwhite market share for expenditures by nonfarm families and single consumers. (Nonwhite consumers = 11.5 percent of population.)

SOURCE: Percentages calculated by the National Industrial Conference Board, based on data from the Bureau of Labor Statistics, U.S. Department of Labor.

TABLE 15   Personal Care, 1966[1]

	MARKET SHARE (PERCENT)
Personal care	10.5
Personal care services	11.5
Haircuts, men and boys	11.0

[1] Estimated nonwhite market share for expenditures by nonfarm families and single consumers. (Nonwhite consumers = 11.5 percent of population.)

	MARKET SHARE (PERCENT)
Personal care services (*cont'd*)	
Haircuts, women and girls	6.0
Shaves	43.0
Waves, shampoos, other hair care	12.5
Other services	4.0
Personal care supplies	10.0
Toilet soap	13.0
Dental needs	10.5
Razors and blades	10.0
Electric shavers and repairs	2.0
Shaving preparations	8.0
Cleansing tissues	9.5
Face powder	10.0
Face and skin creams, lotions	11.5
Shampoos, other hair preparations	6.5
Home permanent kits	2.5
Hairbrushes, combs, nets	10.0
Sanitary supplies	10.5
Other cosmetics	11.0
Other supplies	5.5

SOURCE: Percentages calculated by the National Industrial Conference Board, based on data from the Bureau of Labor Statistics, U.S. Department of Labor.

TABLE 16   Recreation and Equipment, 1966[1]

	MARKET SHARE (PERCENT)
Recreation	7.5
TV, radios, musical instruments	10.0
Television, portable or table	17.5
Other television sets	10.5
Radios, portable or table	13.0
Other radios	9.0
TV and radio repairs	9.5

[1] Estimated nonwhite market share for expenditures by nonfarm families and single consumers. (Nonwhite consumers = 11.5 percent of population.)

	MARKET SHARE (PERCENT)
TV, radios, musical instruments (*cont'd*)	
Phonographs, tape recorders	8.5
Hi-fi components, kits, parts	10.5
Records, magnetic tapes, reels	9.0
Pianos and organs	3.5
Other items	4.5
Spectator admissions	9.5
Movies, indoor	12.0
Movies, drive-in	8.0
Sports events	7.5
Concerts, plays, other admissions	5.0
Participant sports	3.5
Hunting and fishing equipment	5.0
Other sports equipment	4.0
Dues and fees for sports	3.0
Club dues and memberships	4.5
Hobbies	4.5
Cameras	7.0
Other photographic items	4.5
Crafts and other hobbies	1.5
Pets (purchase, supplies, equipment)	2.5
Pet food	6.0
Toys and play equipment	8.0
Dolls and accessories	10.5
Stuffed toys and infant toys	6.5
Tricycles	16.5
Wagons, skates, sleds	8.5
Games, puzzles, mechanical toys	5.5
Other toys and equipment	5.0
Lump-sum expenditures	9.0
Recreation out of home city	4.0
Other recreation	15.0

SOURCE: Percentages calculated by the National Industrial Conference Board, based on data from the Bureau of Labor Statistics, U.S. Department of Labor.

TABLE 17 Reading, Education, and All Other Expenditures, 1966[1]

	MARKET SHARE (PERCENT)
Reading	7.5
Newspapers	8.5
Magazines	6.0
Books (not school or technical)	6.5
Pocket editions	6.5
Comic books	16.5
Hardbound books	5.5
Other reading expenses	8.5
Education	6.0
Tuition and fees	7.0
School and technical books, supplies	7.5
Music and other special lessons	3.0
Other educational expenses	3.0
Other current expenditures	6.5
All expense tours, etc.	2.5
Legal expenses	6.5
Funeral expenses	10.5
Other expenses	7.5
Additional disbursements	7.0
Personal insurance	8.0
Life, endowment, annuity	7.5
Veterans	3.5
Group	6.5
Other	7.5
Other personal insurance	12.0
Retirement funds	8.0
Refunds on insurance	4.0
Gifts and contributions	6.0

[1] Estimated nonwhite market share for expenditures by nonfarm families and single consumers. (Nonwhite consumers = 11.5 percent of population.)

SOURCE: Percentages calculated by the National Industrial Conference Board, based on data from the Bureau of Labor Statistics, U.S. Department of Labor.

TABLE 18   Number of Cars and Other Durables
Purchased per 100 Households, by Race:
1968–1972

	WHITE	NEGRO
New cars	66.1	27.4
Used cars	110.8	72.9
Washing machines	29.2	22.6
Clothes dryers	21.7	7.0
Kitchen ranges	17.9	18.0
Refrigerators and freezers	33.1	29.1
Dishwashers	11.2	1.4
Room air conditioners	17.0	9.7
Black and white televisions	28.5	36.8
Color televisions	37.6	23.7

SOURCE: *Current Population Reports, Consumer Buying Indicators,* U.S.
Department of Commerce.

TABLE 19   Estimated Minority Personal Consumption
Expenditures: 1975–1980[1]
(in millions of dollars)

	1975	1976	1977	1978	1979	1980
Food, alcohol, and tobacco	19,139	20,880	22,780	24,853	27,114	29,581
Clothing, accessories, and jewelry	9,672	10,552	11,512	12,559	13,701	14,947
Personal care	1,538	1,677	1,829	1,995	2,176	2,374
Housing	12,465	13,599	14,836	16,186	17,658	19,264
Household operation	11,887	12,968	14,148	15,435	16,839	18,371
Medical care expenses	4,852	5,293	5,774	6,299	6,872	7,497
Personal business	3,495	3,813	4,159	4,537	4,949	5,399
Transportation	8,450	9,218	10,056	10,971	11,969	13,058
Recreation	4,666	5,090	5,553	6,058	6,609	7,210
Private education	944	1,029	1,122	1,224	1,335	1,456
Total	77,108	84,119	91,769	100,117	109,222	119,157

[1] Assumes a 9 percent increase compounded annually between 1975 and 1980.
SOURCE: Bureau of Domestic Commerce, U.S. Department of Commerce.

TABLE 20 Projected 1980 Minority Population,
by State

REGION AND STATE	NEGRO AS PERCENT OF TOTAL	OTHER RACES AS PERCENT OF TOTAL	1980 NEGRO POPULATION (EST.)	1980 OTHER RACES POPULATION (EST.)
U.S.	1.1	1		
Region				
Northeast	9	1		
North Central	8	1		
South	19	1		
West	5	5		
New England	3	1		
Maine	–	–	–	–
New Hampshire	–	–	–	–
Vermont	–	–	–	–
Massachusetts	3	1	188,007	62,669
Rhode Island	3	1	30,948	10,316
Connecticut	6	–	201,462	–
Middle Atlantic	11	1		
New York	12	1	2,322,228	193,519
New Jersey	11	1	888,833	80,803
Pennsylvania	9	–	1,138,437	–
East North Central	10	1		
Ohio	9	–	1,048,554	–
Indiana	7	–	404,852	–
Illinois	13	1	1,571,817	120,909
Michigan	11	1	1,071,675	97,425
Wisconsin	3	1	142,098	47,366
West North Central	4	1		
Minnesota	1	1	41,194	41,194
Iowa	1	–	29,134	–
Missouri	10	–	507,120	–
North Dakota	–	3	–	17,361
South Dakota	–	5	–	32,725
Nebraska	3	1	44,964	14,988
Kansas	5	1	111,420	22,284
South Atlantic	21	1		
Delaware	14	1	87,710	6,265
Maryland	18	1	805,212	44,734
District of Columbia	71	1	532,500	7,500
Virginia	19	1	1,006,126	52,954

REGION AND STATE	NEGRO AS PERCENT OF TOTAL	OTHER RACES AS PERCENT OF TOTAL	1980 NEGRO POPULATION (EST.)	1980 OTHER RACES POPULATION (EST.)
South Atlantic (*cont'd*)				
West Virginia	4	–	73,284	–
North Carolina	22	1	1,261,986	57,363
South Carolina	30	–	845,550	–
Georgia	26	–	1,338,298	–
Florida	15	–	1,333,960	–
East South Central	20	–		
Kentucky	7	–	252,616	–
Tennessee	16	–	729,088	–
Alabama	26	–	974,142	–
Mississippi	37	–	861,323	–
West South Central	16	1		
Arkansas	19	–	396,454	–
Louisiana	30	–	1,123,290	–
Oklahoma	7	4	193,361	110,492
Texas	13	1	1,581,697	121,669
Mountain	2	4		
Montana	–	4	–	26,788
Idaho	–	2	–	14,158
Wyoming	1	2	3,309	6,618
Colorado	3	1	77,583	25,361
New Mexico	2	8	21,098	84,392
Arizona	3	6	66,777	133,554
Utah	1	2	11,601	23,202
Nevada	6	3	36,936	18,468
Pacific	6	5		
Washington	2	3	70,998	106,497
Oregon	1	2	23,346	46,692
California	7	4	1,568,238	896,136
Alaska	3	18	9,996	59,976
Hawaii	1	60	8,475	508,500

–: Less than 1 percent of population.

SOURCE: Estimated by Bureau of Domestic Commerce from data from the Census Bureau and projections by the Bureau of Economic Analysis, U.S. Department of Commerce.

TABLE 21 Projected 1980 Per Capita Income
for Minorities (in dollars)

STATE (LISTED BY GEOGRAPHICAL AREA)	WHITE PROJECTED 1980 PER CAPITA INCOME	NEGRO PROJECTED 1980 PER CAPITA INCOME	PERSONS OF SPANISH ORIGIN PROJECTED 1980 PER CAPITA INCOME
U.S. average	5,015.2	2,899.4	3,695.9
Maine	4,114.2	2,952.2	4,327.7
New Hampshire	4,487.4	3,138.1	4,487.4
Vermont	4,314.6	3,938.8	5,243.2
Massachusetts	5,332.2	3,287.8	3,530.2
Rhode Island	4,886.9	2,902.2	3,913.3
Connecticut	5,725.5	3,227.9	3,540.1
New York	6,074.2	3,742.8	2,794.1
New Jersey	5,604.7	3,246.2	2,615.1
Pennsylvania	4,942.2	3,338.0	2,372.6
Delaware	5,819.6	2,964.8	4,174.7
Maryland	5,465.4	3,026.8	4,831.9
District of Columbia	12,525.9	5,070.3	6,861.6
Michigan	5,275.2	3,627.0	3,723.6
Ohio	4,999.3	3,326.4	3,622.2
Indiana	4,700.6	3,161.3	3,391.1
Illinois	5,729.3	3,471.3	3,710.7
Wisconsin	4,683.0	2,986.4	3,342.4
Minnesota	4,813.9	3,654.7	3,899.0
Iowa	4,606.3	3,078.5	3,459.3
Missouri	4,767.7	2,935.7	3,966.2
North Dakota	3,996.1	2,790.2	2,983.3
South Dakota	4,089.6	–	2,790.2
Nebraska	4,730.7	2,970.1	3,203.6
Kansas	4,663.9	2,841.2	3,156.4
Virginia	4,896.2	2,337.6	4,405.7
West Virginia	3,769.0	2,375.1	4,255.9
Kentucky	3,966.5	2,539.9	4,074.7
Tennessee	4,079.1	2,111.2	4,113.0
North Carolina	4,468.2	2,110.5	3,976.0
South Carolina	4,474.9	1,812.6	3,775.5
Georgia	4,818.6	2,094.5	4,621.1
Florida	4,910.0	2,132.4	3,606.4
Alabama	4,219.6	1,775.1	4,008.4
Mississippi	4,330.2	1,527.9	4,109.6
Louisiana	4,593.3	1,919.2	3,925.7
Arkansas	3,952.1	1,679.1	3,329.9
Oklahoma	4,280.7	2,170.9	3,087.3
Texas	4,639.0	2,419.8	2,358.7
New Mexico	4,090.9	2,544.6	2,533.0

STATE (LISTED BY GEOGRAPHICAL AREA)	WHITE PROJECTED 1980 PER CAPITA INCOME	NEGRO PROJECTED 1980 PER CAPITA INCOME	PERSONS OF SPANISH ORIGIN PROJECTED 1980 PER CAPITA INCOME
Arizona	4,557.6	2,477.3	2,706.1
Montana	4,303.7	2,839.7	3,134.2
Idaho	4,119.5	2,850.1	2,481.5
Wyoming	4,552.5	2,710.8	2,652.2
Colorado	4,733.1	3,222.4	2,764.1
Utah	4,063.2	2,798.7	2,714.1
Washington	4,962.8	3,506.3	3,290.5
Oregon	4,518.8	2,999.1	2,990.1
Nevada	5,446.3	2,849.1	4,076.9
California	5,475.1	3,369.7	3,475.5
Alaska	6,435.0	4,342.5	4,477.5
Hawaii	5,707.1	3,767.1	3,912.2

–: Base is too small to be shown.

SOURCE: Estimated by Bureau of Domestic Commerce from Bureau of Census and Bureau of Economic Analysis data.

TABLE 22   Per Capita Income of Minorities, 1969

STATE (LISTED BY GEOGRAPHICAL AREA)	TOTAL 1969 (PERCENT)	WHITE	NEGRO	PERSONS OF SPANISH LAN- GUAGE	WHITE AS PERCENT OF TOTAL	NEGRO AS PERCENT OF TOTAL	PERSONS OF SPANISH LAN- GUAGE AS PERCENT OF TOTAL
U.S. average	3,025	3,242	1,884	2,390			
Maine	2,550	2,556	1,835	2,690	100.2	71.9	105.4
New Hampshire	3,023	3,028	2,117	3,027	100.1	70.0	100.1
Vermont	2,776	2,775	2,533	3,370	99.9	91.2	121.4
Massachusetts	3,425	3,469	2,138	2,296	101.2	62.4	67.0
Rhode Island	3,147	3,187	1,892	2,555	101.2	60.1	81.1
Connecticut	3,900	4,008	2,259	2,477	102.7	57.9	63.5
New York	3,650	3,834	2,365	1,764	105.0	64.7	48.3
New Jersey	3,691	3,869	2,243	1,807	104.8	60.7	48.9
Pennsylvania	3,093	3,185	2,152	1,528	102.9	69.5	49.4
Delaware	3,298	3,531	1,786	2,514	107.7	54.4	76.6
Maryland	3,540	3,848	2,134	3,402	108.7	60.2	96.1
District of Columbia	3,859	6,743	2,734	3,693	174.7	70.8	95.7

STATE (LISTED BY GEOGRAPHICAL AREA)	TOTAL 1969 (PERCENT)	WHITE	NEGRO	PERSONS OF SPANISH LANGUAGE	WHITE AS PERCENT OF TOTAL	NEGRO AS PERCENT OF TOTAL	PERSONS OF SPANISH LANGUAGE AS PERCENT OF TOTAL
Michigan	3,373	3,498	2,405	2,469	103.7	71.3	73.2
Ohio	3,221	3,323	2,211	2,406	103.1	68.6	74.7
Indiana	3,093	3,164	2,130	2,283	102.3	68.8	73.8
Illinois	3,512	3,701	2,243	2,396	105.3	63.8	68.2
Wisconsin	3,046	3,086	1,968	2,203	101.3	64.6	72.3
Minnesota	3,052	3,068	2,330	2,485	100.5	76.3	81.4
Iowa	2,894	2,907	1,942	2,182	100.4	67.1	75.4
Missouri	2,983	3,106	1,914	2,586	114.1	64.1	86.6
North Dakota	2,479	2,516	1,757	1,878	101.4	70.8	75.7
South Dakota	2,418	2,480	–	1,694	102.6	–	70.0
Nebraska	2,814	2,852	1,790	1,932	101.3	63.6	68.6
Kansas	2,945	3,007	1,833	2,037	102.1	62.2	69.1
Virginia	3,013	3,340	1,594	3,004	110.8	52.9	99.7
West Virginia	2,338	2,371	1,496	2,679	101.4	63.9	114.5
Kentucky	2,437	2,502	1,601	2,570	102.6	65.7	105.4
Tennessee	2,469	2,673	1,383	2,696	108.2	56.0	109.1
North Carolina	2,492	2,839	1,342	2,522	113.9	53.8	101.2
South Carolina	2,313	2,828	1,145	2,386	122.2	49.5	103.1
Georgia	2,649	3,103	1,350	2,976	117.1	50.9	112.3
Florida	3,092	3,390	1,473	2,491	109.6	47.6	80.5
Alabama	2,352	2,751	1,157	2,614	117.9	49.6	112.0
Mississippi	1,935	2,545	898	2,415	131.5	46.4	124.8
Louisiana	2,345	2,840	1,188	2,428	129.1	50.6	103.5
Arkansas	2,155	2,410	1,024	2,031	111.8	47.5	94.2
Oklahoma	2,723	2,864	1,452	2,066	105.1	53.3	75.8
Texas	2,810	2,992	1,561	1,521	106.4	55.5	54.1
New Mexico	2,449	2,581	1,604	1,597	105.3	65.5	65.2
Arizona	2,945	3,110	1,693	1,847	105.6	57.4	62.7
Montana	2,712	2,775	1,832	2,023	102.3	67.5	74.5
Idaho	2,649	2,665	1,844	1,606	100.6	57.4	60.6
Wyoming	2,920	2,944	1,754	1,714	101.1	60.2	58.9
Colorado	3,118	3,157	2,149	1,843	101.2	68.9	59.1
Utah	2,703	2,729	1,881	1,822	100.9	69.5	67.4
Washington	3,370	3,413	2,411	2,263	101.2	71.5	67.1
Oregon	3,163	3,189	2,117	2,112	100.8	66.9	66.7
Nevada	3,570	3,708	1,940	2,777	103.8	54.3	77.7
California	3,632	3,760	2,314	2,389	103.5	63.7	65.7
Alaska	3,765	4,308	2,907	2,997	114.4	77.2	79.6
Hawaii	3,378	3,588	2,369	2,461	106.2	70.1	72.8

–: Base is too small to be shown.

SOURCE: U.S. Bureau of the Census, Census of Population: 1970, Vol. 1, *Characteristics of the Population*, Table 57. (Individual state parts)

BIBLIOGRAPHY
Advertising and Marketing to the Black Consumer

Bibliographies

BARRY, THOMAS E.; HARVEY, MICHAEL C.; and MCGILL, MICHAEL E., compilers and eds. *Marketing and the Black Consumer, an Annotated Bibliography*. American Marketing Association, 222 S. Riverside Plaza, Chicago, IL, 1976. Bibliography Series #22. 40 pp.

CASHMAN, MARC. *Bibliography of American Ethnology*. Rye, NY: Todd Publications, 1976. 304 pp.

GAGALA, KENNETH L. *The Economics of Minorities*. Detroit, MI: Gale Research Co., 1976. Economics Information Guide Series, vol. 2. 212 pp.

HALLIDAY, THELMA Y. *Minorities in the Field of Business, an Annotated Bibliography*. Howard University, Institute for Minority Business Education, P.O. Box 748, Washington, DC 20059. October 1975. 131 pp. *See* "Marketing," pp. 92–96.

PRESSLEY, MILTON M. *A Selected Bibliography of Readings and References Regarding Marketing to Black Americans*. October 1974. 36 pp. Exchange Bibliography no. 671. Council of Planning Librarians, P.O. Box 229, Monticello, IL 61856.

U.S. DEPT. OF COMMERCE, OFFICE OF MINORITY BUSINESS ENTERPRISE, WASHINGTON, D.C. 20230. *Minority Business Enterprise—A Bibliography*, 1973. 231 pp.

WESTMORELAND, GUY T., JR. *An Annotated Guide to Basic Reference Books on the Black American Experience*. Wilmington, DE: Scholarly Resources, Inc., 1974. 98 pp.

Directories

AFRAM ASSOCIATES. *Directory, National Black Organizations*, compiled by Charles L. Sanders and Linda McLean. AFRAM Associates, Inc., 68–72 East 131st St., Harlem, NY 10037. August 1972. 115 pp. Supplement 1974.

AMERICAN AIRLINES. *American Airlines 1977 Travel Guide to Black Conventions and Conferences*. Prepared by D. Parke Gibson International, Inc. Convention Sales, American Airlines, Inc., P.O. Box 1000, Bellmore, NY 11710. 80 pp. (4″ x 9″, brochure format)

CALVERT, ROBERT, JR. *Equal Employment Opportunity for Minority Group*

College Graduates: Locating, Recruiting, Employing. Minority population statistics, minority newspapers, periodicals, radio stations, associations. Garrett Park Press, Garrett Park, MD 20766. 1972. 247 pp.

COLUMBIA BOOKS, INC. *1976 National Trade and Professional Associations of the U.S. and Canada and Labor Unions*, Craig Colgate, Jr., ed. Columbia Books, Inc., 734 15th St., NW, Rm 601, Washington, DC 20005. Annual. 365 pp.

Gebbie Press All-in-One Directory. Information on more than 22,000 publicity outlets in the U.S., with special sections on the Black press and Black radio stations. Gebbie Press, Box 1000, New Paltz, NY 12561. Annual. 530 pp.

JACKSON, LAWRENCE T., and JACKSON, ALBERT. *The Black Press Periodical Directory, 1975.* 60 pp. Supplement #1, 1976, L. T. Jackson, ed. Black Newspaper Clipping Bureau, Inc., U.B.A., Beatrice Lewis Bldg., 68–72 East 131st St., Harlem, NY 10037.

National Minority Business Campaign, *Guide to Minority Business Directories*, 10th ed. National Minority Business Campaign, 1016 Plymouth Ave. N., Mnneapolis, MN 55411. Local, state, and specialized national or regional directories. February 1975. 15 pp.

————. *Purchasing People in Major Corporations.* National Minority Business Campaign, Minneapolis, MN. 1976.

————. *Try Us: 1976, National Minority Business Directory.* National Minority Business Campaign, Minneapolis, MN. More than 4,000 minority businesses having a national reach. Annual.

U.S. DEPT. OF COMMERCE, BUREAU OF THE CENSUS, SOCIAL AND ECONOMIC STATISTICS ADMINISTRATION, WASHINGTON, D.C. 20233. *Data on Selected Racial Groups Available from the Bureau of the Census*, DAD no. 40. May 1975. 43 pp.

————, BUREAU OF THE CENSUS. *1972 Survey of Minority-Owned Business Enterprises: Minority-Owned Businesses—Black.* Special Report MB72-1, November 1974. 161 pp. (Statistical information. Also available from the Office of Minority Business Enterprise, U.S. Dept. of Commerce.)

————, DOMESTIC AND INTERNATIONAL BUSINESS ADMINISTRATION. *Publications for American Business.* Catalog of publications available from the U.S. Dept. of Commerce. 18 pp.

————, OFFICE OF MINORITY BUSINESS ENTERPRISE, WASHINGTON, D.C. 20230. *American Marketing Association Directory of Marketing Assistance for Minority Business.* September 1976. AMA volunteers by geographical location. 58 pp.

————, OFFICE OF MINORITY BUSINESS ENTERPRISE, WASHINGTON, D.C. 20230. *OMBE-Funded Organizations Directory.* January 1976. 48 pp.

U.S. DEPT. OF LABOR, BUREAU OF LABOR STATISTICS. *Directory of Data Sources on Racial and Ethnic Minorities.* 1975. 83 pp. (Bulletin 1879). Supt. of Documents, GPO, Washington, DC 20402.

Handbooks

EBONY EDITORS, and SAUNDERS, DORIS E. *The Ebony Handbook.* Chicago, IL: Johnson Publishing Co., Inc., 1974. 443 pp.

NATIONAL NEWSPAPER PUBLISHERS ASSOCIATION. *Black Press Handbook.* National

Newspaper Publishers Assn., Washington, DC. Member publications, history, and related information. 116 pp.

SMYTHE, MABEL M., ed. *The Black American Reference Book*. Englewood Cliffs, NJ: Prentice-Hall, Inc., 1976. 1,026 pp. Previous editions by J. P. Davis, published under title, *The American Negro Reference Book*.

U.S. DEPT. OF COMMERCE, BUREAU OF THE CENSUS, SOCIAL AND ECONOMIC STATISTICS ADMINISTRATION. *The Social and Economic Status of the Black Population in the United States 1974.* (1975 bicentennial ed. not yet available.) Current Population Reports, Special Studies Series P-23, no. 54. Issued July 1975. 195 pp.

————, DOMESTIC AND INTERNATIONAL BUSINESS ADMINISTRATION. *Minority Markets*. Available from the Supt. of Documents, GPO, Washington, DC 20402. October 1975. 66 pp.

Books and Pamphlets

ANDREASEN, ALAN R. *The Disadvantaged Consumer*, foreword by Mary Gardiner Jones. New York, NY: Free Press, 1975. 366 pp.

————. *Improving Inner-City Marketing*. Chicago, IL: American Marketing Association, c. 1972. 278 pp.

ARBITRON RADIO. *How Blacks Listen to Radio*. New York, NY: Arbitron Radio, American Research Bureau, sub. of Control Data Corporation, 1350 Avenue of the Americas, NY 10019. October 1974. 21 pp.

BAUER, RAYMOND A., and CUNNINGHAM, SCOTT M. *Studies in the Negro Market*. Cambridge, MA: Marketing Science Institute, 1970. 198 pp.

BELL, DURAN, and ZELLMAN, GAIL. *Issues in Services Delivery to the Ethnic Elderly*. March 1976. 15 pp. (P-5613). Rand Corporation.

BLACKMAN, COURTNEY N. *Black Capitalism in Economic Perspective*. New York, NY: Economic Research Dept., Irving Trust Co., 1973. 40 pp.

BRIMMER, ANDREW F. *Capital Shortage: Real or Imagined?* (10th Annual Wm. K. McInally Mem. Lecture). 1976. Repr. pap. University of Michigan Graduate School of Business Administration, Division of Research, Ann Arbor, MI 48104.

————. *Central Banking and Credit Allocation*. (W. H. Irons Mem. Lecture Series, No. 2). 1975. Paper. University of Texas at Austin, Bureau of Business Research, P.O. Box 7459, University Sta., Austin, TX 78712.

————. "Commercial Bank Lending Abroad and the U.S. Balance of Payments" in *The International Monetary System in Transition*. Chicago, IL: The Federal Reserve Bank, 1972.

————. "The Framework of Industrial Organization in India." MA: Center for International Studies at M.I.T., 1957.

————. *Life Insurance Companies in the Capital Market*. Michigan State University, Public Bureau of Business and Economic Research, 1962.

————. "Structural Changes in the Canadian-American Balance of Payments" in *Canadian-U.S. Financial Relationships*. Boston, The Federal Bank, 1972.

————; WHEELER, OLIVER; and HOLMES, ALLAN. "Preliminary Report on the Origin and Functions of a Central Bank for the Sudan." Khartoum Ministry of Finance and Economics, 1957.

CHRISTIAN, VIRGIL, and MARSHALL, RAY. *Black Economic Progress in the South: The Role of Education.* In J. L. Stern and B. D. Dennis (eds.), Industrial Relations Research Association Series: Proceedings of the Twenty-Seventh Annual Winter Meeting, Dec. 28–29, 1974, San Francisco. Madison, WI: Industrial Relations Research Association, 1975. 372 pp.

COLES, FLOURNOY A., JR. *Black Economic Development.* Chicago, IL: Nelson-Hall, 1975. 222 pp.

DEUTSCH, SHEA & EVANS, INC. *The DS&E Recruitment Manual 1975–76.* New York, NY: Deutsch, Shea & Evans, Inc., 1975. 112 pp.

DYER, LEE W., ed. and author. *Merchandising in Action.* Based on the A&P study researched and written by the editors of *Progressive Grocer Magazine* in cooperation with The Great Atlantic & Pacific Tea Co., Inc. New York, NY: *Progressive Grocer Magazine,* 1972. 304 pp. *See especially* "The Negro Customer" in Ch. II, pp. 57–66.

EBONY MAGAZINE. *How Do You Sell to Urban Negro Customers.* Chicago, IL: Johnson Publishing Co., Sales Promotion Dept., n.d. 16 pp.

EPSTEIN, EDWIN M., and HAMPTON, DAVID R. *Black Americans and White Business.* Encino, CA, Dickenson Publ. Co., 1971. 447 pp.

FERGUSON, RICHARD D., JR., and GITTER, A. GEORGE. *Blacks in Magazine and Television Advertising.* August 1971. 35 pp. (CRC Report, no. 56). Communication Research Center, Boston University, Boston, MA 02215.

GIBSON, D. PARKE. *The Thirty Billion Dollar Negro.* New York, NY: Macmillan Publishing Co., Inc., 1969. 311 pp.

GLOSTER, JESSE E. *Economics of Minority Groups* [United States]. Houston, TX: Premier Printing Co., 1973. 216 pp.

GRAVES [EARL G.] MARKETING & RESEARCH, INC. *A Study of Advertising Responsiveness Among Upscale Blacks and Upscale Whites.* New York, NY: Earl G. Graves Marketing and Research, Inc., 1973. 59 pp.

GROH, GEORGE W. *The Black Migration: The Journey to Urban America.* New York, NY: Weybright and Talley (div. of David McKay), Inc., 1972. 301 pp.

JOHNSON, JOSEPH T. *The Potential Negro Market.* New York, NY: Pageant Press, 1952. 185 pp.

JOYCE, GEORGE, and GOVONI, NORMAN, eds. *Black Consumer: Dimensions of Behavior and Strategy.* New York, NY: Random House, 1971. 369 pp.

KRONUS, SIDNEY. *The Black Middle Class.* Columbus, OH: Charles E. Merrill Publishing Company, 1971. 182 pp.

LEVITAN, SAR A. and others. *Minorities in the United States: Problems, Progress, and Prospects.* Washington, DC: Public Affairs Press, 1975. 106 pp. (George Washington University, Center for Manpower Policy Studies Publication).

MARKHAM, CLARENCE, JR. *Economic Impact of the Negro Traveler.* Chicago, IL: Traveler Research, 1971. 143 pp.

MASTERS, STANLEY H. *Black-White Income Differentials: Empirical Studies and Policy Implications.* New York, NY: Academic Press, 1975. 188 pp. (Institute for Research on Poverty monograph series).

NATIONAL COMMISSION FOR MANPOWER POLICY. *The Economic Position of Black Americans: 1976.* Special Report no. 9, July 1976. National Commission for

Manpower Policy, 1522 K St. NW, Suite 300, Washington, DC 20005. 65 pp.

NATIONAL PLANNING DATA CORPORATION. *Demographics, U.S.A., a Comprehensive Summary of the U.S. Census*. Rochester, NY: National Planning Data Corporation, 65 Broad St., Rochester 14614. 1972 (1970 Census). 180 pp.

NATIONAL URBAN LEAGUE. *Full Employment as a National Goal*. Proceedings of the 64th National Urban League Conference, San Francisco, CA, July 28–31, 1974. New York, NY: National Urban League, 1975. 229 pp.

NEW YORK CITY COUNCIL ON ECONOMIC EDUCATION. *Fact Book on the New York Metropolitan Region, 1976–77*. New York, NY: New York City Council on Economic Education, Pace University, 1976, 144 pp.

———. *Proceedings of the Ninth Annual One-day Institute: Challenges of the Changing Economy of New York City*. NYC Council on Econ. Ed. 1976. 52 pp.

NEW YORK STATE DEPT. OF LABOR, DIV. OF RESEARCH AND STATISTICS, BUREAU OF LABOR MARKET INFORMATION. *Annual Planning Report, Fiscal Year 1977, New York City*. Prepared by Irma Siegal and staff. New York State Dept. of Labor, 1976. 103 pp.

NEW YORK TIMES, NEW YORK CITY PLANNING DEPT., NEW YORK CITY ECONOMIC DEVELOPMENT ADMINISTRATION. *New York Market Analysis; New York City Marketing Districts, Population and Housing, Retail Trade*. New York, NY: *New York Times*, 1973.

PETZRICK, COMDR. PAUL A., U.S.N, compiler. *1976 Energy Fact Book*. Virginia: Tetra Tech, Inc., 1975. Approx. 160 pp. (Tetra Tech Inc, 1911 N. Fort Myer Drive, Arlington, VA 22209).

SOWELL, THOMAS. *Race and Economics*. New York, NY: David McKay, 1975. 276 pp.

STURDIVANT, FREDERICK D. *The Ghetto Marketplace*. New York, NY: The Free Press, 1969. 320 pp.

SWINTON, DAVID H., and JULIAN, ELLISON. *Aggregate Personal Income of the Black Population in the U.S.A., 1947–1980*. New York, NY: Black Economic Research Center, 1973. 75 pp.

Travel Market Yearbook 1975–76. "The Black Travel Market," pp. 89–90. *Travel Market Yearbook*, 31 Wallacks Lane, Stamford, CT 06902. Annual. 100 pp.

U.S. DEPT. OF COMMERCE, BUREAU OF THE CENSUS. *Consumer Income: Money Income in 1974 of Families and Persons in the United States*. Index of Median Family Income in Current and Constant Dollars, for the United States: 1947–1974. Current Population Reports, Series P-60, no. 101. January 1976. 176 pp.

———. OFFICE OF MINORITY BUSINESS ENTERPRISE, WASHINGTON, D.C. 20230. *Developing Marketing Plans as Part of the Loan Packaging Process*. November 1974. 111 pp.

———. *Land and Minority Enterprise: The Crisis and the Opportunity*. Policy Research Study prep. by Dr. Lester M. Salamon, Duke University, for the U.S. Dept. of Commerce. June 30, 1976. 86 pp.

U.S. DEPT. OF HEW, OFFICE FOR CIVIL RIGHTS, DATA BRANCH. *Racial and Ethnic En-*

rollment Data from Institutions of Higher Education. Fall 1972. 136 pp. (OCR-74-13). Supt. of Documents, GPO, Washington, DC 20204.

————. OFFICE OF THE ASSIST. SEC'Y FOR PLANNING AND EVALUATION, OFFICE OF SPECIAL CONCERNS. *A Study of Selected Socio-Economic Characteristics of Ethnic Minorities, Based on the 1970 Census;* v. 4, HEW Regional data. July 1974. 41 pp. [HEW pubn. no. (OS) 75-123]. Supt. of Documents, GPO, Washington, DC 20204. Prepared by Urban Associates, Inc., Arlington, VA.

U.S. DEPT. OF LABOR, BUREAU OF LABOR STATISTICS. *Black Americans; a Decade of Occupational Change.* By Sylvia Small. Rev. 1972. 26 pp. Supt. of Documents, GPO, Washington, DC 20204.

U.S. HOUSE COMMITTEE ON SMALL BUSINESS, SUBCOMMITTEE OF SBA OVERSIGHT AND MINORITY ENTERPRISE. *Minority Enterprise and Allied Problems of Small Business: Hearings,* July 8–10, 1975. 261 pp. (94th Congress, 1st Session).

WRIGHT, JOHN S., and LARSON, CARL. *A Survey of Brand Preferences Among Chicago Negro Families.* College of Business Administration, University of Illinois, Chicago, IL, 1967. 74 pp.

YANCY, ROBERT J. *Federal Government Policy and Black Business Enterprise.* Cambridge, MA: Ballinger, 1974. 166 pp.

Articles

ABBOT, LEANDRA. "Mainway Can Get It for You Wholesale," *Black Enterprise,* November 1975, pp. 49–50.

ADAMS, JAMES RING. "The 'Two Nations' of Black America: Income Distribution Among Blacks Alone Is Far More Unequal Than Income Distribution Among Whites," *Wall Street Journal,* Sept. 19, 1974, p. 18.

ADRIAN, J., and DANIEL, R. "Impact of Socio-economic Factors on Consumption of Selected Food Nutrients in the United States," *American Journal of Agricultural Economics,* February 1976, pp. 31–38.

ALDRICH, H., and REISS, A. J., JR. "Continuities in the Study of Ecological Succession: Changes in the Race Composition of Neighborhoods and Their Businesses," *American Journal of Sociology,* January 1976, pp. 846–866.

ALEXANDER, K. M., JR. "Media Project in Action," *Crisis,* December 1975, pp. 434–5.

"America's Rising Black Middle Class," *Time,* June 17, 1974, pp. 19–24ff.

ANDERSON, BERNARD E. "Full Employment and Economic Equality," *Annals of the American Academy of Political and Social Science,* March 1975, pp. 127–137.

ANGELUS, T. "Black Film Explosion Uncovers an Untapped, Rich Market," *Advertising Age,* July 24, 1972, pp. 51ff.

ARMENDARIS, ALEX. "New Trends in Minority Enterprise Development [United States]," *Journal of Small Business Management,* July 1975, pp. 18–22.

"Avon Aims New Line, Ad Effort at Fast-Growing Black Market," *Advertising Age,* July 28, 1975, p. 57.

BALTERA, L. "Avon Lady Is Changing: New Youth, Black Drive," *Advertising Age,* June 3, 1974, p. 1ff.

BARBAN, ARNOLD M. "The Dilemma of Integrated Advertising," *Journal of Business*, October 1969, pp. 477–496.

BARROW, LIONEL C., JR. "Factors Related to Attention to the First Kennedy-Nixon Debate," *Journal of Broadcasting*, 5, 1961, pp. 229–38. Reprinted in *Issues of Our Time*, H. W. Hildebrandt, ed., New York: Macmillan Publishing Co., Inc., 1963.

———. "Minority Media Means Money," *Contact Magazine*, vol. 5-1, Winter 1973, pp. 46–47.

———. "New Uses of Covariance Analysis," *Journal of Advertising Research*, 7, December 1967, pp. 49–54. Reprinted in *Revista di Statistica Applicata*, vol. 3, no. 1, March 1970, pp. 2–14.

———. "Proposed Theory for the Effect of Educational Television," in *The Impact of Educational Television*, W. Schramm, ed., Urbana: University of Illinois Press, 1960, pp. 229–247.

———, and Westley, Bruce H. "Comparative Teaching Effectiveness of Radio and Television," *Audio-Visual Communications Review*, 7, 1959, pp. 14–23. Reprinted in *The Impact of Educational Television*, W. Schramm, ed., Urbana: University of Illinois, 1960, pp. 143–150.

———. "Intelligence and the Effectiveness of Radio and Television," *Audio-Visual Communications Review*, 7, 1959, pp. 193–208.

———. "An Investigation of News-Seeking Behavior," *Journalism Quarterly*, 36, 1959, pp. 431–38.

———; Beutschmann, Paul J.; and McMillan, Anita. "The Efficiency of Different Modes of Communication," *Audio-Visual Communications Review*, 9, 1961, pp. 263–70.

BARRY, T. E., and HARVEY, M. G. "Marketing to Heterogeneous Black Consumers," *California Management Review*, Winter 1974, pp. 50–57.

BAUER, RAYMOND A.; CUNNINGHAM, SCOTT M.; and WORTZEL, LAWRENCE H. "The Marketing Dilemma of Negroes," *Journal of Marketing*, July 1965, pp. 1–6.

"Beauty Chemicals: The Ethnic Market," *Chemical Marketing Reporter*, June 11, 1973, pp. 35–36.

BECNEL, BARBARA. "Profiling the Black Worker, 1976," *American Federationist*, July 1976, pp. 11–17.

"Black Ad Insert Will Run in Three Women's Magazines," *Advertising Age*, Oct. 4, 1974, p. 53.

"A Black Bank Rides Out Money Market Storms—with Profits, Too [First Independence National Bank, Detroit, Mich.]," *Banking*, March 1975, pp. 66–67.

"The Black Consumer: A Major New Force in the American Economy," *Black Enterprise*, November 1973. Entire issue is devoted to the Black consumer.

"Black Creative Group Formed," *Advertising Age*, August 20, 1973, p. 55.

"Black Economists: Black Economists Help to Shed Light on Economic Plight of Blacks," *Black Enterprise*, June 1976, pp. 87–96ff.

"Black Expo Comes of Age," *Ebony*, December 1971, pp. 64–68ff.

"Black Fund-Raising [Symposium]," *Black Scholar*, March 1976, pp. 2–30.

"Black Image Makers on Madison Avenue," *Black Enterprise*, February 1971, pp. 15–17, 20–22.

"Black Is Bountiful: Firms' Buying Policies Help in Recovery of Minority Businesses; Corporate Purchasers Find Federally Spurred Plans Can Be to Their Benefit; Rual Boles' Wax Firm Cited," *Wall Street Journal*, Jan. 7, 1976, p. 1, col. 1.

"A Black-Led U.S. Group Seeks Business Ties in Africa; Pan-African Business Enterprises, Inc., Based in New York, Has Been Urging Black American Businessmen to Seek New Ventures in African Countries," *Wall Street Journal*, Apr. 28, 1975, p. 6, col. 3.

"The Black Market," *Chain Store Age*, May 1970, pp. 99–138.

"Black Market No Monolith: Ebony Chief," *Advertising Age*, May 13, 1974, p. 62.

"Black Population in Dramatic Market Shifts," *Sales Management, The Marketing Magazine*, July 21, 1975, p. A-20. (1975 Survey of Buying Power.)

"Black Retailing: The Cash Registers Ring," *Black Enterprise*, November 1974. (Issue is devoted almost entirely to black retailing.)

"Black Shopping Centers: Finding Money and AAA Tenants Is Hard, but Having the Right Location Helps," *Black Enterprise*, September 1972, p. 43ff.

"Blacks Avoid Main White Travel Spots, Survey Indicates," *Advertising Age*, Mar. 17, 1975, p. 62.

"Blacks, Upscale Trends..." *Sales & Marketing Management* (formerly *Sales Management, the Marketing Magazine*), July 26, 1976, p. A-16. (1976 Survey of Buying Power.)

BLOCK, CARL E. "White Backlash To Negro Ads: Fact or Fantasy?" *Journalism Quarterly*, Summer 1972, pp. 258–262.

BONEPARTH, ELLEN. "Black Businessmen and Community Responsibility [based on interviews with sixty Black businessmen in the New York metropolitan area]," *Phylon*, March 1976, pp. 12–25.

BOORMAN, JOHN T., and KWAST, MYRON L. "The Start-Up Experience of Minority-Owned Commercial Banks: A Comparative Analysis [concentrates on the experience of the eight minority-owned banks founded between 1963 and 1965 and compares their performance with that of a sample of similarly situated nonminority banks], *Journal of Finance*, September 1974, pp. 1123–1141.

BRADFORD, W. D., and OSBORNE, A. E., JR. "The Entrepreneurship Decision and Black Economic Development," *American Economic Review*, May 1976, pp. 316–319.

BRIMMER, ANDREW F. "The Banking System and Urban Economic Development." Remarks at annual meetings of American Real Estate and Urban Economics Association and the American Finance Association, Chicago, IL, Dec. 28, 1968.

———. "The Black Banks, An Assessment of Performances and Prospects." Remarks, American Finance Association, Detroit, MI, Dec. 28, 1970.

———. "The Business Community and the Tasks of Urban Reconstruction, National Business League, Atlantic City, NJ, Sept. 15, 1967. (Remarks.)

———. "An Economic Agenda for Black Americans, Atlanta, GA, Oct. 16, 1970. (Remarks.)

———. "Economic Progress and Community Aspirations," Los Angeles Metropolitan Council of the National Association for the Advancement of Colored People, Biltmore Hotel, Los Angeles, CA, Oct. 27, 1967. (Remarks.)

———. "Economic Situation of Blacks in the United States," JEC, statement, Feb. 23, 1972.

———. "Economic Trends in the Negro Market," *Marketing Guide*, May 1964, pp. 2–7.

———. "Economic Trends in the United States and the Outlook for Developing Countries." (Remarks.) Chamber of Commerce, Monrovia, Liberia, July 23, 1970.

———. "Education and the Economic Advancement of Minority Groups in the United States." Remarks at Phi Epsilon Pi Fraternity Convention, Miami Beach, FL, Aug. 28, 1969.

———. "Equal Opportunity in Banking: An Urban Perspective." Remarks at Equal Employment Opportunity Conference Sponsored by U.S. Treasury Dept., American Bankers Assn., and California Bankers Assn., Los Angeles, CA, July 11, 1968.

———. "Employment Patterns and the Quest for Equal Opportunity in Banking." Remarks at Conference on Bank Employment Practices sponsored by U.S. Treasury Dept. and Michigan Human Relations Commission, Lansing, MI, May 22, 1968.

———. "Euro-Dollar Flows and the Efficiency of U.S. Monetary Policy," remarks at New School for Social Research, New York, NY, Mar. 8, 1969.

———. "Financial Institutions and Urban Rehabilitation." Remarks at National Bankers Convention, Kansas City, MO, Sept. 22, 1967.

———. "The Negro in the American Economy." Remarks opening a symposium at the Memorial Dedication Festival of the North Carolina Mutual Life Insurance Company, Durham, NC, Apr. 1, 1966.

———. "Opportunity and Responsibility in Urban Financing," National Association of Real Estate Brokers, New York, NY, Feb. 16, 1968. (Remarks).

———. "Outlook for Black Business," *Black Enterprise*, June 1976, pp. 26–30.

———. "Recent Developments in Black Banking: 1970–1971," Report, Washington, DC, July 31, 1972.

———. "Recent Trends in Black Banking," Press Conference at Convention of National Bankers Association, Washington, DC, Oct. 6, 1971.

———. "The Road Ahead: Outlook for Blacks in Business." Remarks, Cincinnati, OH, Oct. 19, 1972.

———. "Small Business and Economic Development in the Negro Community," Statement before House Committee on Small Business, July 25, 1969.

BROWNE, ROBERT S. "Economics and the Black Community in America," *The Review of Black Political Economy*, Spring 1975, pp. 302–313. Reprinted from *The Black Collegian*, September/October, 1974.

BULLOCK, HENRY ALLEN. "Consumer Motivation in Black and White," *Harvard Business Review*, May–June 1961, Part I, p. 89; July/August 1961, Part II, p. 110.

"The Business of Travel: Restaurants, p. 18; Boating, p. 19; Hotels, p. 28; Airlines, p. 35; Travel Writing, p. 46; Sporting Goods, p. 49; Beach Resorts, p. 50; Travel Agencies, p. 53 . . ." *Black Enterprise*, April 1975.

CARUTH, DONALD L. "Media and the Negro Market," *North Texas State University Studies*, Spring 1969, pp. 35–39.

CHAPKO, MICHAEL K. "Black Ads Are Getting Blacker," *Journal of Communication*, Autumn 1976, pp. 175–178.

CHOUDHURY, P. K., and SCHMID, L. S. "Black Models in Advertising to Blacks," *Journal of Advertising Research*, June 1974, pp. 19–22.

CICARELLI, J. "On Income, Race, and Consumer Behavior," *American Journal of Economics and Sociology*, July 1974, pp. 243–247.

CLAY, W. L. "Socio-economic Status of Blacks," *Ebony*, September 1975, p. 29.

CLOTFELTER, C. T. "The Effect of School Desegregation on Housing Prices," *Review of Economics and Statistics*, November 1975, pp. 446–451.

COALE, ANSLEY J., and RIVES, NORFLEET W., JR. "A Statistical Reconstruction of the Black Population of the United States 1880–1970: Estimates of True Numbers by Age and Sex, Birth Rates, and Total Fertility," *Population Index*, January 1973, pp. 3–36.

"Coalition of Civil Rights Groups Charged Federal Banking Regulators with Failing to Act Against Race and Sex Discrimination in Home-Mortgage Lending," *Wall Street Journal*, Apr. 27, 1976, p. 13, col. 1.

COLE, LEONARD A. "Electing Blacks to Municipal Office: Structural and Social Determinants [focuses on New Jersey municipalities, relating governmental forms and population characteristics to the likelihood of electing blacks]," *Urban Affairs Quarterly*, September 1974, pp. 17–39.

"Consumer Studies Place Emphasis on Young Blacks." Special Report, *Television/Radio Age*, Feb. 18, 1977, pp. A1-32.

CORNEHLS, JAMES V., and TAEBEL, DELBERT A. "The Outsiders and Urban Transportation [the poor, the elderly, the handicapped and especially those from minority groups can be classified as 'the outsiders' in regard to our auto-oriented transportation system]," *Social Science Journal* (Fort Collins), April 1976, pp. 61–73.

COTTINGHAM, PHOEBE H. "Black Income and Metropolitan Residential Dispersion [1970 census data for the Philadelphia metropolitan area is used to estimate Black and non-Black suburban selection functions, holding income levels constant]," *Urban Affairs Quarterly*, March 1975, pp. 273–296.

CULLEY, JAMES D., and BENNETT, REX. "Selling Women, Selling Blacks," *Journal of Communications*, Autumn 1976, pp. 160–173.

D. PARKE GIBSON INTERNATIONAL INC. "Important Developments in the Minority Marketplace," *The Gibson Report*, vol. 17, no. 2, July 1976, 4 pp.

"Daniels & Bell, Inc., Black-Owned New York Stock Exchange Member Firm, Announced Formation of Daniels & Bell (Africa) Ltd., with Offices in Monrovia, Liberia, and Lome, Togo," *Wall Street Journal*, Sept. 23, 1976, p. 35, col. 4.

DARDEN, NORMAN. "The New Breed of Negro Male in the Ghetto [Clean-Cut Black Business Men in Harlem]," *Michigan Quarterly Review*, Fall 1971, pp. 287–290.

DAVIS, KING E. "Socio-Economic Feasibility of Black Fund Raising," *Black Scholar*, March 1976, pp. 5–9. (Adapted from his book *Fund Raising in the Black Community*.)

"DDB: Education Key to Black Market Potential," *Advertising Age*, Mar. 15, 1976, p. 56.

"The Dealers [art dealers]," *Black Enterprise*, December 1975, pp. 43–45.

DECKER, C. RICHARD, and WINN, PAUL R. "Discriminatory Food Pricing: A Comment [on studies that have focused on whether discrimination in food pricing is specifically directed at poor people and/or Blacks]," *Business and Society*, Fall 1975, pp. 19–24.

DEMSETZ, H. "Advertising in the Affluent Society," *Modern Age*, Winter 1974, pp. 14–20.

DEWITT, KAREN. "Black Business in a New Town," *Black Enterprise*, November 1974, pp. 41–43ff.

———. "The Small Business Administration: Hey, Buddy, Can You Spare Me a Share in the System [Aid to Minority Entrepreneurs]," *Black Enterprise*, January 1975, pp. 25–27.

DIETRICH, R. F. "Know Your Black Shopper: Race May Be One of Your Least Important Clues," *Progressive Grocer*, June 1975, pp. 44–46.

———. "When Blacks Choose a Super, Some Departments Matter More," *Progressive Grocer*, August 1975, p. 34.

DOCTORS, SAMUEL I. and others. "The Impact of Minority Banks on Communities [a study of the impact of two such banks in the fictitiously named 'Midwest City']," *Bankers Magazine* (Boston), Spring 1975, pp. 84–91.

DONATH, B. "Dr. Tichenor Uses Negro Markets as Springboard for Metro Franchise," *Advertising Age*, Feb. 18, 1974, p. 3ff.

DONOHUE, T. R. "Effect of Commercials on Black Children," *Journal of Advertising Research*, December 1975, pp. 41–47.

DUKER, JACOB M., and HUGHES, CHARLES E. "The Black-Owned Life Insurance Company: Issues and Recommendations," *Journal of Risk and Insurance*, June 1973, pp. 221–230.

DURAND, R. "Some Dynamics of Urban Service Evaluations Among Blacks and Whites," *Social Science Quarterly*, March 1976, pp. 698–706.

DURKIN, THOMAS A. "Consumer Awareness of Credit Terms: Review and New Evidence [summarizes the findings of recent studies and reports the results of new research on credit-term awareness among those previously thought to have benefited least from Truth in Lending: low-income, minority-group members]," *Journal of Business*, April 1975, pp. 253–263.

"The Economics of Black Media: for Newspapers and Radio Stations, It's Getting a Bigger Share of the Ad Dollar; in TV It's Gaining the Initial Foothold," *Black Enterprise*, September 1974, pp. 16–20.

"Editorial Page Article on Missing Numbers in the Census: Government Head-counters Missed Counting One in Every Ten Black Males in 1970; Some Evidence Links High Mobility, Unconventional Living Arrangements as Reasons 9.9% Not Counted," *Wall Street Journal*, Aug. 31, 1976, p. 10, col. 4.

"Ethnic HABA, a Way to Win Black Customers," *Progressive Grocer*, vol. 55, no. 11, November 1976, pp. 83–86.

"Ethnic Marketing—So Much Opportunity, So Much to Learn," *Product Marketing Magazine*, June 1977, pp. 29–34.

FALLIS, DIANA S. "Black Executives' Wives: A Survey," *MBA: the Master in Business Administration*, March 1973, pp. 46–47.

FEDLER, FRED. "The Media and Minority Groups: A Study of Adequacy of Access; study of Minneapolis [Minn.] media finds that minority groups receive more, not less, publicity than comparable established groups," *Journalism Quarterly*, Spring 1973, pp. 109–117.

FORKAN, J. P. "N.Y.'s Inner City Going Strong with AM, FM Combo," *Advertising Age*, Oct. 13, 1975, p. 20.

———. "Who's Who in $350,000,000 Black Grooming Market," *Advertising Age*, Nov. 20, 1972, pp. 96–97.

"FTC Weïghing Consent Order Against Revlon Inc. in Dispute Involving Hair-Straighteners; 'Racism' Alleged in Agency's Moving Against Black Company, but Not Revlon," *Wall Street Journal*, Aug. 6, 1976, p. 21, col. 3.

GALLIMORE, R. and others. "Cultural Differences in Delay of Gratification: A Problem of Behavior Classification," *Journal of Personality and Social Psychology*, July 1974, pp. 72–80.

GARFINKLE, STUART H. "Occupations of Women and Black Workers, 1962–1974: Detailed Data from the Current Population Survey Reveal Substantial Improvement in the Occupational Standing of Women and Blacks," *Monthly Labor Review*, November 1975, pp. 25–35.

GENSCH, DENNIS H., and STAELIN, RICHARD. "The Appeal of Buying Black," *Journal of Marketing Research*, May 1972, pp. 141–148.

GIFFORD, JOHN B. "Integrated Advertising," *Miami Business Review*, April 1973, pp. [1–4].

GILLIAM, DOROTHY, and SOJOURNER, SUSAN. "The History of a Black S&L," *Black Enterprise*, October 1974, pp. 49–52.

GLASSER, G. J., and METZGER, G. A. "Radio Usage by Blacks," *Journal of Advertising Research*, October 1975, pp. 39–45.

GOODLOE, J. W. "Black-Operated Firm: the Men, Markets and Myths." Address, May 12, 1971, *Vital Speeches*, Sept. 15, 1971, pp. 709–715.

GOULD, JOHN W. and others. "Black Consumer Reactions to 'Integrated' Advertising: An Exploratory Study," *Journal of Marketing*, July 1970, pp. 20–26.

GREGORY, W. H. "Airlines Focus on Special Interest Groups," *Aviation Week & Space Technology*, Aug. 2, 1971, pp. 32–34.

HAIL, W. "Boom in Black Spending [South Africa]," *The Banker*, September 1975, pp. 1115–1119.

HAWKINS, HOMER C. "Trends in Black Migration from 1863 to 1960 [largely out-migration from the South]," *Phylon*, June 1973, pp. 140–152.

HILLS, G. E. and others. "Black Consumer Perceptions of Food Store Attributes," *Journal of Marketing*, April 1973, pp. 47–57.

HILTZ, STARR ROXANNE. "Why Black Families Own Less Life Insurance," *Journal of Risk and Insurance*, June 1971, pp. 225–235.

HODGSON, PETER. "Sampling Racial Minority Groups," *Journal of the Market Research Society*, April 1975, pp. 104–106.

"House Banking and Currency Committee Voted to Make It Illegal for a Lender to Refuse Loans to Someone Because of Race, Color, Religion, National Origin or Age," *Wall Street Journal*, May 7, 1975, p. 5, col. 3.

"How Associations Can Impact on Black America," *The Gibson Report*, D. Parke Gibson International, Inc., May 1977, 4 pp.

"How Blacks Are Faring: Latest Official Report," *U.S. News & World Report*, Aug. 11, 1975, p. 27.

"HUD, in Line with Recent Supreme Court Decision, Took First Step Toward Moving Racially Mixed Public Housing into White Suburban Areas, Chiefly in Chicago," *Wall Street Journal*, June 8, 1976, p. 4, col. 2.

HUNT, DERYL G. "The Viable Black Community," *Black Politician: A Journal of Current Political Thought*, October 1971, pp. 35–39.

HUNTER, VICKY. "Retailing on 125th Street: The Road's Not Paved with Gold but Curbside Merchants Are Turning the Sidewalk into Dollars," *Black Enterprise*, November 1975, pp. 30–31.

HURWOOD, DAVID L. "More Blacks and Women in Sales and Marketing? [responses and experiences of 110 manufacturing and service firms in the face of pressure to increase representation by minorities and women]," *Conference Board Record*, February 1973, pp. 38–44.

"Industries: The employment picture for Blacks varies considerably from industry to industry and from occupation to occupation. In order to define a clear pattern of how Blacks are faring in finding employment in the major sectors of the economy, *Black Enterprise* has asked the Black Economic Research Center in New York City to make a survey of some of the country's major industries...," *Black Enterprise*, January 1976, pp. 46–47; Public Administration, February 1976, pp. 45–46; Public Education, March 1976, pp. 46–47; Lumber and Wood Products, July 1976, p. 39.

"Interview with Barbara Proctor," *Media Decisions*, April 1977.

IRONS, EDWARD D. "Black Entrepreneurship; Its Rationale, Its Problems, Its Prospects [conference paper]," *Phylon*, March 1976, pp. 12–25.

"Jackson's Expo; Black Expo Trade Fair," *Newsweek*, Oct. 4, 1971, pp. 24.

JOHNSON, J. H. "Greening of the Black Consumer Market," *Crisis*, March 1976, pp. 92–95.

JOHNSON, T. B., and DILLINGHAM, M. "Quest of the Black Man," *Intellect*, March 1973, pp. 366–370.

KAIN, J. F., and QUIGLEY, J. M. "Housing Market Discrimination, Home Ownership, and Savings Behavior," *American Economic Review*, June 1972, pp. 263–277. Reply with rejoinder: J. F. McDonald, March 1974, pp. 225–231.

KASSARJIAN, WALTRAUD M. "Blacks as Communicators and Interpreters of Mass Communication; Data on Black Media Use Patterns Are Mixed; Content Studies Document Increased Presence of Blacks in Ads in All Media," *Journalism Quarterly*, Summer 1973, pp. 285–291.

KATZ, PHYLLIS A., and ZALK, SUE R. "Doll Preferences: An Index of Racial Attitudes?" *Journal of Educational Psychology*, October 1974, pp. 663–668.

"Key Aspects of a Comprehensive Minority Relations Program," *Public Relations News*, Oct. 17, 1977, pp. 3–4.

LARSON, C. M., and WALES, H. G. "Brand Preferences of Chicago Blacks," *Journal of Advertising Research*, August 1973, pp. 15–21.

LEE, ROY F. "A Strategy for Minority Business Development," *Journal of Small Business Management*, January 1975, pp. 46–51.

LIEBERSON, S., and WILKINSON, C. A. "Comparison Between Northern and Southern Blacks Residing in the North," *Demography*, May 1976, pp. 199–224.

LINDEN, FABIAN. "Consumer Markets: the Economics of Cities and Suburbs [employment patterns, the occupation mix, and the distribution of buying power of the city and suburban family, 1974; United States]," *Conference Board Record*, March 1976, pp. 42–45.

LINK, C. R., and RUTLEDGE, E. C. "The Influence of the Quantity and Quality of Education on Black-White Earnings Differentials: Some New Evidence," *Review of Economics and Statistics*, August 1975, pp. 346–350.

LONG, LARRY H. "How Racial Composition of Cities Changes [focuses on sources of racial change between 1950 and 1970 in eleven of the twelve cities with the largest Black populations (250,000 or more in 1970) and their metropolitan areas; United States]," *Land Economics*, August 1975, pp. 258–267.

MAGGARD, JOHN P. "Negro Market—Fact or Fiction," *California Management Review*, November 1971, pp. 420–426.

"Making Good in the Ghetto [Wrigley Super Markets, Detroit]," *Progressive Grocer*, June 1975, pp. 49ff.

"Making It with the Black Consumer," *Sales Management*, November 26, 1973, p. 3.

MARSHALL, R. "The Economics of Racial Discrimination: A Survey," *Journal of Economic Literature*, September 1974, pp. 849–871.

MARTICORENA, C. "Ethnic Market: Biggest Potential for Growth in Cosmetics Industry," *Chemical Marketing Reporter*, June 23, 1975, pp. 37–39.

MASSON, ROBERT TEMPEST. "Costs of Search and Racial Price Discrimination [develops a model to analyze racial price discrimination and interprets empirical studies which indicate that Blacks often pay more for the same goods than do whites]," *Western Economic Journal*, June 1973, pp. 167–186.

"MCA Inc. to Boost Minorities in Field of Entertainment; Concern's New Ventures Unit to Receive $3 Million Backing, Matching Aid from U.S.," *Wall Street Journal*, Aug. 20, 1976, p. 3, col. 4.

"Military Exchanges Think Black," *Ebony*, July 1971, pp. 54–56.

"Minority Vendor Programs Feel the Pressure of the Recession... Some 400 Large Corporations Have Instituted Programs in Which Special Efforts Are Made to Buy Supplies from Businesses Owned by Blacks and Other Minority Group Members," *Wall Street Journal*, Jan. 23, 1975, p. 1, col. 5.

"Miracle of Supreme Life," *Ebony*, October 1973, pp. 116–124.

"Moving Ahead in Style: Blacks in the Fashion Industry," *Black Enterprise*, September 1976, pp. 35, 36ff.

NATHANSON, C. A. "Moving Preferences and Plans Among Urban Black Families," *American Institute of Planners Journal*, September 1974, pp. 53–59.

"New Look at the Black Consumer," *Sales Management*, Aug. 6, 1973, p. 13.

"New Starch Study Shows Blacks Have Fewer Misgivings About Advertising," *Advertising Age*, Apr. 16, 1973, p. 30.

ORPHEN, C. "Reactions to Black and White Models," *Journal of Advertising Research*, October 1975, pp. 75–79.

"Outlook for Black Business," *Black Enterprise*, June 1976, p. 30.

PARVIN, J. "The Effect of Race on the Flight to the Suburbs," *Journal of Political Economy*, August 1975, p. 865.

PATTERSON, PAT. "A Profile of Richard Gidron: Within Fifteen Years He Moved from Car Jockey to Car Dealer and Now Owns One of Cadillac's Most Successful Agencies," *Black Enterprise*, April 1975, pp. 45–47ff.

PERETTI, P. O., and LUCAS, C. "Newspaper Advertising Influences on Consumers' Behavior by Socio-economic Status of Customers," *Psychological Reports*, December 1975, pp. 693–694.

"Perspectives on the Political Economy of Racism [United States]," *Review of Radical Political Economics*, Fall 1975, pp. 1–99.

PETROF, JOHN V. "Customer Strategy for Negro Retailers," *Journal of Retailing*, Fall 1967, pp. 30–37.

———. "Minority Representation in French Advertising," *Marquette Business Review*, Spring 1973, pp. 9–12.

———. "Newspaper Advertising and the Negro Market," *Journal of Retailing*, Spring 1970, pp. 20–31.

———. "Reaching the Negro Market: A Segregated vs. a General Newspaper," *Journal of Advertising Research*, June 1968, pp. 40–43.

———. "The Role of Ethnic and General-Use Publications vs. Communication Tools in Marketing Strategies Aimed Toward Minority Markets," *Southern Journal of Business*, Jan. 1968, pp. 45–51.

"A Place on the Platform," *Advertising News of New York*, October 7, 1977, pp. 9–11.

POLITE, C. K. and others. "Ethnic Group Identification and Differentiation," *Journal of Social Psychology*, February 1974, pp. 149–150.

PRUDEN, H. O., and LONGMAN, D. S. "Race, Alienation, and Consumerism," *Journal of Marketing*, July 1972, pp. 58–63. Reply with rejoinder, by E. L. Landon, Jr., and W. J. Lunds, *Journal of Marketing*, April 1973, pp. 67–70.

"Reaching the Black Consumer," *Black Enterprise*, June 1973, pp. 125–126ff.

ROEDER, RICHARD A. "Integration in Business Advertising," *The MBA: The Master in Business Administration*, October 1970, pp. 26–29.

ROISTACHER, E. A., and GOODMAN, J. L., JR. "Race and Home Ownership: Is Discrimination Disappearing?" *Economic Inquiry*, March 1976, pp. 59–70.

ROSSER, L., and WHITE, B. "Answer to Housing Discrimination; the Need for Unitary Marketing System," *Civil Rights Digest*, Winter 1975, pp. 10–19.

SAMPSON, WILLIAM A., and MILAN, VERA. "The Interracial Attitudes of the Black Middle Class: Have They Changed? [Effects of the civil rights movements of the 1960s on their sense of group solidarity]," *Social Problems*, December 1975, pp. 153–165.

SCOTT, GIL. "Blacks in the Liquor Industry," *Black Enterprise*, September 1975, pp. 33–37ff.

SEARING, DANIEL A. "Discrimination in Home Finance [types of discrimination practiced against minorities and response of each of the four federal financial regulatory agencies to complaints]," *Notre Dame Lawyer*, June 1973, pp. 1113–1144.

SELBY, EDWARD B., and LINDLEY, JAMES T. "Black Customers—Hidden Market Potential [as users of commercial bank services]," *Bankers Magazine* (Boston), Summer 1973, pp. 84–87.

"Session Told: Redirect Ads to Black Buyer," *Advertising Age*, July 29, 1974, p. 56.

"Selling to the Black Consumer: A Round-table Discussion of the Increasing Black Impact on Corporate Economies," *Black Enterprise*, November 1973, pp. 31–33.

SEXTON, DONALD E., JR. "Black Buyer Behavior [surveys research on Black buying behavior and provides information needed to market more effectively to Black consumers]," *Journal of Marketing*, October 1972, pp. 36–39.

———. "Differences in Food Shopping Habits by Area of Residence, Race, and Income," *Journal of Retailing*, Spring 1974, pp. 48ff.

———. "Do Blacks Pay More?" *Journal of Marketing Research*, November 1971, pp. 420–426.

SHARON, A. T. "Racial Differences in Newspaper Readership," *Public Opinion Quarterly*, Winter 1973–1974, pp. 611–617.

SIEMBIEDA, W. J. "Suburbanization of Ethnics of Color," *Annals of the American Academy of Political and Social Science*, November 1975, pp. 118–128.

SPRATLEN, THADDEUS H. "The Black Consumer Response to Black Business," *The Review of Black Political Economy*, Fall 1973, pp. 73–105.

STRANG, W. A. "Blacks in Sales: Why Are There So Few?" *The Review of Black Political Economy*, Winter 1976, pp. 200–212.

STRASZHEIM, M. R. "Housing Market Discrimination and Black Housing Consumption," *Quarterly Journal of Economics*, February 1974, pp. 19–43.

SUCSY, LEONARD G. "Marketing's New Role in the Ghetto," *Sales Marketing Today*, February 1970, pp. 9–11.

SWINTON, D. H. "Factors Affecting the Future Economic Prospects of Minorities," *American Economic Review: Papers and Proceedings*, May 1975, pp. 53–58.

———, and ELLISON, J. "Aggregate Personal Income of the Black Population in the USA, 1947–1980: Excerpts," *The Review of Black Political Economy*, Winter 1974, pp. 113–122.

TAYLOR, THAYER C. "Black Middle Class: Earn, Baby, Earn," *Sales Management, The Marketing Magazine*, July 8, 1974, pp. A5–A28. (1974 Survey of Buying Power).

TERRELL, ANGELA. "The Beauty Business Is Still Bullish," *Black Enterprise*, November 1975, pp. 40–42ff.

TIMMONS, J. A. "Black Is Beautiful: Is It Bountiful?" *Harvard Business Review*, November 1971, pp. 81–94.

"Today's Black Shopper: Not What You Think," *Progressive Grocer*, vol. 54, no. 6 (June 1975), pp. 44–46, 49–52.

TOLSON, ARTHUR L. "Historical and Modern Trends in Black Capitalism [conference paper]," *Black Scholar*, April 1975, pp. 8–14.

TOPPING, JOHN C., JR. "Minority Business Development in a Community Revitalization Strategy [based on a conference paper]," *Ripon Quarterly: Journal of Republican Politics and Policy*, Fall 1974, pp. 23–30.

"Trend and Analysis of Black Economic Development [conference papers]," *American Economic Review*, May 1976, 316–331.

TUCKER, C. J. "Changes in Age Composition of the Rural Black Population of the South, 1950–1970," *Phylon*, September 1974, pp. 268–275.

TUSKEGEE INSTITUTE BUSINESS DEVELOPMENT CENTER. "Minority Consumer Expenditures: Growth of Minority Markets," *Exchange*, monthly publication, Tuskegee Institute, Alabama, April 1976, vol. IV, no. IV, p. 2.

"A View from the Top: Chief Executives Discuss the Economic War and Strategies for Winning," *Black Enterprise*, June 1975, pp. 79ff.

UNNI, V. K. "A Study of Selected Characteristics of Consumption, Life Style, and Social Class Concepts Among Wives of Negro Blue-Collar Industrial Workers in Selected Louisiana Parishes," *Dissertation Abstracts International*, April 1974, p. 6194.

UNWIN, STEPHEN, J. F. "How Culture, Age and Sex Affect Advertising Response: Study of Responses to Magazine Ads by American Students, Their Parents and Foreign Students Suggest [sic] Cultural Differences Larger than Generation Gap," *Journalism Quarterly*, Winter 1973, pp. 735–743.

WALL, KELVIN A. "The Great Waste: Ignoring Blacks," *Marketing/Communications*, February 1970, pp. 42–50.

———. "New Market: Among Blacks, the Haves are Overtaking the Have-Nots," *Advertising Age*, Feb. 11, 1974, pp. 35–36.

———. "Positioning Your Brand in the Black Market," *Advertising Age*, June 18, 1973, pp. 71ff.

———. "Why Products Fail in a Negro Market," *Media/Scope*, May 1970, pp. 55–61.

WEATHERS, DIANE. "Boutiques, The Fashionable Way to Sell Fashion," *Black Enterprise*, pp. 25–30.

"What to Do When the Neighborhood Goes Black," *American Druggist*, July 15, 1973, pp. 28–31.

"When Black Is Beautiful: Johnson Products Co.," *Business Week*, Sept 8, 1973, p. 51.

WHITE, JOYCE. "Black Travel on the Upsurge," *Encore American & Worldwide News*, July 7, 1975, pp. 36–38.

"White Markets for a Black Insurer," *Business Week*, Nov. 11, 1972, pp. 66ff.

"Why Black Enterprise?" *Black Enterprise*, August 1975, pp. 23–25ff.

WILSON, F. D. "Ecology of a Black Business District," *The Review of Black Political Economy*, Summer 1975, pp. 353–375.

WONG, JIM and others. "Marketing Assistance Models for Minority Enterprise [based on conference paper]," *Atlanta Economic Review*, October 1974, pp. 49–54.

WOODSIDE, A. G. "Credibility of Advertising Themes Among Blacks and Whites," *Marquette Business Review*, Fall 1975, pp. 134–142.

WORTHAM, JACOB. "Retailing in the Seventies," *Black Enterprise*, November 1974, pp. 25–29.

INDEX